HISTORICAL LINGUISTICS

AND

GENERATIVE GRAMMAR

PRENTICE-HALL INTERNATIONAL, INC., *London*
PRENTICE-HALL OF AUSTRALIA, PTY. LTD., *Sydney*
PRENTICE-HALL OF CANADA, LTD., *Toronto*
PRENTICE-HALL OF INDIA PRIVATE LIMITED, *New Delhi*
PRENTICE-HALL OF JAPAN, INC., *Tokyo*

ROBERT D. KING
DEPARTMENT OF LINGUISTICS
UNIVERSITY OF TEXAS

HISTORICAL LINGUISTICS
AND
GENERATIVE GRAMMAR

PRENTICE-HALL, INC., ENGLEWOOD CLIFFS, NEW JERSEY

TO MARTIN JOOS

Current printing (last number):

10 9 8 7 6 5 4 3 2

PREFACE

The new insights into language provided by generative grammar have led to new ways of looking at historical linguistics. I have tried to present here a comprehensive picture of historical linguistics as currently understood by linguists who share the view of language and grammar associated with Noam Chomsky and Morris Halle.

This is not a theory of historical linguistics—we do not have one—but an effort to suggest profitable ways of thinking about historical linguistics and to treat subjects on which generative grammar has had an impact. Some topics customarily included in historical linguistics, such as the genetic model and language families, are absent from the book except insofar as they call for reinterpretation within the model proposed here or are otherwise relevant.

Much of what I say about historical linguistics is tentative and doubtless will prove with time to be incomplete, perhaps wrong. I caution the reader that nothing in this book was passed down from Mount Sinai, and I urge each reader to test critically these ideas and claims in light of his own knowledge of languages.

I have tried to avoid the polemical tone that is almost inevitable given a linguistic subject. Perhaps it is not desirable to avoid polemics; certainly a text purged of every trace of polemic would not accurately echo the tenor of linguistics in the 1960's.

My reverence for the tradition of historical linguistics is great, as is my debt to it. Let that be well understood. No one in historical linguistics today can fail to be acutely conscious of the accomplishments of his predecessors and contemporaries, whatever their theoretical position.

The supplementary reading suggestions closing each chapter furnish background, additional discussion in the generative framework of the topics treated, or a different and often opposing point of view. The supplementary reading selections are intended not to be exhaustive but only to guide the reader who wants to read more.

A number of people have helped this book to completion. I would like to thank Emmon Bach and William S-Y. Wang for reading the manuscript at various stages and giving me the benefit of criticism. To Paul Kiparsky I am indebted for stimulation and insight as well as for criticism of the manuscript. I particularly wish to thank Stanley Peters for his discussion and comments. I am grateful to G. H. Matthews for the data on Crow and Hidatsa used in the discussion of comparative reconstruction. Correspondence with William G. Moulton and Herbert Penzl helped clarify my position on certain issues. And I thank my wife Janet for everything, not least for ignoring the tedious business of writing a book.

Finally, I wish to acknowledge a debt to two men who had no direct participation in this book but who, indirectly, influenced its creation. One is Roe-Merrill S. Heffner, my first teacher of linguistics. The kind of debt I owe Professor Heffner will be perhaps sufficiently hinted at if I relate that he used to insist, to the exasperation of almost everyone, on calling himself "The Last of the Neogrammarians."

My largest debt of gratitude is to Martin Joos, to whom this book is fondly dedicated, for an education in some ways peculiar, always idiosyncratic, often mystifying—but highly useful.

R. D. K.

CONTENTS

1

PROLOGUE

To define historical linguistics is not taxing. One might say that historical linguistics is the study of all aspects of language development through time, or that historical linguistics is the investigation of language change. The average linguist would accept such definitions without much disagreement, perhaps adjusting them here and there in the direction of his private interest in the field. But to define the relation of historical linguistics to general linguistics is not an easy or obvious matter. This is a seminal question having no answer to which all linguists readily assent. Nor is it obvious why historical linguistics is of interest to the linguist, who can do linguistics without caring in the least what historical linguistics is all about.

This has not always been so. There was a time when the position of historical linguistics was quite well defined and when its study was as much a matter of course as that of any other reasonable subject. The reason was simple:

main stream linguistics *was* historical linguistics—what you did if your interest was language rather than politics or the cavalry. The place was Europe, particularly Leipzig in Germany, and the time was the last quarter of the nineteenth century, a period of enthusiastic and valuable activity (valuable even today) in the still nascent discipline of historical linguistics. In that cultural and historical context to have asked one of the great linguists of the time, say Karl Brugmann or Hermann Paul, why he was involved in historical rather than general linguistics would have elicited for the sophisticated questioner a puzzled look but not much of an answer. Historical linguistics was where the action was: if you studied languages, you were involved in historical linguistics, and few scholars engaged in linguistic research stopped long enough to wonder whether their work properly belonged to historical linguistics or to the larger field of general linguistics, or indeed to ask what the difference was.

Only an intellectual climate like this could have produced the famous statement made by Hermann Paul in defense of the title of his book *Prinzipien der Sprachgeschichte* (*Principles of the History of Language*), published in 1880: "The objection has been raised that the historical approach to language is not the only scientific method available for the study of language. I am forced to deny this" (Paul 1960:20). Such simplicity is not possible now. Few linguists today would care to argue for the advantages of making historical linguistics coterminous with linguistics in general.

Though most of our predecessors in the late nineteenth century (including both Neogrammarians and linguists like Hermann Collitz and Hugo Schuchardt who were not Neogrammarians) merged what we today might call *descriptive* and *historical* practice, at least one of them, Ferdinand de Saussure, came to perceive clearly the fact that the two disciplines are different in several crucial respects. It was Saussure who first insisted in stringent fashion on the distinction between what he called *synchrony* (the study of language in its static states) and *diachrony* (the study of language in its evolutionary stages). And the degree to which we now observe the separation of the two betokens the extent to which modern linguistics continues to profit from certain of Saussure's insights. He wrote:

> For a science concerned with values the distinction [between synchrony and diachrony] is a practical necessity and sometimes an absolute one. In these fields scholars cannot organize their research rigorously without considering both coordinates and making a distinction between the system of values per se and the same values as they relate to time (Saussure 1959:80).

As with Saussure's writings in general one may quarrel with certain aspects of this statement, or subject it to reinterpretation within whatever theory of language one subscribes to. By and large, however, most linguists today recognize the necessity of the distinction between synchrony and diachrony, though as Roman Jakobson perceptively remarks, "The uniting of static and dynamic processes in language is one of the fundamental dialectic antinomies which serve to characterize the concept of language. The dialectic of language development cannot be understood without observance of this antinomy" (1931:267).

Saussure's sharp separation of the two aspects of language study continues to have many implications for linguistics. One of its effects was to spoil the easy answer which Hermann Paul and others of his time might have given to the question "Why be concerned with historical linguistics?" After Saussure it was necessary to make a choice, so to speak: if you were interested in languages you studied linguistics, and you could if you liked study historical linguistics.

The unfortunate result was a deflection of historical linguistics from the center of the stage in linguistic research—a state of affairs which has continued to the present. Most of the considerable work in structural linguistics done during and since the second quarter of the twentieth century has been primarily devoted to problems of synchronic analysis: refinement of the notion "phoneme," problems of phonological and morphological analysis, immediate constituent cuts, the adequacy of phrase-structure grammars, the role of transformations, and so on. Many European scholars continued to devote most of their time to historical linguistics, but the emphasis in mainstream American linguistics lay very much more on the side of synchrony. The main reason for this, of course, was that under the influence of Boas, Sapir, and Bloomfield, American linguists had been primarily concerned with describing living languages, especially the native American languages, and they required the development of a body of analytical techniques for the synchronic description of language. If diachrony came into the picture, as it did in Bloomfield's Algonquian studies and in much of Sapir's work, so much the better; but synchrony had the prior claim.

One should not leap to the conclusion that historical linguistics in America had necessarily to suffer on account of this shift of attention. On the contrary, the predominant feeling in the forties and fifties was that historical linguistics had everything to gain from assimilating the sophisticated tools being devised for synchronic analysis. It was, as Hall says regarding one branch of historical linguistics, "the goal of some present-day workers to return to comparative reconstruction and to revivify it with an infusion of descriptive (synchronic) analysis" (1950:6). A number of well-known papers illustrate this: Twaddell (1938), where the notions of allophone and phoneme are related to scribal practice in the attempt to explain a long-standing problem in the orthographic representation of High German umlaut; Hall (1950), which is a case study in careful application of the comparative method with constant reference to what earlier would have been called "the phonemic principle"; Hoenigswald (1950), where the problem of comparative reconstruction is shown to parallel the problem of assigning phones to phonemes on the basis of phonetic similarity and complementary distribution. Hoenigswald (1960) represents in some ways the culmination of such trends. *Language Change and Linguistic Reconstruction* summarizes the directions historical linguistics had been moving under the aegis of American structural linguistics, and it codifies a great deal of what seemed to be best in the emergent techniques.

Meanwhile, in Europe, work in historical linguistics had gone right on, though on lines hardly parallel to those developing in America. Some linguistic scholars had remained outside the structuralist schools altogether. Linguists of the Prague Circle were not primarily interested in historical linguistics, though some of them, notably Roman Jakobson, made important contributions. Jerzy Kuryłowicz continued to publish significant work dealing with theoretical problems in historical linguistics, as did Émile Benveniste; and all over Europe scholars carried on research in historical linguistics either guided by Neogrammarian or "idealistic" precepts or influenced by Prague (e.g. André Martinet and Jean Fourquet).

But all of this has not brought us any closer to answering the second of our initial questions: what is the position of historical linguistics? Or more directly: why should anyone be concerned with historical linguistics? Merely observing that linguistics since the Neogrammarians has not been identical with historical linguistics does not provide a *raison d'être* for the latter. The observation that historical linguistics has been revitalized by new insights from synchronic linguistics is not necessarily calculated to win students for historical linguistics.

More than this, our question seems to gain in seriousness the further away we move from the certainties of the nineteenth century, where so much, not only questions in linguistics, seems to us to have had such easy answers. Throughout the twentieth century linguistics has expanded its horizons (occasionally to its own disadvantage) to include or touch on an ever increasing number of previously excluded subjects: anthropology, psychology, mathematics, sociology, and so on, and we have come to expect, perhaps too optimistically, that linguistics will continue to grow in relevance to mankind's problems and the human condition.

So too with historical linguistics. It is not quite sufficient today to assert that one should study historical linguistics because it is intrinsically interesting (though no doubt that is sufficient reason for the majority of scholars busily engaged in historical linguistics). Similarly, it is not enough to claim that historical linguistics is useful because it gives us new perspectives about present-day languages and how they came to be that way.

The purpose of this book is to present historical linguistics as it is understood and practiced by linguists committed to the conception of language and grammar implicit in the theory of generative grammar. The book's larger purpose, however, is to point out some of the ways in which the theory of generative grammar has made historical linguistics more relevant to general linguistics. We will be able to discuss such matters critically only after we have examined the form of historical linguistics as it appears within the theory of generative grammar. Suffice it to remark here that historical linguistics and the evidence of historical change have a good deal to say about the ultimate shape of our model of what a speaker knows in order to speak his language.

In other words, we shall see how historical linguistics stands to profit from the new insights into language that have come with the development of generative grammar. But the gains are not all one-sided: the theory of grammar too is enriched by the inclusion of data from historical linguistics.

We are, in a sense, riding out a pendulum swing from earlier positions in which historical linguistics was receiving much and returning little vis-à-vis linguistic theory. Today we find that material from historical linguistics figures prominently in many discussions principally concerned with questions of synchrony, and often the historical data are crucial in deciding questions about the form of grammar rules (cf. Bach 1968 and Kiparsky 1968b). In the 1950's such cooperation between synchrony and diachrony would have been almost unthinkable.

Our more immediate concern, however, is not so much to justify the existence of historical linguistics or to emphasize its pertinence in regard to general linguistics as it is to examine historical linguistics from within the theory of generative grammar. What do we mean when we say that language changes? How does it change? What changes? In particular, what is sound change, and what is the mechanism by which it takes place? Is sound change regular? What is analogy within generative grammar? What can we say about syntactic change? Does generative grammar have any implications for internal and comparative reconstruction? Why does change occur? What, if anything systematic, do scribes write?

But in delving into these and related subjects, let us not lose sight of our main goal in historical linguistics—to say all that we can about the processes that take place in language through time and space. It is emphatically not our job to provide a number of gimmicks which somehow make language change look easy, nor is it even, primarily, to show that a given theory of language and grammar renders a better accounting of the facts of language change than do other theories. Of course, it is impossible to discuss any set of linguistic data in a vacuum: data do not explain themselves, only an associated theory can explain them; and success in explaining the data is directly proportional to the relative correctness of our theory of language. We cannot discuss language change without discussing the ways in which our theory of grammar gives us richer insights into the nature of change than do other theories. This is proper, but let us not forget that our primary goal is to deepen understanding of the mysterious phenomenon of linguistic change.

First, we must state clearly the theoretical position from which we shall be examining the data from the history of languages. What are the goals of linguistic theory, and how are we to account for observable facts about language?

SUPPLEMENTARY READING

Hoenigswald, Henry M. 1960. *Language Change and Linguistic Reconstruction.* Chicago: University of Chicago Press.

Lehmann, Winfred P. 1962. *Historical Linguistics: An Introduction.* New York: Holt, Rinehart & Winston, Inc.

Lehmann, Winfred P., ed. 1967. *A Reader in Nineteenth-Century Historical Indo-European Linguistics.* Bloomington: Indiana University Press.

Meillet, Antoine. 1921. *Linguistique historique et linguistique générale.* Paris: Champion (= Collection linguistique publiée par la Société de Linguistique de Paris, 8).

Paul, Hermann. 1960. *Prinzipien der Sprachgeschichte* (6th ed.). Tübingen: Max Niemeyer. Available in English as *Principles of the History of Language,* trans. Herbert A. Strong. London: Longmans, Green & Co. Ltd., 1891.

Pedersen, Holger. 1962. *The Discovery of Language,* trans. John W. Spargo. Bloomington: Indiana University Press.

Waterman, John T. 1963. *Perspectives in Linguistics.* Chicago: University of Chicago Press.

Whitney, William D. 1883. *The Life and Growth of Language.* New York: D. Appleton and Company.

2

BACKGROUND

Most branches of science that obtain their data from the observation of human behavior draw a distinction between what the human organism _knows_ and what it _does_. In linguistics this is referred to as the difference between the _competence_ and the _performance_ of the speaker-hearer. Competence is the intrinsic, largely unconscious knowledge underlying our ability to speak and to understand what is spoken. Performance is the way this intrinsic knowledge is applied in a given case. The study of competence may be regarded as the study of the potential performance of an idealized, "perfect" speaker-hearer. The actual performance of a speaker-hearer is affected by nonlinguistic factors such as distraction, memory limitation, and emotions. The difference is crucial to an understanding of what a generative grammar is supposed to represent, and such understanding in turn is necessary for the material on historical linguistics to be presented in the remainder of the book.

2.1 COMPETENCE AND PERFORMANCE

Let us consider a nonlinguistic example. Suppose we wished to formulate a theory of arithmetic ability based on observation of educated adults. For simplicity's sake we shall deal with addition only.

The starting point toward such a theory of addition is the observation of humans in the act of doing sums. We note that our subjects can add certain integers with no apparent difficulty, e.g. $9 + 8 = 17$, $3 + 2 = 5$, that they have some slight trouble with larger pairs of integers, e.g. $128 + 52 = 180$, and that for still larger integers they resort to pencil and paper to keep track of inter- mediate results, e.g.

$$\begin{array}{r} 658 \\ + 1798 \\ \hline 2456 \end{array}$$

Observations such as these are the raw material—the *primary data*— available to us in developing a theory that correctly accounts for the exact form and substance of the underlying knowledge involved in addition. By "correctly" we mean that our theory not only gives the right sum for any pair of integers but also is the psychologically correct version of this intrinsic knowledge.

In this sense, certain theories of arithmetic competence in humans are clearly wrong—for example, the theory that the human brain has large addition tables stored within its cells, and that the competence underlying addition consists of a table-lookup procedure. Given any two integers, we just look through these tables until we find the one appropriate for the two integers and read off the result. This theory might be taken seriously at least in the initial stages of our work since it could be made to predict the right answers. Moreover, it would reasonably account for one aspect of the primary data: that our subjects tend to take more time carrying out addition as the numbers become larger. Under our tentatively proposed theory the longer time could be attributed to the need to look through more of the internalized tables.

But this theory of competence is falsified (i.e. shown to be incontrovertibly wrong) by at least one crucial piece of evidence: the competence of human beings to produce an infinite number of arithmetic results. There is simply no upper limit to the sums we can in principle produce. No matter what two integers we are supplied with, we can calculate their sum in a finite amount of time. Suppose someone were to claim that the upper limit to the sums a human being can produce is 145,987,823,975,576. I could merely add 1 to this, obtaining 145,987,823,975,577. Since the brain, though it has immensely many cells, does not have an infinite number, and since human beings *can* in principle generate a number of sums in excess of any finite number, it is obvious that we can produce more sums than can be stored in the brain. Our rather simple-minded table-lookup theory of arithmetic ability must be wrong.

Various theories that do not entail infinite brain capacity can be envisioned. For example, we might assume that addition is based on a combination of two basically simple operations: one is a table-lookup within a finite, even small, table; the other is a recursive (i.e. repeatable) process requiring a small amount of temporary storage capacity. We assume that the brain has in permanent storage an addition table of the form $m + n$, where m and n are integers from 0 to 9. Addition of two integers each of which is less than 10, say 6 and 3, is carried out by table-lookup within this small table (small since it has only 100 entries). Addition of integers larger than 9 consists of a lookup in this table, temporary storage of this result as well as of the "carry," repeated table-lookup, and so forth with repeated application of these two processes. This procedure, which resembles what children are taught to do in school, can best be illustrated with a simple example.

Suppose we add 29 and 34. First we obtain $9 + 4 = 13$ by table-lookup since both 9 and 4 are integers less than 10. We store the 3 in our result cell in the rightmost position and store the 1 in a temporary "carry" cell. This corresponds to the initial step "9 plus 4 equals 3 carry 1" in the language of the elementary schoolroom, or

$$
\begin{array}{r}
1 \\
34 \\
+\ 29 \\
\hline
3
\end{array}
$$

Next we obtain $3 + 2 = 5$ by table-lookup, and this 5 is added (via table-lookup) to the 1 left over from the previous addition, yielding 6. This result is then entered in the position second from left in the result cell, which now contains the final answer 63.

Such an account of arithmetic facility is not incorrect in the way that the theory of mere table-lookup was. It assumes only a finite amount of storage capacity, yet can reasonably account for our ability to produce arbitrarily large sums by finitely many applications of simple processes. We must ask ourselves, however, whether this is an account of competence in the technical sense of that word. Our proposed theory is free, to be sure, of gross performance factors such as whether the subject shouted or whispered his answers when asked to add, whether he mumbled them, whether he made a mistake when momentarily distracted by a pretty girl. All these things are clearly performance factors: they affect given acts of addition, but they have nothing to do with the intrinsic knowledge of a person who has learned to add.

But in a more interesting sense it is by no means obvious that our theory is one of competence and not of performance. Is it not possible and even likely that we have a quasi-performance model, stripped of the grossest performance factors but in reality far removed from what actually goes on psychologically when someone adds two numbers? Haven't we done what is usually done as the first step in the history of any science—namely, haven't we simply equated appearance with reality, assuming that what we see on the surface is really what *is*? All we can assert is that our account meets the level of *observational adequacy*: it describes the data on which it is based (Chomsky and Halle 1965:99). Let us now briefly consider another possible candidate for a theory.

We might assume that the correct account of the tacit knowledge underlying addition is more abstract, less tangible, than assumed in the previous theory. We might assume further that arithmetic involves repetition of a procedure which we may call the "successor operation." The "successor" of an integer is the next larger integer: the successor of 2 is 3, the successor of 298 is 299. Therefore, given two integers, for example 28 and 52, we may propose that their sum is obtained by means of 52 consecutive applications of the successor operation to 28: $28 + 1 = 29$ (one application), $29 + 1 = 30$ (two applications), . . . , $78 + 1 = 79$ (fifty-one applications), $79 + 1 = 80$ (fifty-two applications and halt). This account also requires only a finite amount of storage capacity and permits the addition of any two integers in finitely many steps.

Again, we note that this theory meets the level of observational adequacy and that it is not a performance model in the trivial sense of performance: it makes no predictions about how a particular act of addition is carried out (i.e. whether accompanied by grunting, whether pencil and paper are used, whether the subject said "81" when he meant to say "80"). This account of arithmetic ability is more abstract, further from the primary data of observation, from the surface aspect of addition, and closer to an account of what really takes place when we add two integers.

Both theories lay claim to our consideration since there is no immediately apparent piece of data which falsifies either one. Both are simple, fairly plausible accounts of the ability to add. Either is falsified if it violates some known external constraint on the human neural system or if data exist that are incompatible with the theory. Whether either is anywhere near psychologically correct is outside the bounds of the present discussion. If we were interested in pursuing the question further, we would have to marshal a great deal of collateral evidence relevant to the following questions. Does one theory accord better with our set of intuitions about addition? Are there psychological experiments that might let us penetrate deeper? Does the time required to do a sum lend reasonableness to one theory but not the other? Further, have we been misled by external appearances to incorporate performance factors in what we intended to be a theory of competence?

Let us turn to linguistics, to which much of the preceding discussion is immediately relevant, though arithmetic ability and linguistic ability are crucially different in a number of essential and interesting ways. Our goal in linguistics is the construction of a grammar: the correct account of the linguistic competence of the native speaker-hearer of a language. Note well that this goal is a matter of choice. Other choices of goals are possible and in fact have been made. It might be proposed that the goal of linguistic inquiry is to devise the best way of reducing languages to writing, though it is doubtful whether anyone ever has made any such outlandish suggestion. In principle there is no objection to a choice like this; one can only observe that it seems overly limiting and not very interesting.

We take then as our immediate goal in linguistics the formulation of a correct account of the speaker's intrinsic knowledge of his language—the system of rules that determine a connection of sound and meaning for each sentence in the language. This account is of the speaker's *competence*, not his *performance*. Whether he enunciates sloppily, whether he breaks off in mid-sentence and starts on a new topic, whether he (as a speaker of English) varies the amount of aspiration on his word-initial *p*'s—all these matters of performance are not within the accountability of the grammar.

This is not to imply that linguistics is unconcerned with questions of performance. Rather, we consider a performance theory as contingent on a competence theory, and consequently, since so much remains to be done even in the area of competence, we regard accounts of competence as the immediate goal. The testability of a linguistic theory, however, requires that linguists and psycholinguists determine precisely what belongs to performance and what to competence. After all, it is through performance and the judgments associated with performance that we gain insight into competence, and it would not be surprising to find aspects of performance carried over by error or oversight into our accounts of competence. As with arithmetic ability, it is not always apparent where competence leaves off and performance begins.

The distinction between competence and performance, a necessary dichotomy in the investigation of any aspect of complex human behavior, has always existed in linguistics. It has in fact been observed almost universally, though only recently has it been so explicitly formulated and insisted upon. Saussure's famous distinction between *langue* and *parole* is partially analogous to competence and performance, though one need not accept those aspects of his *langue* (competence) that are essentially social, nor subscribe to Saussure's larger conception of language as a system of elements whose values are determined by all other elements in the system. In any case, when writing grammars, linguists have always stripped away at least the grossest of performance factors. No one has ever written parallel accounts of Hindi entitled *A Grammar of Hindi*; *A Grammar of Hindi As Spoken When Excited*; and so on.

Rather, linguists have always tried to describe what a speaker intuitively "knows," not how he uses that knowledge in this or that set of circumstances. This knowledge has universally been assumed to be present in some form or other, though not always consciously available to the speaker. A grammar—

i.e. a formal account of competence—should provide a starting point for formulating and testing theories of performance, but the grammar qua formal account of competence makes no direct commitment vis-à-vis performance.

We may now determine from our arithmetic example to what extent theory construction for arithmetic ability parallels construction of a grammar. What are the data of linguistics? They are in part quite similar to those involved in arithmetic: observations, usually in the form of phonetic transcription. But in linguistics there are other kinds of less tangible observations which are nonetheless relevant data. These are intuitive judgments of the native speaker, of which statements like the following are a tiny sample: "The sentences *John saw Mary* and *Mary was seen by John* are related, whereas *John saw Mary* and *Harry eats apples* are not." "There is something peculiar about the plurals of English nouns like *foot, goose, child*, and *woman*." "The sentence *Martin found the boy studying in the library* has several different interpretations." In other words, the native speaker of a language has acquired intuitions about his language that, along with his observable phonetic behavior, constitute an area of accountability of a theory of linguistic competence.

In common with accounts of arithmetic competence, a grammar must permit an infinity of results (sentences) with only finite means. For: (1) there is no upper bound to the number or length of sentences that a human being can in principle produce and understand (i.e. speakers can produce and hearers can understand new and novel sentences without any particular difficulty, and given most declarative sentences one can make a longer sentence by, for instance, preceding the sentence with *It is a fact that*), and (2) the brain is finite in capacity.

A grammar in the sense of "formal account of competence" must, given any particular sentence, state precisely and mechanically the steps involved in connecting meaning and sound. Such grammars are called *generative grammars*. Examples of grammars that are not explicit are abundant: for example, any school grammar of German, French, or Russian. Rather than describing the competence that underlies speech and linguistic judgments, pedagogical grammars generally give the paradigms and lexical items from which the reader can generalize to produce utterances not given in the paradigms and examples. Such a procedure is effective enough for learning languages, but it is obviously inadequate as an explicit account of the knowledge underlying the speaker-hearer's ability to use and produce an infinity of utterances.

The given substance for our work as linguists consists then of the primary data (roughly equivalent with phonetic observations about speech), linguistic judgments, and the external constraint that our theory must have a recursive property—i.e. must give explicit directions for producing an infinite set of utterances given only a finite number of rules and lexical entries (morphemes). Parts of all this have obvious analogues in our discussion of arithmetic competence, and we will now proceed to the framing of first accounts of linguistic competence, but not before one crucial difference between arithmetic and linguistic investigation has been pointed out.

Arithmetic ability, because it is taught, can be consciously recreated to some extent: we can simply ask a subject how he does sums and he will tell us exactly what steps he goes through. This is not possible in linguistics. No linguist would get anywhere by asking someone exactly how he produces the sentence *John and Mary are going to get married.* Linguistic ability is acquired unconsciously as one part of the maturation process of a child, as is visual perception and crawling. We aren't taught such things the way arithmetic is taught and the knowledge underlying these processes is not available to our consciousness.

Notwithstanding this essential difference between arithmetic and linguistic ability, much of our account of arithmetic competence carries over easily to linguistics. We exclude performance data where possible and consider various plausible accounts of linguistic competence. An account that describes a finite corpus of primary data is said to meet the level of *observational adequacy.* A grammar that gives a correct account of the primary data *and* of the speaker's tacit knowledge—his intuitions and judgments about his language—is said to meet the level of *descriptive adequacy.* A descriptively adequate grammar, then, is both a physically correct account of the primary data and the psychologically correct account of the knowledge underlying these data and the linguistic judgments of the speaker-hearer. A linguistic theory (not a grammar) is said to meet the level of *explanatory adequacy* if it provides a principled basis for the selection of descriptively adequate grammars. Given any number of observationally adequate grammars, explanatory adequacy selects the descriptively adequate grammar.

To decide which of two observationally adequate grammars (or even grammar fragments) is closest in form and substance to the descriptively adequate account of the competence of the speaker is in practice extremely difficult, and in particular much more difficult than determining whether observational adequacy has been met. The latter problem is essentially a matter of goodness-of-fit between what the grammar predicts and the primary data, whereas the determination of descriptive adequacy is bound up with language acquisition and its numerous psychological factors. Hence no entirely explanatorily adequate theory is likely to be forthcoming in the near future. At any stage of psychological research and linguistic knowledge, we are not apt to know which grammar best recapitulates our true linguistic competence. Nevertheless, it is crucial to the development and refinement of linguistic theory to have in it an evaluation measure to enable us to pick out of any number of observationally adequate grammars the one that best attains the level of descriptive adequacy.

This conception of the goals of linguistic theory clearly moves linguistics into an intimate relationship with psychology, especially cognitive psychology that deals with the child's acquisition of language. Given a finite set of heard utterances, a child develops a system of internalized rules which we call his linguistic competence. Similarly, under conditions such as those of the elementary classroom he develops a system of rules which we call his arithmetic competence. As linguists (or as students of arithmetic cognition) we can devise many observationally adequate accounts of the primary data. But which of these most closely resembles the one that has actually been constructed in his mind in the form of rules, elements, and so on? A theory approaches explanatory adequacy to the extent with which it offers a principled (i.e. not ad hoc) basis for making such a choice. Obviously we are very far removed from attaining explanatory adequacy on a large scale, and in fact we are very happy when we can bring it to bear even in a gross way on a given decision in linguistics; but this should not dim the insight that the relevance of linguistics to the other fields of human behavior grows in direct proportion to the degree of attainment of explanatory adequacy. And in linguistics proper our success in determining the descriptively adequate grammar of a language is directly proportional to the degree of explanatory adequacy of our linguistic theory.

Here and elsewhere in this book a systematic ambiguity is often used in speaking of a "grammar" (cf. Chomsky and Halle 1968:3–4). On the one hand, we mean the speaker's internally represented and organized body of intrinsic linguistic knowledge—his competence. On the other hand, we mean by "grammar" also the linguist's account of this competence—his formal, explicit, written account. The latter is a set of rules, elements, and so on, often written on paper; the former is immensely abstract and complex knowledge contained in the human organism. Until our evaluation measures are vastly more refined and explicit than they are now, there is no reason to suppose that there is point for point correspondence between the two.

In other words, the speaker has an internalized grammar—a competence—and the linguist's grammar is a *model* of this competence. The difference between these two uses of the word "grammar" will become important when we speak of linguistic change, for we will make statements of the sort, "Clearly what has happened here is that a rule has been added to the grammar of the speaker of Quechua." We do not mean that the speaker of Quechua has somehow consciously stuck a rule into his head thereby changing his (internalized) grammar. What we mean is that the primary data have become different between two types of Quechua, say two dialects or two chronologically distinct stages of the language; that is, the data—the phonological alternations in the languages, the positions of elements in the sentence, perhaps some judgment of the speaker—are different in a systematic way. *Our* account of this difference is best described in terms of rule addition to the grammar. When we add the rule, our model of the competence of the Quechua speaker becomes current.

The distinction of competence and performance is crucial not only to our notion of what a generative grammar is and is not, but in historical linguistics is specifically crucial to our conception of linguistic change. Within generative grammar, change is regarded as change *in competence*, not just in performance. Change occurs because the grammar of the language has changed, and the largely random effects of performance have nothing to do with it. It is perhaps this empirically based conviction, rather than others which might be mentioned, that sets off the conception of historical linguistics within generative grammar from its conception within other linguistic traditions. This point will be argued and illustrated in Chapter 5. See also Postal (1968:271–281).

Finally, let us take brief cognizance of the role of linguistic universals in both general and historical linguistics. It is often observed that languages from all over the world share a surprisingly large number of common features. In phonology many five-vowel languages have the vowels /i u e o a/, but few if any have /i e ü œ æ/. The consonants /p t k s n/ are rarely absent in a language. Such properties of language, such " linguistic universals," determine the class of possible natural languages and the class of potential grammars for some particular language. We assume that these universal properties are in some way available to the child and that they are an integral part of the evaluation measure that selects for the child the best (descriptively adequate) grammar of his language. In this sense the search for linguistic universals is almost coterminous with the study of the innate ability that makes language acquisition in children possible in so short a time under conditions far from ideal (Chomsky and Halle 1968:4).

It is obvious to anyone acquainted with the state of current general linguistic theory that we are far from secure in our knowledge of any large body of linguistic universals. But their importance is not lessened nor should our concern for them be diminished. These assertions are equally valid for historical linguistics, where every aspect of work draws on our knowledge of what is universal in language—what is possible and likely in a natural language, what processes of change may be assumed as plausible.

Appeals to universals are most patent in linguistic reconstruction, where at every step toward the recovery of earlier structure we must ask ourselves whether the reconstructed stage is possible in terms of what we know to be generally true of natural languages—i.e. to be linguistic universals or near-universals. Any linguist who found himself reconstructing a proto-language with the two-vowel system /ɨ e/ would do well to keep the news to himself unless the evidence for his reconstruction was uncommonly good. Why? Because the languages we know do not have vowel systems like this. Similarly, we would have a lot more faith in the reconstructed five-vowel system /i u e o a/ than /u ɨ ʌ œ æ/, because the latter is more highly marked, more complex than the former (Chomsky and Halle 1968:409).

In another subfield of historical linguistics, that of genetic relationship, our judgments are obviously heavily influenced by knowledge of the universal properties of language. For example, no linguist is likely to be impressed by the argument that two languages are genetically related because the word for 'father' in each begins with a labial obstruent such as [p]. Jakobson (1941) has shown that children, whatever their language, acquire sounds in a largely predictable order ([p] being one of the first) dependent not on external factors like frequency of exposure but only on the intrinsic complexity of sounds. For universal reasons, therefore, totally unrelated languages may have words beginning with [p] or [m] to designate those beings on whom a child is initially most dependent.

Our work as historical linguists is narrowly constrained by our judgments of what is and what is not a universal property of natural language, and we can expect the progress of historical linguistics to be closely connected with the search for linguistic universals.

2.2   THE FORM OF A GRAMMAR

Following Chomsky (1965:15–18) and Chomsky and Halle (1968:6–7), we shall assume that the grammar of any language must have the following major components:

(1) a syntactic component, consisting of
   (a) a base component, and
   (b) a transformational component;

(2) a semantic component;

(3) a phonological component.

The position of these components in the grammar may be represented schematically as in Figure 2.1.

The *base rules* and the *lexicon* make up the *base component* of the grammar. Various other rules, such as the "readjustment rules" which relate syntax to phonology (Chomsky and Halle 1968:10), are not discussed here.

THE BASE RULES.   This system of rules generates the restricted set of basic sentence types in the language together with the structural description that is associated with each basic sentence type. The base rules thus correspond in part to the phrase-structure rules or constituent-structure rules of earlier formulations of transformational grammar (Bach 1964:33–53 and Chomsky 1957:26–33). The structural description may be represented in part by a labeled branching diagram or phrase-marker, as in Figure 2.2.

The output of the base component is the deep structure of the sentence. Figure 2.2 represents a portion of the deep structure of the sentence whose ultimate phonetic representation would be approximately [a·y tʰo·wl jæk tʰə kʰʌ·m] 'I told Jack to come'. A number of operations would have to be performed on the deep structure of Figure 2.2 to obtain from it this

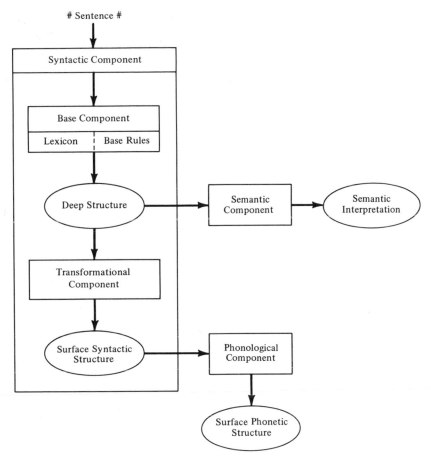

FIGURE 2.1

ORGANIZATION OF A TRANSFORMATIONAL GENERATIVE GRAMMAR

phonetic surface structure. Transformational rules would delete the second occurrence of *Jack*, convert Pres to *to*, and carry out various other rearrangements in the string produced by the base component. The phonological component contains rules that specify the final phonetic form of this utterance.

THE LEXICON. This component of the base is identifiable in part with the traditional notion of dictionary. It consists of a list of the morphemes of the language and the information that characterizes the behavior of each morpheme at all levels. A partial statement of such information for each morpheme would be the redundancy-free underlying phonological shape expressed as a matrix of distinctive features, its syntactic category, information required for the semantic interpretation of the sentence, any individual peculiarities that

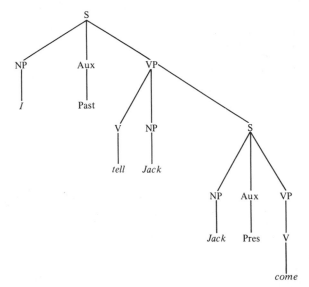

(The abbreviations used here are as follows: S = Sentence, NP = Noun Phrase, Aux = Auxiliary, VP = Verb Phrase, V = Verb. The italicized items such as *I*, *tell*, and *Jack* are taken from the lexicon.)

FIGURE 2.2

PHRASE-MARKER FOR *I told Jack to come.*

make the morpheme violate constraints normally placed on morphemes of its general type. To illustrate a typical entry in the lexicon, and at the same time to emphasize the abstract nature of the phonological representation of morphemes, consider the deep structure for the sentence *Divinity may frighten the boy* (cf. Chomsky 1965:108–109 for a similar example), shown in Figure 2.3.

Entries such as *divinity*, *may*, *frighten*, and *boy* in this deep structure come from the lexicon. The item *divinity* has a lexical representation that the following approximates:

(divīn + i + ty   [+ Noun, + Determiner ____, − Count,

+ Abstract, . . .])

That is, the noun *divinity*, whose underlying phonological representation is representable informally as /divīn + i + ty/ where + stands for "morpheme boundary," is not a Count Noun but an Abstract Noun, and so on. The three dots ... cover the host of other properties that characterize the behavior, syntactic, semantic, and phonological, of the particular noun *divinity*.

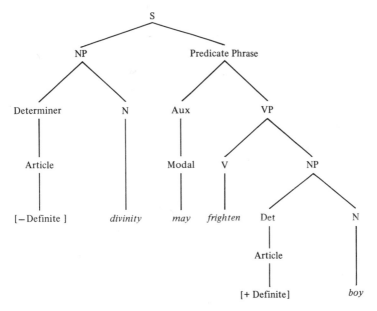

FIGURE 2.3
PHRASE-MARKER FOR *Divinity may frighten the boy.*

The spelling /divīn+i+ty/ is, as mentioned, only an informal representation of the phonological shape. Its true representation in the lexicon is a sequence of bundles of distinctive features—the minimum set of distinctive feature specifications needed to account for the final phonetic shape of this word, namely [dĭvínĭtiy]. Thus, *divinity* appears in the lexicon in a representation that Figure 2.4 approximates.

The distinctive features used in specifying these segments and boundaries are taken from Chomsky and Halle (1968). Further discussion of distinctive features will follow under the rubric of the phonological component.

Associated with the lexicon is a set of *contingency statements*, which fill out redundant feature specifications in the lexical representations of morphemes (cf. Stanley 1967). These statements, which correspond to the rules of the morpheme-structure component of earlier formulations of generative phonology (Harms 1968), specify two kinds of redundancy. First, they specify segmental redundancies of the sort embodied in statements such as: all vowels, nasals, and resonants in English receive the specification [+ voice]; vowels specified as [+ back] in English are redundantly [+ round]. Second, they fill out the redundancies that result from sequential constraints on the occurrences of segments. In English, if the second C in the morpheme-initial sequence +CC is an obstruent, then the first C must be [s] (as in *spin*); if the second consonant is a liquid, then the first C must be an obstruent (*play*, *crime*).

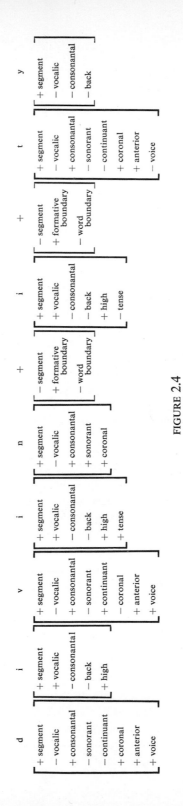

FIGURE 2.4

PHONOLOGICAL REPRESENTATION OF *divinity* IN THE LEXICON

The phonological representation of morphemes in the lexicon is thus extremely abbreviated and quite abstract. Redundancy statements add features to the redundancy-free representations and produce fully specified distinctive feature matrices which then are the input to the phonological component of the grammar.

It should be noted that the structure of the lexicon is currently subject to much debate. For example, for a variety of reasons phonological representations in the lexicon should be stated in terms of *marked* and *unmarked* values of features rather than strictly in terms of pluses and minuses, as was done above in accordance with phonological practice current through the mid 1960's. For a preliminary discussion of this question see Chomsky and Halle 1968:400–435).

THE SEMANTIC COMPONENT. This component assigns semantic interpretations to the deep structure generated by the base component. These interpretations, called "readings," correspond to the traditional notion of "possible meanings of an utterance." Although semantic change is of great intrinsic interest in historical linguistics, this book has nothing to say about it. For discussion of the semantic component of a grammar see Katz and Fodor (1963) and Katz and Postal (1964).

THE TRANSFORMATIONAL COMPONENT. The rules in this part of the grammar convert the deep structure generated by the base component into the surface syntactic structure. Some transformations have been alluded to in the discussion of the base. In general, transformations effect changes in the order of elements in the underlying string produced by the base, insert elements into the string, delete others—in short, all changes required in producing the surface syntactic structure from the deep structure of a sentence. Literature on the transformational component is now voluminous, cf. Bach (1964), Katz and Postal (1964), and Chomsky (1957, 1965), and acquaintance with its operation is assumed.

THE PHONOLOGICAL COMPONENT. The rules in this component of the grammar act on the surface-structure syntactic string produced by the syntactic component and provide a phonetic interpretation for the sentence represented by this string. Let us consider again the example *Divinity may frighten the boy* (cf. Figure 2.3).

Rules in the transformational component are required to specify the shape of [− Definite] in various contexts. [− Definite] is realized as null before the [− Count] noun *divinity*, and [+ Definite] is realized as *the*, phonologically /ði/, before *boy*, which is [+ Count]. When these and any other required transformations have been carried out, the string which leaves the syntactic component as input to the phonological component will have a structure as in Figure 2.5:

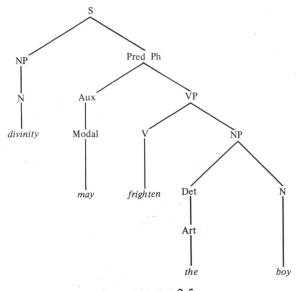

FIGURE 2.5

SURFACE SYNTACTIC STRUCTURE OF
Divinity may frighten the boy.

or equivalently as:

$$[_S[_{NP}[_N + divinity +]_N]_{NP}[_{Pred\text{-}Ph}[_{Aux}[_{Modal} + may +]_{Modal}]_{Aux}[_{VP}[_V +$$
$$frighten +]_V[_{NP}[_{Det}[_{Art} + the +]_{Art}]_{Det}[_N + boy +]_N]_{NP}]_{VP}]_{Pred\text{-}Ph}]_S$$

In addition to the syntactic information retained in this representation, any data relevant to a single morpheme are carried over from the lexicon. If, for example, some lexical item in this string is an exception to a particular phonological rule (perhaps because that item has recently been borrowed from a foreign source, or for any reason whatsoever), then this information is retained in the string entering the phonological component and treated as a signal that the aberrant morpheme is not to undergo the rule that would normally apply.

In general, syntactic information is necessary for the operation of at least certain phonological rules. English, as well as German and various other languages, has a set of rules that assign stress. These rules operate cyclically, in "the transformational cycle," and syntactic bracketing is required for their operation. On the transformational cycle see Chomsky and Halle (1968:59–162) and Harms (1968).

Rules that require syntactic information are applied as the first set of rules in the phonological component. As they are applied, the syntactic bracketing is "erased" from the underlying representation. After the last phonological rules in the cycle have been applied, syntactic information is not available for the phonological rules which follow. At this point in the derivation of the sentence *Divinity may frighten the boy*, we are left with a string of phonological elements which may be represented as

$$\# \# \text{div}\bar{\imath}\text{n}+\text{i}+\text{ty} \# \# \text{m}\bar{\text{æ}} \# \# \text{fr}\bar{\imath}\text{t}+\text{n} \# \# \eth\text{i} \# \# \text{b}\bar{\text{æ}} \# \#$$

The symbol # represents *word boundary*, the symbol + represents *morpheme boundary*, and formatives such as *divinity* and *may* are presented in an orthography intended to convey their underlying phonological representations. For explanation of the not immediately obvious aspects of these phonological base forms, e.g. /bǣ/ for surface phonetic [bəy], see Chomsky and Halle (1968).

The remaining phonological rules may be divided into two blocks: (1) the phonological rules proper, which convert the underlying systematic phonological representation into a "low-level" phonetic representation, and (2) phonetic rules that assign detailed phonetic specifications to the previously obtained string of phonological segments. The rules in the first block of rules are assumed to operate on and produce segments stated in terms of *binarily specified* (either + or −, but no other value) distinctive features. The second block of rules produces segments whose intersecting set of distinctive features may contain *n-ary* values of these features: not necessarily only + and −, but values specified in terms of a sequence of integers.

Returning to the underlying phonological representation of *Divinity may frighten the boy*, phonological rules will carry out many kinds of changes needed to obtain the surface phonetic structure. These rules are discussed and motivated in depth in Chomsky and Halle (1968), and here they will be only indicated in brief. Phonological rules would diphthongize /ī/ > [ay], as in /frīt+n/ > [fraytn], another rule would lax /ī/ > [ɪ] under certain conditions, as in /divīn+i+ty/ > [dɪvɪnitiy], and so on. (Here a condition has been introduced and will be followed concerning the use of solidi / / and square brackets [ ]. Solidi enclose systematic phonological segments—the informally designated symbols used to spell items in the lexicon. Square brackets enclose segments that have been produced by rules in the phonological component of the grammar.)

We will state phonological rules in terms of distinctive features, but for convenience each rule will be followed by a plain English statement of what the rule does. The present book depends on a particular set of phonological features only in a rather peripheral way. Mostly we will be concerned with rules and various sorts of rule phenomena. It is understood that the basic units manipulated by these rules are distinctive features, but the use of any particular set of features is not crucial. For this reason, the features used throughout this book are (with one or two exceptions) chosen to minimize difficulty for the reader who has not undergone and mastered the vicissitudes of shifting feature terminology during the 1960's. For vowels, for example, the familiar features *high, low, back, round, tense,* and *long* are used. For consonants the features used in the majority of rules should not create problems for anyone acquainted with phonetic terminology: e.g. *nasal, continuant, lateral, palatalized,* and *voiced.* The features *obstruent, vocalic,* and *consonantal* are used to define the major natural classes of segments as follows:

	vowels	*obstruents*	*nasals*	*resonants*	*glides*
obstruent:	−	+	−	−	−
vocalic:	+	−	−	+	−
consonantal:	−	+	+	+	−

Thus, the class of vowels is defined by $\begin{bmatrix} + \text{ vocalic} \\ - \text{ consonantal} \end{bmatrix}$; the class of obstruents (true consonants such as *p d k s ǰ*) is defined by [+obstruent]; *r* and *l* are $\begin{bmatrix} + \text{ vocalic} \\ + \text{ consonantal} \end{bmatrix}$; and glides such as *j* and *w* are $\begin{bmatrix} - \text{ vocalic} \\ - \text{ consonantal} \end{bmatrix}$.

The features *anterior* and *coronal* (adopted from Chomsky and Halle 1968) for consonants require some explanation. *Anterior,* which is identical with *diffuse* for consonants in earlier distinctive feature theory, describes sounds produced with an obstruction located in front of the palato-alveolar region of the mouth. Thus, the following classes of sounds are [+ anterior]: labials (*p b m*), alveolar and dental consonants (*t d n*); and the following are [− anterior]: palato-alveolars (*č ǰ ñ*), velars and uvulars (*k g ŋ x*). Coronal sounds are produced with the blade of the tongue raised from the neutral position. Labials, velars, palatals, and uvulars are [− coronal], whereas dentals and palato-alveolars are [+ coronal]. Dental [r] is [+ coronal], and uvular [R] is [− coronal].

Often, for the sake of convenience, we will write V and C to denote respectively the natural classes of "vowels" and "consonants." Thus, the segment

$$\begin{bmatrix} V \\ + \text{ high} \\ + \text{ round} \\ + \text{ back} \\ - \text{ long} \end{bmatrix}$$

designates a vowel which is high, round, back, and short—i.e. [u]. The feature columns

$$
\begin{bmatrix}
\text{C} \\
+\text{ anterior} \\
-\text{ coronal} \\
+\text{ nasal}
\end{bmatrix}
\quad
\begin{bmatrix}
\text{C} \\
+\text{ anterior} \\
+\text{ coronal} \\
-\text{ continuant} \\
+\text{ voice}
\end{bmatrix}
\quad
\begin{bmatrix}
\text{C} \\
-\text{ anterior} \\
-\text{ coronal} \\
+\text{ continuant} \\
-\text{ voice}
\end{bmatrix}
$$

could refer (depending on the language and what segments occur in the language) respectively to [m], [d], and [x].

The segments or natural classes stated so far contain distinctive features marked either plus or minus. The n-ary rules, the rules that assign detailed phonetic specification to segments, will assign more than binary specifications of features where needed. In English, for example, both [a] and [ɔ] are [+ back], but [ɔ] is typically more back than [a]. Hence, a rule in the last block of rules in the phonological component—the set of rules that assign final, detailed phonetic specifications—will assign [ɔ] a higher backness value than [a]. The conventions for such assignments are not well established, but the principle involved may be indicated by assuming that a phonetic rule will assign the value [+2 back] to [ɔ] and [+1 back] to [a].

For a detailed discussion of the phonological component of a grammar see Harms (1968) and Chomsky and Halle (1968). Putting aside questions of the formal appearance of the phonological component, we may say that its content represents a set of generalizations about the phonological structure of a language. These generalizations are stated in the form of rules that act on underlying abstract representations of sentences to produce a phonetic interpretation.

The chief source of evidence for deciding which rules to posit is provided by phonological alternation—or, as it is often called, morphophonemic alternation—in the language. The presence of phonological alternation is usually an indication that a generalization can be extracted by positing a common underlying form and positing a rule or set of rules that accounts for the phonetic realizations of the members of the alternation. In German, voiceless obstruents word-finally alternate with voiced obstruents in non-word-final position: *Rad* [ra:tʰ] 'wheel' versus *Rades* [ra:dəs] 'of the wheel', *Tag* [tʰa:kʰ] 'day' versus *Tage* [tʰa:gə] 'days', *Gras* [gra:s] 'grass' versus *Grases* [gra:zəs] 'of the grass'. This completely general phonological alternation supports the decision to derive both forms participating in such alternations from common phonemic sources; that is, both the [tʰ] in *Rad* and the [d] in *Rades* should be derived by rule from a single phonological segment. Whether this segment should be /d/, /t/, or a segment different from either must be determined by simplicity. In the German case, we take the voiced member of the alternation as basic and derive the voiceless member by means of the rule:

$$[+ \text{ obstruent}] \rightarrow [- \text{ voice}]/\underline{\quad\quad} \#$$

(Obstruents are devoiced in word-final position.)

This solution provides derivations like the following:

Underlying Form:	/rad	rades	tag	tage	graz	grazes/
Devoicing:	rat	....	tak	....	gras	....
Phonetic Form:	[ra:tʰ	ra:dəs	tʰa:kʰ	tʰa:gə	gra:s	gra:zəs]

(This partial derivation is presented only to show how the voiceless/voiced alternation arises. Other phonological rules would be required to account for the lengthening of the vowel, for the occurrence of [ə], and for the aspiration occurring in various positions.)

It is crucially important to understand that the devoicing rule is included in the synchronic grammar of German because of certain facts about German today, not because terminal devoicing occurred in the historical development of German. Given the voiced/voiceless alternations found in modern standard German, the simplest way of accounting for them is to include a rule of terminal devoicing in the grammar. We may call this a "late" rule meaning that it need not necessarily precede certain rules in German and must in fact be placed close to the end of the set of ordered rules comprising the phonological component. It just so happens that the devoicing rule entered the grammar of German a long time ago—slightly less than a thousand years. Chronologically, this makes devoicing a rather early rule compared with others found in the grammar of modern German, but this does not alter our judgment that terminal devoicing is a rule in the synchronic sense and a late rule at that.

2.3 POSTSCRIPT

It should be emphasized that what has been said here about the internal make-up of a transformational generative grammar is tentative in many of the details. Like any serious effort to describe complex modes of human behavior, the theory of generative grammar is not static and unchanging. New perceptions, new data, and old data seen in a new light lead to revisions and corrections in one or the other component. The new predictions, general and particular, created by the new grammar and the theory may in turn bring new data to light, and these data may again suggest new revisions in the grammar and the theory.

This is a natural process in the development of any science. It is natural, it is unavoidable, it is not cause for grief. The general picture presented here of the form of transformational generative grammar is adequate in most points, so far as we know at present, though a considerable lack of clarity exists in details. The line of demarcation between the syntactic and the semantic components, the form of the lexicon, the set of distinctive features—these raise questions as yet unanswered. But despite these uncertainties, this chapter's theory of language and grammar provides much insight into language and, as well, into historical linguistics, to which we now turn.

SUPPLEMENTARY READING

Bach, Emmon. 1964. *An Introduction to Transformational Grammars*. New York: Holt, Rinehart & Winston, Inc.

Chomsky, Noam. 1964. "Current Issues in Linguistic Theory," in *The Structure of Language*, eds. Jerry A. Fodor and Jerrold J. Katz. Englewood Cliffs, N.J.: Prentice-Hall, Inc.

Chomsky, Noam. 1965. *Aspects of the Theory of Syntax*. Cambridge, Mass.: The M.I.T. Press.

Chomsky, Noam, and Morris Halle. 1968. *The Sound Pattern of English*. New York: Harper & Row, Publishers.

Harms, Robert T. 1968. *Introduction to Phonological Theory*. Englewood Cliffs, N.J.: Prentice-Hall, Inc.

Jacobs, Roderick A., and Peter S. Rosenbaum. 1968. *English Transformational Grammar*. Waltham, Mass.: Blaisdell Publishing Company.

Katz, Jerrold J., and Paul M. Postal. 1964. *An Integrated Theory of Linguistic Descriptions*. Cambridge, Mass.: The M.I.T. Press.

Langacker, Ronald W. 1968. *Language and Its Structure*. New York: Harcourt, Brace & World, Inc.

Postal, Paul M. 1968. *Aspects of Phonological Theory*. New York: Harper & Row, Publishers.

3

PRIMARY CHANGE

The topic of central interest in historical linguistics is linguistic change. If languages never changed, clearly no one would be interested in the historical development of languages except in connection with political and social events. Whatever else we may do in the name of historical linguistics, at bottom we are dealing in matters at first or second remove from change in a language or language family. But before saying what we can about linguistic change, we shall make what at first glance seems a detour to concern ourselves with the question of dialects and their differences. This is really not a digression because any change—our paramount concern—is ultimately rooted in the process of two dialects having become different. Dialects, in other words, provide the most direct evidence regarding change at our disposal. Thus, our immediate job is to clarify the notion of difference between related dialects of the same language, for without understanding dialect differences we cannot hope to determine with any precision how those differences have arisen; that is to say, we cannot determine what has changed or indeed for that matter what change really is.

3.1 ON THE DIFFERENTIATION OF DIALECTS

The problem of describing the differences between dialects, especially at the phonological level, was given much attention by linguists during the 1950's, and a great deal of agonizing went on in its behalf. The crux of the dilemma was that dialects seemed to be essentially nondichotomous in structure. They blend almost imperceptibly into one another within a given language area. In fact, dialects seem to constitute a perfect example of the kind of continuity that, as Martin Joos remarked, is "shoved outside of linguistics in one direction or another" (1950:702). Typically, structural linguistics dealt with this sort of continuity by quantizing—by assigning continuous data to a discrete unit such as the autonomous phoneme. (Cf. Postal 1968 on the "autonomous" phoneme.) Thus, the autonomous phoneme /a/ in English was regarded as a discrete abstract unit realized in countless ways all clustering around a phonetic norm [a]. The data on performances of /a/ make up a continuum of observations, yet as structural linguists we would have focused our concern first on procedures which allow us to deal with a finite, and fairly small, number of discrete units such as autonomous phonemes that have a functional role in language. The continuity would be left to phoneticians.

Quantization of this kind is a characteristic and crucial part of American descriptive ("Neo-Bloomfieldian") linguistics, and it is precisely this sort of dichotomous procedure that dialects seem to be the least amenable to. That is to say, dialects seemed inherently beyond the procedures of Saussurean and Bloomfieldian linguistics, both of which assumed that typical units of structural description (phonemes, morphemes) were defined *within an idiolect* by their relationships to all other units in the system of that idiolect.

Let us consider an example. Within autonomous phonemics, the vowel /a/ is a phoneme in my idiolect because it contrasts with the vowels of *pet, pat, put*, and so on. Another speaker of American English may have an autonomous phoneme /a/ that likewise is defined by contrast with other units in his speech. In what sense can one "compare" /a/ in the two idiolects? In what sense is it legitimate to assert that this other speaker and I have the "same" phoneme /a/ in our speech? The only allowable answer in strict descriptive linguistics is "None" unless we have speech patterns that are identical in every single respect, a condition that has never been observed in the speech of any two people anywhere. For the autonomous phoneme /a/ is determined not by the fact that it generally sounds like [a] and thus is similar in realization to /a/ in other idiolects, but by the units it contrasts with in the whole of my speech.

Since the whole of my speech is different, though perhaps only in minute details, from that of anyone else, it necessarily follows that nobody else can possibly have a comparable phoneme /a/. The situation is made more apparent if we assume that I have no barred-*i* phoneme /ɨ/ in my autonomous phonemic inventory whereas the other speaker does. In this case my /a/ is clearly different from his since mine does not have an /ɨ/ to contrast with, and there is no basis for comparison of the "same" sound /a/ in the two idiolects.

In other words, how can we speak of dialect differences and dialect similarities? If we are strict about it, there seems to be no way of incorporating the "emic" units of descriptive linguistics into the description of dialect differences without violating the fundamental proposition of Saussure (which is implicit, though not always explicitly stated, in all schools of descriptive linguistics) that structural units are defined within an idiolect by the web of relationships locking them into the system.

From this strict point of view a number of things desirable in linguistics become impossible. It is impossible to compare two dialects, or two idiolects for that matter. It doesn't even make much sense to say that two dialects are different, since by definition a linguistic description is good for one, and for only one, speaker. And since what is true of dialect differences applies *mutatis mutandis* to differences between chronologically different stages of the same language, then how can we compare the differences between two stages of a language, say between Middle English and Modern English?

If we relax our observance of the Saussurean dictum (though exactly how this can be done is not immediately apparent), then the methods of structural linguistics (and specifically of autonomous phonemics) can be applied to dialects, but this always requires compromise with Saussure's fundamental principle. Several attempts at dissolving the inherent antinomy between dialects and structuralism emerged from the dialogue of the 1950's, and we shall discuss briefly two of these attempts here.

One solution widely subscribed to for a time was the "overall pattern." This was constituted by the minimal set of autonomous phonemes that taken together would account for all of the contrasts found in the speech of any speaker in a given language area. Each dialect, and by implication each idiolect, would then choose some subset of the maximal set of phonemes in the overall pattern.

This way of reconciling structuralism and dialectology has numerous bad consequences, which need not be enumerated here. The theoretical objections are obvious: besides violating the cardinal tenet that each dialect must be analyzed in its own terms without reference to or data from other dialects, what sense does it make to say that someone has in the overall pattern of his language a phoneme that he does not use? Merely because someone in some dialect of American English has phonemic /ɨ/—say on the basis of the usual minimal pair [jɨst] 'just (adverb)' ≠ [jʌst] 'just (adjective)'—must I accept barred-*i* in the description of my speech and transcribe, say, [bɪznɨs] 'business' as /bɪznɨs/, even though for me [ɨ] is an allophone of some other vowel under weak stress and not phonemic? This seems radically counter-intuitive to the notion of "phoneme."

Practically speaking, too, the notion of overall pattern leads to conclusions that seem out of line with our intuitions about language and its structure. Consider the vowel nucleus in a word like *ride*. For a Wisconsinite this might be pronounced [aɪ̯], for the Mississippian [aˤ·ə̯]. In the Trager-Smith (1957) overall pattern we would transcribe these /ay/ and, with a slight modification of the Trager-Smith system, /Ah/, where /A/ stands for a vowel approximately midway between /æ/ and /a/. Thus, the Wisconsinite has phonemic /rayd/ and the Mississippian /rAhd/. The overall pattern transcription shows that the two dialects pronounce the diphthong differently. But what is not stated is that both the Wisconsinite and the Mississippian have in their phonemic inventories only a single diphthong /ay/ contrasting with other diphthongs /aw/ and /oy/, so writing /ay/ for one dialect and /Ah/ for another implies a greater phonemic difference in the structure of the dialects than seems warranted by the data. Indeed, the two dialects have very similar phonemic inventories, and the main differences between them are at the phonetic level. That is, the phonemicizations /ay/ and /Ah/ emphasize dialect difference at the expense of the considerable dialect similarity. One could better say that both dialects have phonemic /ay/ which is realized by the Wisconsinite as [aɪ̯] and the Mississippian as [aˤ·ə̯]. But this shoves whatever systematic pattern exists down into the phonetics of the description, and the eminently *structural* level of description—the phonemic level—fades in relevance to the characterization of the differences between these dialects.

A somewhat different approach to resolving the conflict between dialectology and structural linguistics was proposed in the article "Is a Structural Dialectology Possible?" by Uriel Weinreich (1954). (To be precise, we should say that Weinreich's goal was not so much to reconcile the two as it was to devise ways of accommodating the interests of dialectologists *and* linguists within the field of general linguistics.) His principal contribution was the concept of "diasystem." This is similar to, and in some senses a generalization of, the concept of overall pattern, but with the crucial difference that it characterizes dialect differences by the use of phonemic correspondences and not by the idea that dialects choose from among a set of abstract elements.

To illustrate the idea of diasystem, let us return to our *ride* example. We assume that, except for the difference in pronunciation of the diphthong in words such as *ride*, the Wisconsin and Mississippi dialects are identical; e.g. for *bit* both have [bɪt]. Thus, the two dialects share (in some sense or other which is not specified exactly) the phonemes /b/, /ɪ/, /t/, and all the others, but [aɪ̯] in Wisconsin corresponds to [aˤ·ə̯] in Mississippi. There is only one /ay/

phoneme in either dialect, but its realization is different. The diasystem abstracted from this would be

$$/\!/\,b \approx \text{I} \approx t \approx \cdots \approx \frac{w[a\underline{i}]}{M[a\ulcorner\cdot\underset{\,}{\varrho}]}\,/\!/$$

In this way we obtain a comparison between the two dialects that displays their points of agreement *and* their points of dissimilarity; and this is done without obscuring either the phonetics or the phonemics of the situation. Several objections, however, have been raised against the diasystem. It does not, nor did Weinreich claim that it did, get around the Saussurean riddle. But even if we ignore this forbidding crisis of theory, serious problems in application arise. The chief question is whether we take account of cognate items in the two dialects when we determine the diasystem. Ignoring cognates altogether leads to the absurdity that any two languages with identical phoneme inventories share the same diasystem. For example, Spanish and Standard Yiddish could be regarded as sharing the identical (phonemic) vowel diasystem $/\!/\text{ i} \approx e \approx a \approx o \approx u\,/\!/$. This is obviously an undesirable result since the two are not dialects of the same language. On the other hand, requiring the two dialects to have their variants of the same diaphoneme in cognate items rules out the possibility of setting up a diasystem for different languages like Spanish and Yiddish, but again we are led to counter-intuitive results. This has been demonstrated by Moulton (1960:176–177). By imposing this condition he showed that two Swiss German dialects not fifty miles apart and mutually completely intelligible have no more than three shared diaphonemes (the dialects separately have eleven phonemes each), only one of which is fully shared.

This excursus into the problems of structural dialectology was made in order to point up the fact that it is by no means obvious how structural linguistics (or any theory of linguistics) is relevant to the description of the differentiation of dialects. Our real problem is how to account within a single linguistic theory for the essential fact about dialects—that they are in many ways similar—without unduly emphasizing the undeniable fact that they are in some ways different. The task is not an easy one, as the weaknesses of the overall pattern and the diasystem illustrate.

3.2   DIALECT DIFFERENTIATION IN GENERATIVE GRAMMAR

We shall now examine the implications that the goals and form of generative grammatical theory have for the description of dialect differences—a topic that, let it again be emphasized, is as pertinent to historical linguistics as it is to dialectology.

For the time being we shall confine our attention to phonology. We saw in Chapter 2 that our paramount concern as linguists is with the grammar of a language—the system of rules that account for the native speaker's intuitions about his language and for the primary data. In particular, as regards the phonological component of a grammar, our main questions are (1) what is the set of underlying systematic phonemes?, and (2) what is the set of rules that capture with the greatest generality and economy the observable facts about the phonology of a given language? We saw also that the most direct way of getting at these rules was through the evidence of phonological (morphophonemic) alternation.

Let us now consider a hypothetical example in which two dialects of a language differ in a very minor way. In Dialect A there is an underlying set of five (systematic phonemic) vowels /i e a o u/. The only alternation of any interest at the present is $a : æ$. [æ] occurs after palatalized consonants, [a] elsewhere, e.g. [ap] 'dog' : [t,æp] 'to the dog', where t,– is a prefix for indirect objects (t, denotes a palatalized t). We classify the five underlying segments as follows, where redundant features are enclosed in parentheses:

	i	e	a	o	u
consonantal:	−	−	−	−	−
vocalic:	+	+	+	+	+
high:	+	−	−	−	+
back:	−	−	+	+	+
low:	(−)	(−)	+	−	(−)
round:	(−)	(−)	(−)	(+)	(+)

To account for the $a : æ$ alternation we have the rule:

$$3.1 \quad \begin{bmatrix} - \text{consonantal} \\ + \text{vocalic} \\ + \text{low} \end{bmatrix} \rightarrow [- \text{back}] \, / \, [+ \text{palatalized}] \underline{\hspace{2cm}}$$

(A low vowel is fronted following a segment which is palatalized.)

Next let us assume that Dialect B of this hypothetical language is identical in every respect with Dialect A except that forms having the $a : æ$ alternation in Dialect A have an alternation $o : æ$ in Dialect B before labial consonants, e.g. [op] 'dog' : [t,æp] 'to the dog'. Note that Rule 3.1 affects only the low vowel /a/ in Dialect A. It does not apply to /o/, which is [− low], so that /o/ undergoes no fronting after palatalized consonants in Dialect A, e.g. [op] 'cat' : [t,op] 'to the cat'. Similarly, in Dialect B words containing /o/ corresponding to /o/'s in Dialect A do not enter into any alternation after palatalized consonants; only those pre-labial [o]'s corresponding to [a]'s in Dialect A do this. Thus, Dialect B also has [op] 'cat' : [t,op] 'to the cat'.

How shall we describe the situation in Dialect B? The only real trouble is that some [o]'s alternate with [æ]'s while others do not. It would not do to write 'dog' /op/ in Dialect B and assume operation of Rule 3.1 since this would not yield the correct form [t,æp] 'to the dog'; Rule 3.1 does not affect /o/, so we would get the wrong form *[t,op]. One conceivable solution would be to have two different kinds of /o/ segments in the underlying forms: /o/'s which do not alternate will be a plain /o/, those which do will be marked with an apostrophe, /o'/. To distinguish the two, as we must do in order to make them distinct in lexical morphemes, we will posit a feature "alternating" and classify the segments in Dialect B as follows:

	i	e	o'	o	u
consonantal:	−	−	−	−	−
vocalic:	+	+	+	+	+
high:	+	−	−	−	+
back:	−	−	+	+	+
alternating:	(−)	(−)	+	−	(−)
round:	(−)	(−)	(+)	(+)	(+)

We must now have a more complicated version of Rule 3.1, namely:

$$3.1' \quad \begin{bmatrix} - \text{ consonantal} \\ + \text{ vocalic} \\ + \text{ alternating} \end{bmatrix} \rightarrow \begin{bmatrix} - \text{ back} \\ - \text{ round} \\ + \text{ low} \end{bmatrix} / \, [+ \text{ palatalized}] \, \underline{\quad\quad}$$

(/o'/ becomes [æ] after palatalized segments.)

This solution does seem to account for the intrinsic knowledge of the native speaker of Dialect B that words containing certain kinds of /o/ sounds have grammatically related forms with [æ] when a palatalized consonant precedes. What is wrong with this solution? First, the feature "alternating" is strictly ad hoc, invented for this problem. It is used only to set off one kind of /o/ from another, and it has no discernible physical manifestation since there is no phonetic difference in the two /o/'s. This gives us a completely abstract phonemic representation divorced from the phonetic substance of which phonological alternations consist. The feature "alternating" imposes no natural constraints on phonemic representations like those implicitly imposed by our use of the features "high," "continuant," "back," and so on. A second, related objection to Rule 3.1' is that it disguises tne basic phonetic naturalness of the process taking place in Dialect B. Rule 3.1 in Dialect A expresses a natural process frequently encountered in the languages of the world: a vowel is fronted after a palatalized consonant (Russian has such a rule). Rule 3.1' does not express any such natural process. It states only that a vowel of a certain, not phonetically defined type is fronted, unrounded, and lowered after a palatalized consonant. This is the inevitable result of the use of ad hoc features like "alternating." With them anything is possible, nothing excluded, and no phonological rule is more or less natural than any other.

Let us consider an alternative way of describing the vowel alternation in Dialect B. We posit for this dialect the same five underlying vowels as for Dialect A, and we classify them according to the same specifications for distinctive features. Likewise we include in the grammar of Dialect B the Rule 3.1 (not 3.1'). Up to this point the grammars of the two dialects are identical, but we include additionally in the grammar of Dialect B *after* Rule 3.1 has operated the rule:

$$3.2 \quad \begin{bmatrix} - \text{ consonantal} \\ + \text{ vocalic} \\ + \text{ back} \end{bmatrix} \rightarrow \begin{bmatrix} - \text{ low} \\ + \text{ round} \end{bmatrix} / \underline{\quad\quad} \begin{bmatrix} + \text{ consonantal} \\ + \text{ anterior} \\ - \text{ coronal} \end{bmatrix}$$

(Any back vowel must be not low and must be round preceding labial consonants, i.e. *a* > *o* before labials.)

In Dialect B we will then have the derivations:

Underlying Forms:	ap	t,ap	op	t,op	ep	t,ep
Rule 3.1:	....	t,æp	....	....	....	....
Rule 3.2:	op	....	....	....	....	....
Final Forms:	op	t,æp	op	t,op	ep	t,ep
Glosses:	'dog'	'to the dog'	'cat'	'to the cat'	'fly'	'to the fly'

The word /ep/ 'fly' with its dative form /t,ep/ has been included for the purpose of a later illustration. The grammar of Dialect A has only Rule 3.1; hence the output of this rule gives the proper forms of these words in Dialect A. The output of Rule 3.2, acting on the forms produced by the operation of Rule 3.1, gives the correct forms in Dialect B. For comparison we have:

Dialect A	Dialect B	
ap	op	'dog'
t,æp	t,æp	'to the dog'
op	op	'cat'
t,op	t,op	'to the cat'
ep	ep	'fly'
t,ep	t,ep	'to the fly'

What have we done in analyzing these two dialects and, more important, what have we not done? Our sole aim was to construct a grammar fragment that correctly accounts for certain kinds of vowel alternations in these two dialects. In Dialect A we found that five vowel phonemes are needed to specify the lexical shape of morphemes, and we have posited for that grammar a rule (3.1) that fronts /a/ after a palatalized consonant. We found that Dialect B also has in its inventory of systematic phonemes five underlying vowels—the same five as Dialect A with respect to their distinctive feature specifications—and we have included in the grammar of Dialect B a rule (3.2) that raises and rounds /a/ to [o] and that applies after Rule 3.1.

We have come closer to a treatment of dialect difference that in justice to the intuitive notion of dialect shows a great amount of relatedness between these two dialects: they share similar sets (in this case identical sets) of systematic phonemes; their grammars contain identical rules (Rule 3.1 and by assumption all the other phonological rules); and the final phonetic forms generated by the two grammars are similar and to some extent identical. This latter point is the most salient common-sense characterization of dialect relatedness: they sound pretty much alike, and there is considerable mutual intelligibility. Yet even though we have found that the grammars of the two dialects have much in common, there are differences between the two, which can be stated precisely. Using terms that dialectologists might traditionally apply, the isogloss between these two dialects is defined by a difference in their grammars: one dialect has a rule absent in the other.

There are several noteworthy things we did not do and indeed would not care to do. We did not assume that the two dialects were in some ways similar—that, for example, they had the same set of underlying vowels or that they shared a number of identical rules. Economy and the naturalness of rules (as well as considerations about what distinctive features should be present in a natural language) would induce us to posit an underlying /a/ in the grammar of Dialect B even though there is no [a] sound in the paradigm for 'dog' and irrespective of the fact that Dialect A has a systematic phonemic /a/ which happens to be realized as phonetic [a]. We were led to derive [æ] from underlying /a/ rather than /o/ or /o'/ because we could do so with fewer features and with natural rules. In principle, our linguistic theory would have led us to the same grammars even if we knew only of the existence of the one dialect and not the other. In practice, of course, our expectation of what to find in one dialect is conditioned by what we know of other related dialects, and we use anything we can get our hands on to come up with a good analysis. But in our role of linguist qua constructor of grammars we are concerned only with accounting for the intrinsic knowledge underlying speech in one dialect, and the existence of a second dialect is absolutely irrelevant to this goal. In short, the similarities (and divergences) between the two grammars are a result of purely synchronic analyses carried on for each dialect individually and are in no way an assumption upon which our analysis is based.

Finally, in regard to what was said earlier about overall patterns and diasystems, it is instructive to see what kind of dialect comparison emerges from application of one of these constructs. We have minimal pairs for /e/, /a/, and /o/ in Dialect A—[ep] : [ap] : [op]; and minimal pairs for /e/, /æ/, and /o/ in Dialect B—[t,ep] : [t,æp] : [t,op]. Assuming in addition then that /i/, /u/, and /a/ are (autonomous) phonemic in both dialects, we might have the following inventories of autonomous (as distinct from systematic, or underlying) phonemes in the two dialects:

Dialect A		Dialect B	
i	u	i	u
e	o	e	o
a		æ	a

Following Weinreich we can establish the diasystem:

$$ /\!/ \; i \approx e \approx a \approx \frac{_A/a \sim o/}{_B/æ \sim o/} \approx o \approx u \; /\!/ $$

This diagram says both too much and too little. It indicates much dissimilarity between the dialects in regard to the correspondences $_A/a \sim o/ : {}_B/æ \sim o/$, yet we have seen that the dialects correspond with total regularity in this area if we derive [æ] from an underlying /a/ in Dialect B and do not set it up as a separate phoneme. The diasystem does not inform us that there is a general rule predicting [æ] in both dialects, so that the correspondences $_A/a \sim o/ : {}_B/æ \sim o/$ are not so much indications of structural (that is to say, phonemic) disparity between the dialects as they are a slightly peculiar set of partially phonetic, partially phonemic correspondences between them. Thus, while the diasystem does serve to elucidate some of the relationships between the dialects, it also renders them more disparate than the facts justify without telling us specifically where and how they differ.

Our example is hypothetical, but not atypical or pathological. A quite similar example from Russian dialects is cited in Halle (1962:69–70), and there seems to be no reason for assuming that comparable cases are unusual, quite the contrary. One example of this sort has been given by Lamb (1966:542) for Monachi, a Uto-Aztecan language of California. In the dialect of Bishop, California, there is an alternation between [m] and nasalized [w̃]: [w̃] occurs only after vowels, [m] never occurs after vowels, and both segments are always followed by vowels. Example: [miyawai] 'will go', [taw̃iyawai'na] 'our future going'. In the dialect of North Fork the corresponding alternation is between [m] and non-nasalized [w]: [miyawai], [tawiyawai'na]. There is in both dialects a phone [w] which does not alternate with [m] and is in contrast with it. Example: [wiya] 'acorns', [tawiya] 'our acorns'.

To account for this tiny portion of data in our grammar of the Bishop dialect we posit two systematic phonemes /m/ and /w/ classified by at least the features:

	w	m
vocalic:	−	−
consonantal:	−	+
nasal:	−	+
coronal:	−	−

And we include in the grammar of the Bishop dialect the rule:

$$3.3 \quad \begin{bmatrix} + \text{ nasal} \\ - \text{ coronal} \end{bmatrix} \to [- \text{ consonantal}] \ / \ \text{V} \underline{}$$

(/m/ > [w̃] following a vowel.)

The North Fork dialect is similar in having underlying /m/ and /w/ as well as Rule 3.3, but its grammar has a rule that applies after Rule 3.3 and states that any glide (such as [w] or [w̃]) is not nasal:

$$3.4 \quad \begin{bmatrix} - \text{ vocalic} \\ - \text{ consonantal} \end{bmatrix} \to [- \text{ nasal}]$$

(A glide has the feature minus nasality.)

The difference between the two dialects in this one respect can be described by assuming the presence of a rule in the grammar of the North Fork dialect that is absent in the grammar of the Bishop dialect. The underlying segments for this little piece of the grammar are in both dialects the same, /w/ and /m/. (The analysis given here might require modification in the presence of additional data on the dialects. It might, for example, be economical to combine Rules 3.3 and 3.4 into a single rule. For further discussion see Section 3.3 under SIMPLIFICATION.)

The diasystem for this subpart of the autonomous phonemic systems of the two dialects would be // m ≈ w //, which reveals exactly nothing of the way in which the dialects differ. In autonomous phonemic terms the *m* : *w̃* alternation in Bishop is allophonic since the phone [w̃] can be assigned to the phoneme /m/; in North Fork the *m* : *w* alternation is morphophonemic since a phone [w] must be assigned to the phoneme /w/ irrespective of whether it alternates under statable conditions with [m] or not. If we recognize an autonomous phonemic level intermediate between the systematic phonemic and phonetic levels in our grammar, then the two grammars differ at two levels: the morphophonemic and the allophonic. We have seen that the difference can be described simply as the addition of a single rule in a generative grammar that posits no level of representation intervening between the systematic phonemic and the systematic phonetic. In particular, this example demonstrates that meaningful dialect comparison does not necessarily emerge from comparing the phonemic inventories of two dialects, for in this case the phonemic inventories—whether autonomous or systematic phonemic—are identical, and whatever differences there are arise via rules that state realizations of phonemes.

The moral to be drawn from this discussion is that to gain any insight into dialect differences we must concern ourselves with the *grammars* of languages, not their vowel or consonant systems, lists of morphemes, and so on. That is, the study of dialect differences is the study of how the grammars of the dialects differ. By implication, the study of linguistic change is the study of how the grammars of languages change in the course of time. We have nothing to gain from comparing phoneme inventories at two different stages of a given language and seeing what sound has changed into what other sound. Such a comparison gives as little insight into linguistic change as a comparison of before-and-after pictures of an earthquake site gives into the nature of earthquakes.

3.3 TYPES OF CHANGE

For the present we shall be concerned with drawing the consequences of the statement made earlier that all change can be traced to the situation in which two dialects of a language have become different. This includes the possibility that one of these dialects is the immediate chronological predecessor of the other, e.g. Old English and Early Middle English, or Late Proto-Indo-European and Early Proto-Germanic. To say that dialects have become different is to say that the grammars of these dialects are different, and we shall now discuss the ways in which this can happen. Our examples will be taken from phonology; syntactic change will be discussed in Chapter 6. The types of change we shall discuss in the remainder of this chapter are all what we will call *primary change* (change in the rule component) as distinct from *restructuring* (change in underlying representations), which will be discussed in Chapter 4.

RULE ADDITION. The examples of dialect differences given in Section 3.2 involve two dialects which differ by the presence in one of the grammars of a rule absent in the other. Transposed into terms of historical linguistics, this means that one of the ways for sound change to take place is by the addition of a rule to the grammar. Instances of this kind are commonplace, and many well-known sound changes are best described by rule additions.

Thus, the change of Vulgar Latin $\bar{u}$ > Old French $\ddot{u}$ was presumably of this kind. To the grammar of Vulgar Latin was added the rule:

$$3.5 \quad \begin{bmatrix} V \\ + \text{ high} \\ + \text{ long} \end{bmatrix} \rightarrow [- \text{ back}]$$

(A vowel which is high and long becomes front; its roundness value is unchanged. Hence, high back round $\bar{u}$ becomes high front round $\bar{\ddot{u}}$.)

Palatal umlaut—the fronting of back vowels that are followed in the next syllable by i, $\bar{\imath}$, or j—in the Germanic languages is a second example of rule addition. There is no reason to assume that umlaut was present in the grammar of Gothic, the oldest attested of the Germanic languages. (Early Germanic loanwords in Finnish show no umlaut, e.g. Finnish *patja* 'mattress', not *pätjä* or *petja*, from *badja*, cf. Gothic *badi* 'bed'.) We thus have Gothic *gasts* : *gasteis* 'guest (nom. sing. and plu.)', where *ei* spells [i:], and there is no documentary indication of umlaut in the form *gasteis*. In Old High German and Old Saxon, on the other hand, umlaut of short *a* is clearly present and indicated in the manuscripts, so that we have *gast* : *gesti* ($a > e$ under influence of the following *i*). Similarly, corresponding to Gothic *fotus* : *fotjus* 'foot (nom. sing. and plu.)' without umlaut in *fotjus*, we have Old English *fōt* : *fēt* and Old Norse *fótr* : *fótr*. Old Norse points up the older situation, in which $\bar{o}$ is umlauted to $\bar{\ddot{o}}$ (spelled *ǿ* in Old Norse) under the influence of a following *j*, which since had become lost; and most dialects of Old English have unrounded their front rounded (umlaut) vowels, thus $\bar{\ddot{o}} > \bar{e}$. We account for this by assuming the addition of an umlaut rule to the grammar of a dialect (or dialects) of Germanic from which Old English, Old Saxon, Old High German, and Old Norse (but not Gothic) derive. This rule has the general shape:

$$3.6 \quad V \rightarrow [- \text{ back}] / \underline{\hspace{1cm}} C_1 \begin{bmatrix} - \text{ consonantal} \\ + \text{ high} \\ - \text{ back} \end{bmatrix}$$

(A vowel is fronted when followed by one or more consonants plus a vowel or glide segment that is front and high, i.e. $\breve{u} \; \breve{o} \; \breve{a} > \breve{\ddot{u}} \; \breve{\ddot{o}} \; \breve{\ddot{a}}$ when followed by one or more consonants and $\breve{\imath}$ or *j*. Details of this rule would have to be modified in order to account for dialect-specific developments such as the fact that in the West Germanic dialects of Old High German and Old Saxon the umlaut of short *a* is *e* and not *ä*. Also, certain consonants and consonant clusters prevented umlaut from occurring in various dialects.)

The rule that subsequently unrounds front rounded vowels in most dialects of Old English can also be regarded as a case of rule addition. (It is better considered as simplification—the "activation" of the universal marking convention that the unmarked value of roundness for front vowels is [− round], cf. Chomsky and Halle 1968:405. For illustration, however, this change is treated here as rule addition.) In the early documents of Old English 'king' is spelled *cyning* (*y* is high front round *ü*), and in the later documents *cining*, indicating that unrounding has taken place. Likewise, in the older Old English documents and regularly in Anglian manuscripts, isolated occurrences of *ōē* are found for the palatal umlaut of *ō*, e.g. *bōc*: *bōēc* 'book (nom. sing. and plu.)', but in the later writings we find only *ē*, as in *bōc*: *bēc* (cf. similar *foot:feet*). We assume that a rule requiring front vowels to be unrounded was added to the grammar of the unrounding dialects of Old English:

$$3.7 \quad \begin{bmatrix} V \\ - \text{back} \end{bmatrix} \rightarrow [- \text{round}]$$

(Front vowels must be nonround, i.e. *ŭ ŏ* > *ĭ ĕ*. Note that Rule 3.7 applies *after* Rule 3.6.)

As a final example of rule addition let us take one step in the Germanic Consonant Shift (Grimm's Law), namely *b d g* > *p t k*. Corresponding to *b d g* in most of the Indo-European languages, the Germanic languages have, in their earliest reconstructible stages at least, *p t k*. Examples: Greek *déka*, Latin *decem* versus Gothic *taihun*, English *ten*; Greek *génos*, Latin *genus*, Sanskrit *janas* versus English *kin*, Old High German *kunni*, Old Norse *kyn*. We assume that a rule making stops voiceless was added to the grammar of the Northwesterly Indo-European dialect from which Germanic developed:

$$3.8 \quad \begin{bmatrix} + \text{obstruent} \\ - \text{continuant} \end{bmatrix} \rightarrow [- \text{voice}]$$

(Any noncontinuant obstruent—a stop—must be voiceless.)

So far we have discussed rule additions with little reference to *where* the rule is added. In general we must be more precise than this, for it can make a difference at which point a rule is added to the grammar of a language, as is implicit in the notion that the phonological component of a grammar is constituted as a system of rules, some or all of which may be ordered with respect to each other. In all natural languages previously investigated it has been found to be the case that at least some phonological rules must be ordered with respect to each other.

As a concrete example, let us consider Rules 3.6 (umlaut) and 3.7 (unrounding) in Old English. Since Rule 3.6 (umlaut) is present in all of the early Germanic dialects except Gothic and since Rule 3.7 (unrounding) is present only in dialects of Old English and sporadically elsewhere, we are quite certain that Rule 3.6 (umlaut) was added to the grammar of Old English earlier in time than Rule 3.7 (unrounding). The manuscript evidence supports this. Let us suppose then a stage of Old English the grammar of which contains Rule 3.6 (umlaut) but not Rule 3.7. We would then have such derivations as the following:

Base Form:	kuning	dūstiġ	hōrjan
Rule 3.6:	küning	düstiġ	hȫrjan
Early OE Spelling:	cyning	dӯstiġ	hōēran
Gloss:	'king'	'dusty'	'to hear'

(The -j- in hōrjan is lost subsequent to its triggering of umlaut.)

If the unrounding rule (3.7) is added now, *after* Rule 3.6, we will obtain the correct forms for later Old English:

Base Form:	kuning	dūstiġ	hōrjan
Rule 3.6:	küning	düstiġ	hȫrjan
Rule 3.7:	kining	dīstiġ	hēran
Late OE Spelling:	cining	dīstiġ	hēran
Gloss:	'king'	'dusty'	'to hear'

If, conversely, Rule 3.7 were added to the grammar of Early Old English *before* Rule 3.6, then there would be absolutely no change in the final phonetic forms. Rule 3.7 states that front vowels must be nonround; thus Rule 3.7 will change segments only if the language has front rounded vowels. But since the only front rounded vowels in Old English arise through the operation of umlaut, Rule 3.7, if added prior to umlaut, would have no forms to change:

Base Form:	kuning	dūstiġ	hōrjan
Rule 3.7:	....	....	....
Rule 3.6:	küning	düstiġ	hȫrjan
Phonetic Form:	küning	düstiġ	hȫrjan
OE Spelling:	cyning	dӯstiġ	hōēran

If, therefore, Rule 3.7 had been added to the grammar of Early Old English before Rule 3.6, we could not obtain the correct Late Old English forms *cining, dīstiġ,* and *hēran.*

In most cases of rule addition where we have all the necessary documentary and comparative information to determine rule chronologies with precision, the rules are added late in the grammar, at the end of the phonological component. This is not necessarily universal, however; it is entirely possible that our impression that rules tend to be added relatively late rests on insufficient evidence: few languages have written records, and even in those few that do we seldom can determine beyond question the relative chronology of two rules. We are lucky in the case of Old English, which has extensive documentation from circa A.D. 700, and in a few other cases from Indo-European languages.

One of the more certain cases of the addition of a rule not at the end of the phonological component is provided by Lachmann's Law in Latin (extensively discussed in Kiparsky 1965). Indo-European had a regressive voicing assimilation rule of the form:

$$3.9 \quad [+ \text{ obstruent}] \rightarrow [\alpha \text{ voice}] / \underline{\hspace{1cm}} \begin{bmatrix} + & \text{obstruent} \\ \alpha & \text{voice} \end{bmatrix}$$

(An obstruent takes on the voicing value of the immediately following obstruent: it is voiceless if the following obstruent is voiceless, it is voiced if the following obstruent is voiced.) Thus, via Rule 3.9, to the Sanskrit root *vid-* 'to know' we have *vēt-tha* 'you know' from underlying /vēd-tha/; to the Greek root *leg-* (*légō* 'I say') we have *lek-tó-s* 'gathered' from underlying /leg-tó-s/; and to the Latin root *scrīb-* 'to write' we have *scrīp-s-ī* 'I wrote' and *scrīp-t-um* 'having been written' from underlying /skrīb-s-i/ and /skrīb-t-um/. In these cases voicelessness is assimilated regressively, but voicing too could be assimilated (α is + in Rule 3.9): to the Sanskrit root *śak-* 'to be able' we have the second plural middle imperative form *śagdhvam* from underlying /śak-dhvam/. Rule 3.9 was inherited in the grammar of Latin, where it is needed as a synchronic rule to account not only for forms such as *scrībō* : *scrīpsī* : *scrīptum* but also for those like *appellō* 'I call' from underlying /ad-pellō/ and *accipiō* 'I receive' from underlying /ad-kapiō/.

Latin has quantity alternations among vowels of the following sort: *agō* 'I drive, lead' : *āctum* 'having been driven, led'; and *regō* 'I rule' : *rēctum* 'having been ruled'. Yet this short : long vowel alternation is not found in other forms such as *faciō* 'I make' : *factum* 'having been made'; and *capiō* 'I take' : *captum* 'having been taken'. The solution seems clear. The underlying forms of *āctum, rēctum*, and so on are /agtum/, /regtum/ (cf. *agō, regō*), and there is a rule that lengthens vowels when followed by an obstruent cluster, the first member of which is voiced, though analogy has disturbed the effects of this rule. The underlying forms of *factum, captum*, and so on have only voiceless obstruents (i.e. /faktum/, /kaptum/) since no other forms in the paradigm have voiced obstruents, and this rule will not lengthen vowels in these words. The rule, *Lachmann's Law*, can be stated as follows:

$$3.10 \quad V \rightarrow [+ \text{ long}] / \underline{\hspace{1cm}} \begin{bmatrix} + \text{ obstruent} \\ + \text{ voice} \end{bmatrix} \begin{bmatrix} + \text{ obstruent} \\ - \text{ voice} \end{bmatrix}$$

(A vowel is long before the sequence voiced-obstruent-plus-voiceless-obstruent.)

Now the question is: "Where was Rule 3.10 added in the grammar of Latin?" We might first assume that it was added at the end of the phonological rules. In this case it would apply *after* Rule 3.9, the voicing assimilation rule, since the latter rule is an old rule inherited from Indo-European and since Rule 3.10, Lachmann's Law, is a Latin innovation not shared by the other Indo-European languages. This assumption would give derivations such as the following:

Base Form:	agō	agtum	fakiō	faktum
Rule 3.9:	....	aktum	....	....
Rule 3.10:	....	....	....	....
Final Form:	agō	aktum	fakiō	faktum
Latin Spelling:	*agō*	*actum*	*faciō*	*factum*

We see that this assumed order of the two rules does not give the right results for forms such as *āctum, rēctum, lēctum* 'having picked out' (cf. *legō*). The point is that if Rule 3.10 is added at the end of the grammar, then it must apply vacuously (i.e. without effect) since Rule 3.9 will already have made obstruent clusters like the -*gt*- in *agtum* voiceless throughout. In this event, the structural analysis of Rule 3.10 will never be met, and the rule will never apply.

If, on the other hand, we assume that Lachmann's Law was added as a rule of grammar *prior to* Rule 3.9 (voicing assimilation), then we will obtain the following correct results:

Base Form:	agō	agtum	fakiō	faktum
Rule 3.10:	....	āgtum	....	....
Rule 3.9:	....	āktum	....	....
Final Form:	agō	āktum	fakiō	faktum
Latin Spelling:	*agō*	*āctum*	*faciō*	*factum*

A second example of nonchronological rule addition may be taken from the history of German, where the sequence [xs] became [ks] within morphemes: *oxs > oks* 'ox', *zexs > zeks* 'six', *laxs > laks* 'salmon'. However, [x] remained when separated from [s] by a morpheme boundary: *maxst* 'you make', *neːxst* 'next', *laxst* 'you laugh'. Accounting for this by rule addition at the end of the phonological component would require a rule of the sort:

xs > ks only if no morpheme boundary intervenes

This rule violates the apparently valid empirical hypothesis (Chomsky and Halle 1968:364) that processes operating within morphemes normally also apply across morpheme boundaries. The simpler explanation is that this change was added as a morpheme-structure constraint—not, in other words, at the end of the phonological component, but as a condition on the configuration of morphemes.

As these examples show, one must not facilely make the assumption that rules are added only at the end of the phonological component. Perhaps that is the more common occurrence (though this is only an assumption), and for reasons that have to do with the disruption of communication. As Halle (1962:66) has pointed out, "Language change is normally subject to the constraint that it must not result in the destruction of mutual intelligibility between the innovators—i.e. the carriers of the change—and the rest of the speech community." All things being equal, a rule that is added late in the grammar will disrupt communication less than a rule added early in the grammar, though in some cases it will make no difference. Such was the case in Old English discussed earlier: if Rule 3.7 (unrounding) had been applied early —specifically before Rule 3.6, the umlaut rule—then it would not change the previous output of the grammar in the slightest.

It can, however, make a very great difference, depending on the grammar and the rule which is inserted. Suppose, for example, that a rule raising [æ:] > [e:] were added at the end of the phonological component of American English. Instead of [bæ:d] 'bad' and [kæ:n] 'can', we would say [be:d] and [ke:n]. Communication would hardly be impaired at all. In fact, there are many speakers of American English, located primarily in New York City, who have done just this (Labov 1965:102–113), and a great many immigrants pronounce [æ:] as [e:], yet those of us who don't do this have no trouble talking to those who do. It is simply registered as some kind of accent: urban New York, German immigrant, or whatever.

If this rule had been inserted very early in the set of phonological rules, the effect it would have on the final phonetic output of the grammar would be much greater. There is in the grammar of English a rule raising underlying /ǣ/ to [ē] (the macron denotes tenseness, or length). Thus, the underlying forms of *compare* [kʰʌmpe:r] and *comparison* [kʰʌmpærəsin] contain [æ], and the vowel-raising rule operates on the /ǣ/ in *compare* to give [e:]. Also, in its present-day grammar English has a vowel shift rule that (among other things) raises underlying /ē/ to [ī]. This rule is needed to account for such alternations as *keep* [kʰi:p] : *kept* [kʰɛpt], both of which have underlying /ē/. The laxing rule gives /kēpt/ > [kept] which later rules take to [kʰɛpt], and the vowel shift rule gives /kēp/ > [kīp] (> [kʰi:p]). (Note that here and elsewhere the vowels in English *beet, bait, pod, boat, boot,* and so on are written as simple vowel plus [:]. This implies not that "length" is the only relevant feature phonetically present but that a variety of phonetic features such as tenseness, length, and offglide are involved.) For the details of this analysis see Chomsky and Halle (1968).

Now let us suppose that the rule raising /ǣ/ to [ē] were added at the very beginning of the phonological component. We would then have

Underlying:	ē	ǣ
ǣ > ē	.....	ē
Vowel Shift:	ī	ī

Under these conditions *compare* would come out [kʰʌmpiːr] and *comparison* would come out [kʰʌmperəsin]. The degree to which changes of this sort would adversely affect communication is open to speculation and could be tested experimentally, but clearly adding the rule /ǣ/ > [ē] at the beginning of the phonological component has brought about a greater deviation from normal pronunciation than results when the same rule is added at the end of the phonological rules.

At present not a great deal is known about the "disruption of mutual intelligibility" criterion. We know that some such tolerance point exists; otherwise we would expect to find cases of radical communication breakdown between speakers belonging to successive generations. But just how to formulate a formal constraint that captures the notion of a point at which mutual intelligibility is disrupted by change is neither easy nor obvious. (It may well be that this constraint should not be stated as a constraint on the grammar at all, but rather should be accounted for elsewhere in the theory.) Languages, or rather their speakers, seem to be able to tolerate seemingly radical changes without slackening their stride to any great extent, yet we know of no language that anywhere in its history has undergone really pathological changes such as "All high vowels become low, all front vowels become back, and all back vowels become mid."

In any case, though evidence is not conclusive, it is plausible to assume that rules tend to be added at the end of the phonological component rather than earlier because communication is thereby less affected. Yet our impression that late rule addition is statistically favored may be due not to some universal principle but merely to insufficient knowledge of sound changes. Numerous instances of rule insertion at points other than the end are attested. Others are shown for Mohawk and Oneida by Postal (1968:245–260).

Before leaving rule addition, it should be observed that this kind of primary change corresponds to what has traditionally been known as *innovation.* Each case presented—Vulgar Latin *ū > ü*, Germanic umlaut, Grimm's Law *b d g > p t k*, and Lachmann's Law—falls in the category of innovations in the individual languages.

RULE LOSS. Another kind of primary change can be deduced from the fact that grammars of dialects sometimes differ by the presence or absence of a single rule: it may be that a rule has been lost from the grammar. We shall discuss two such cases here—one from Yiddish, the other from Gothic. We begin with the Yiddish example since the spoken language is still available to us. (Cf. Kiparsky 1965 and Kiparsky 1968b.)

Middle High German, from which Yiddish dialects derive ultimately though not directly, had a rule that devoiced final obstruents: we posit this rule on the basis of Middle High German alternations such as *gap* 'he gave' : *gāben* 'we gave', *tac* 'day' : *tage* 'days', *sneit* 'he cut' : *snīden* 'to cut'. In word-final position the contrast between voiced and voiceless stops (and probably fricatives too, though the orthography is less clear on this point) is neutralized in favor of the voiceless member. The obvious way to handle such alternations is to posit underlying voiced obstruents in the forms involved and include a terminal devoicing rule in the grammar. The underlying representations of the forms just cited would then be /gab : gāben, tag : tage, sneid : snīden/, and the following rule would convert word-final voiced obstruents to voiceless ones:

3.11 $[+ \text{obstruent}] \rightarrow [- \text{voice}] / \underline{\qquad} \#$

(Obstruents are devoiced word-finally.)

Earliest attested Old High German, the predecessor language of Middle High German, had no such rule in its grammar; the Old High German forms of the words cited were *gab : gābum(es), tag : taga, sneid : snīdan*. It is clear from the written records that Rule 3.11 was added to the grammar of Old High German between A.D. 900 and 1200 depending on the dialect. The terminal devoicing rule is present in the vast majority of the modern German dialects, including Standard German, though in some dialects it is limited to word-final fricatives. Some German dialects, however, do not have such a rule in their synchronic grammars, and in particular many Yiddish dialects do not have this rule. We may cite examples from Standard Yiddish, whose grammar lacks Rule 3.11 in any form: *hob* 'I have' : *hobm* 'we have', *lid* 'song' : *lider* 'songs', *tog* 'day' : *teg* 'days', *noz* 'nose' : *nezer* 'noses', *rov* 'rabbi'.

Two explanations of this are possible. One, which we reject, is that Yiddish never added to its grammar a rule that devoiced final obstruents. Evidence still in the language argues against this, for Standard Yiddish has numerous words which show that Rule 3.11 was operative in the language at some earlier stage: *avek* 'away', *hant* 'hand', *gelt* 'money'. All of these words had underlying *voiced* obstruents earlier, cf. the Middle High German cognates *hant : hende, wec : weges, gelt : geldes*. The final *voiceless* obstruents in the Yiddish forms could only have resulted from a stage in the development of Yiddish when Rule 3.11 was present in the grammar. In addition to purely internal evidence such as this, there is direct textual evidence for such a rule in a Yiddish rhyme of the thirteenth century (Röll 1966). This rhyme begins with the phrase *gūt tak* in Hebrew letters where the *k* in *tak* is spelled with the Hebrew letter for *k* (kuf) and not *g* (gimel). The Standard Yiddish expression for this is *a gutn tog*, cf. Standard German *Guten Tag* 'good day'. Furthermore, many Yiddish dialects still maintain final devoicing (Herzog

1965:220–223). This evidence, taken together, leads us to reject the proposal that Yiddish never had a terminal devoicing rule in its grammar.

One might, of course, try to account for the presence versus the absence of devoicing in Yiddish dialects by appeal to borrowing or to areal influence. There are insurmountable difficulties in such explanations, as Weinreich (1963) has demonstrated, and the various alternative explanations will not be investigated here.

It is more reasonable to assume that the earliest Yiddish dialects had in their grammars Rule 3.11 as an inheritance from Middle High German, but that most of the dialects since lost this rule from their grammars. The underlying voiced final obstruents in *tog*, *hob*, *lid*, *noz*, and so on have been carried along unchanged through the lexicons of successive generations of Yiddish speakers. As long as Rule 3.11 was present in the grammar to act upon these forms, they would have voiceless final obstruents in their phonetic realizations —*tok*, *hop*, *lit*, *nos*, and so on—rather like Standard German *Tag* [tʰa:k], *hab'* [ha:p], *Lied* [li:t]. With the loss of Rule 3.11 the underlying forms come through unaltered as regards their final obstruent; that is, voiced word-final obstruents at the underlying level are realized phonetically as voiced.

Instances of rule loss from a grammar are by no means uncommon. As we shall see in Chapter 4, rule loss is concomitant with the type of change we call restructuring, and restructuring is frequent enough in the history of languages. Let us investigate another case of simple rule loss where the evidence is reasonably clear.

All the early Germanic dialects except Gothic have an original alternation between voiceless and voiced fricatives that shows up with particular regularity in the principal parts of strong verbs. This phenomenon is known as *grammatical change*. It is a result of Verner's Law, which states that "Germanic voiceless spirants remained voiceless if the preceding syllable had the Indo-European accent, but became voiced in voiced surroundings if the preceding syllable had been unstressed in Indo-European times" (Prokosch 1939:61). Verner's Law may be stated as:

$$3.12 \quad \begin{bmatrix} + \text{ obstruent} \\ + \text{ continuant} \end{bmatrix} \rightarrow [+ \text{ voice}] / \begin{bmatrix} + \text{ voice} \\ - \text{ accented} \end{bmatrix} \underline{\quad\quad} [+ \text{ voice}]$$

(Fricatives become voiced in voiced surroundings following an unaccented segment.) Examples of grammatical change are:

	Inf.	*Past Sg.*	*Past Pl.*	*Past Part.*	*Gloss*
OE:	snīþan	snāþ	snidon	sniden	'to cut'
ON:	kiósa	kaus	kørom	kørenn	'to choose'
OS:	tiohan	tōh	tugun	gitogan	'to pull'
OHG:	ziohan	zōh	zugum	gizogan	'to pull'

In the early dialects of Germanic, stress is localized on the root syllable, so that the cited forms reflect the place of original Indo-European accent only in alternations of the sort *þ : d, s : r, h : g*, which show secondary changes from the original Proto-Germanic set of alternations which were voiceless : voiced, e.g. *þ : ð, s : z, x : g*. To see the reason for such differential treatment in the principal parts of verbs, consider these same principal parts as they would have appeared in Indo-European, e.g. IE **dewk-* 'to pull' (Latin *dūcō*):

	Inf.	*Past Sg.*	*Past Pl.*	*Past Part.*
IE:	déwkono	dówke	dwkńt	dwkóno
Early Proto-Gmc:	téwxana	táwxe	tuxúnþ	tuxána
Late Proto-Gmc:	téwxan	táwx	túgun	túgan

Here, the difference between "Early Proto-Germanic" and "Late Proto-Germanic" is that the former stage still has Indo-European accent placement, while the forms in the latter stage have undergone Verner's Law (Rule 3.12) and the accent (or stress) has shifted uniformly to the root vowel.

In order to account for these alternations in the synchronic grammars of the Germanic dialects (not including Gothic), we need a rule that voices fricatives in the requisite environments. It is no longer possible to assume that Rule 3.12 is present in these synchronic grammars, for there is no motivation for assuming different placements of the accent in the principal parts of verbs, and Rule 3.12 crucially requires us to accent the infinitive (and all present tense forms) and the past singular forms on the root vowel, and to accent the past plural and the past participle on the suffix vowel. For these reasons we include in the grammars of the earliest Germanic dialects the rule:

$$3.13 \quad \begin{bmatrix} + \text{ obstruent} \\ + \text{ continuant} \end{bmatrix} \rightarrow [+ \text{ voice}] \; / \; \left[\overline{\left\{ \begin{matrix} + \text{ Past Plural} \\ + \text{ Past Participle} \end{matrix} \right\}} \right] \; +)$$

(Fricatives are voiced in the past plural and past participle when stem-final.)

We may regard Rule 3.13 as the altered synchronic survival of the Germanic innovation (i.e. rule addition) of Rule 3.12, which is Verner's Law. Thus, starting with /snīþ-/ 'to cut' in the lexicon of Old English, the voiceless fricative *þ* would remain unchanged in the present and past singular, but would be voiced in the preterite plural and preterite participle—giving the correct forms *snīþan snāþ snidon sniden* (a rule applying subsequent to Rule 3.13 would convert the *ð* from *þ* into the stop *d*).

We have been careful to exclude Gothic from all of the foregoing comments, for Gothic alone among the Germanic dialects does not have grammatical change in the principal parts of its strong verbs. For the three verbs 'to cut', 'to choose', and 'to pull', cited earlier in their Old English, Old Norse, Old Saxon, and Old High German shapes, Gothic has:

Inf.	Past Sg.	Past Pl.	Past Part.
sneiþan	snaiþ	sniþum	sniþans
kiusan	kaus	kusum	kusans
tiuhan	tauh	tauhum	tauhans

with voiceless fricatives throughout.

What are we to assume has happened? Internal evidence from Gothic inclines us strongly to the assumption that the grammar of Gothic once included Rule 3.12 (Verner's Law) and likely for a time its synchronic guise Rule 3.13, but that the rule was deleted from the grammar. There are relic forms in the language that point to an original voiceless : voiced alternation precisely of the kind found elsewhere in Germanic: examples are *aih* 'I possess' : *aigum* 'we possess', *weihan* 'to fight' : *du wigana* 'to the battle', *frawairþan* 'to perish' : *frawardjan* 'to ruin', *wisan* 'to feast' : *wizon* 'to revel', *þarf* 'I need' : *þaurbum* 'we need', *filhan* 'to hide' : *fulgins* 'hidden'. In these data there are enough past plurals (*aigum*, *þaurbum*) to justify the assumption that Rule 3.13 was once in the grammar of Gothic, presumably as part of its common Germanic heritage, but that it was lost. We assume that while this rule was part of the grammar, past plural and participle forms containing underlying voiceless fricatives were realized with voiced fricatives: e.g. *sniðum sniðans, kuzum kuzans, taugum taugans* parallel to *aigum* and *þaurbum*. But this was at the level of surface phonetic realization. The underlying systematic phonemic forms retained voiceless fricatives. With the loss of Rule 3.13, the great majority of strong verbs came to show at the phonetic level the structure all along present at the systematic phonemic level—voiceless fricatives in all the principal parts.

The relic forms are those in which the morphophonemic identification of related forms had presumably become so weak that a minor sort of restructuring had occurred in the lexicon. For example, *du wigana* 'to the battle', though originally derived from the verb *weihan* 'to fight', was no longer associated synchronically with it in the same close morphophonemic relationship as principal parts of strong verbs. Hence the *wigana* of *du wigana* was changed in the Gothic lexicon from original /wihana/ to /wigana/; similarly for the other relic forms, such as *wizon* 'to revel', which had lost its original transparent relationship with its lexical source *wisan* 'to feast' and had been altered in the lexicon to /wizon/ with /z/ in place of /s/. Two of the verb forms still demonstrating the original phonetic alternations—*aih* : *aigum*, *þarf* : *þaurbum*—have defective distributions in Gothic (and in the other Germanic dialects) as well as an aberrant set of endings. Both these verbs belong to the fossil class of "preterite-present verbs" from which we get our modal verbs in English: *can, may, dare*, and so on. In the third verb in Gothic with a remnant of the original distribution of voiceless : voiced fricatives—*filhan* 'to hide' : *fulgins* 'hidden'—the form *fulgins* had come to be regarded as an adjective rather than the past participle of *filhan*, and had been restructured in the lexicon to a separate adjective entry with /-g-/ no longer derived from the verb *filhan* with phonemic /-h-/. Similarly for *frawairþan* : *frawardjan*.

On balance, the evidence of the relic forms in Gothic points strongly to rule loss. Such relic forms are our best evidence in making a case for loss of a rule, just as the relic form *avek* 'away' in Yiddish supports the assumption that the terminal devoicing rule was lost in that language. In this case, the adverb *avek* had been dissociated from its historical source *veg* (with retained morphophonemic final *g*) and restructured in the lexicon to /avek/.

To be sure, the claim for restructuring rests on reasonable probability, not certain fact: no one knows for sure what took place in a Yiddish or Gothic speaker's lexicon. But one is usually safe in appealing to restructuring when the process of deriving one form from another cannot be synchronically motivated as a rule for the grammar in question, yet the two forms are known to be related etymologically. Gothic *filhan* and *fulgins* are known to be from the same source in pre-Gothic. Yet one cannot motivate a rule for the synchronic grammar of Gothic which would derive adjectives from verbs, among them *fulgins* from *filhan*. Presumably the speaker of pre-Gothic derived *fulgins* and *filhan* from a single lexical source, as English speakers do for *divine* and *divinity*; but the speaker of recorded Gothic learned two separate lexical entries, much as we learn *drink* and *drench* as separate lexical items, even though the two have the same etymological origin.

RULE REORDERING.   Another way dialects differ is in the ordering of certain of their rules. Thus, Dialect A contains in its grammar rules X and Y, which must apply in the order X first and Y second. Dialect B contains the same two rules but in the opposite order: Y first and X second. If the rules are crucially ordered in both dialects, a difference of output results. The number of attested examples of such reorderings increases as more and more languages are investigated from a generative point of view; and our present knowledge of relatively few reorderings indicates not so much their infrequency as the facts (1) that we have detailed histories of relatively few languages and (2) that researchers have not in general been on the lookout for reorderings.

Nevertheless, cases where two or more dialects differ in the order of application of the same or similar rules have been found for American English by Keyser (1963:310–311), for modern Rumanian by Vasiliu (1966), for Swiss German and Finnish by Kiparsky (1965 and 1968b), and for modern German dialects by Becker (1967:87–92). Corresponding to the synchronic cases, a number of instances of rule reorderings in historical linguistics have recently been unearthed, and we shall analyze two of these here.

The phonology of Modern Standard German contains two rules of interest here: one is a terminal devoicing rule (given already as Rule 3.11); the other lengthens vowels followed by voiced obstruents. The latter rule expresses a generalization about German phonology with only a few exceptions, such as

Ebbe 'low tide', *Widder* 'ram', and *Egge* 'harrow', mostly of Low German origin. This rule can be stated as:

$$3.14 \quad V \rightarrow [+ \text{ long}] \, / \, \underline{\hspace{2em}} \begin{bmatrix} + \text{ obstruent} \\ + \text{ voice} \end{bmatrix}$$

(A vowel must be long before a voiced obstruent.)

Rule 3.14 accounts for the long vowels in such words as *Hagel* 'hail', *sagen* 'to say', *Tage* 'days', *fragt* 'he asks'. No prediction of vowel length can be made before voiceless obstruents, where both long and short vowels occur freely: *Betten* [bɛtən] 'beds', in contrast with *Beeten* [be:tən] 'beetroots'.

Rule 3.11, which devoices obstruents in word-final position, accounts in present-day German for voiceless : voiced phonological alternations of the following sort: [lo:p] : [lo:bəs] = *Lob* : *Lobes* 'praise, of praise'; [ra:t] : [ra:dəs] = *Rad* : *Rades* 'wheel, of the wheel'; [ve:k] : [ve:gə] = *Weg* : *Wege* 'path, paths'; [gra:s] : [gra:zəs] = *Gras* : *Grases* 'grass, of the grass'. For such morphemes with allomorphs differing in voice in the final obstruent, we set up base forms containing final voiced obstruents, and those in word-final position will correctly be devoiced by Rule 3.11. Thus, from /lob/ we would have among the formatives that are input to the phonological rules /lob/ 'praise' and /lobəs/ 'of praise'; the former would become [lo:p] by Rule 3.11, the latter would remain [lo:bəs] since /b/ here is not in word-final position. (Cf. the discussion in Section 2.2.)

The lexical entry for 'praise' will then be /lob/, similarly /rad/ 'wheel', /veg/ 'path', /graz/ 'grass', where the vowels are unspecified for length. This solution requires the two rules 3.11 and 3.14 to be crucially ordered: Rule 3.14, for vowel lengthening before voiced obstruents, must apply *before* Rule 3.11, for terminal devoicing. We will have the typical derivations:

Underlying Forms:	lob	lobəs	veg	vegə	graz	grazəs
Vowel Lengthening:	lo:b	lo:bəs	ve:g	ve:gə	gra:z	gra:zəs
Final Devoicing:	lo:p	....	ve:k	....	gra:s	....
Phonetic Shape:	lo:p	lo:ɒəs	ve:k	ve:gə	gra:s	gra:zəs

(The underlying forms cited in these derivations are intended to facilitate presentation of the analysis at hand. They would not be the correct base forms if we were attempting to account for more of the generalizations in German phonology. In particular, /ə/ is not among the systematic phonemes of German —it is a reduction form of other vowels. Likewise, [v] is derived from underlying /u/, so that *Weg* 'path' has the lexical representation /ueg/.)

The order of these two rules in the synchronic grammar of modern German is not their chronological order. A grammar at an earlier stage in the history of German had the two rules crucially ordered in precisely the opposite order. We know this because the reordering occurred within the period of written records, because certain archaic dialects have preserved the original ordering, and because relic forms in the standard language reflect the earlier order.

As was mentioned earlier, final devoicing (Rule 3.11) was an innovation in the grammar of most German dialects around A.D. 1000, in any case not later than 1200. Lengthening of vowels before voiced obstruents was an innovation in the grammar of Early Modern German; that is, the documents indicate that it was a rule added around A.D. 1400, several centuries later than the final devoicing rule was added. Grammars of German immediately subsequent to this, in the fifteenth and sixteenth centuries and even later, had the two rules in the chronological order of their addition: Final Devoicing followed by Vowel Lengthening. In such a grammar the derivations given earlier would have different phonetic outcomes:

Underlying Forms:	lob	lobəs	veg	vegə	graz	grazəs
Final Devoicing:	lop	....	vek	....	gras	....
Vowel Lengthening:	....	lo:bəs	....	ve:gə	....	gra:zəs
Phonetic Shape:	lop	lo:bəs	vek	ve:gə	gras	gra:zəs

Comparing these final phonetic shapes with those given earlier for the grammar of modern German, we see that certain changes have taken place: some short vowels have become long, e.g. *lop > lo:p, vek > ve:k, gras > gra:s*. In traditional presentations this change would be called *analogical leveling*, here leveling under pressure from other forms in the paradigm that have long vowels. In Chapter 5 we shall discuss the problem of analogy in detail, and in Chapter 4 we shall ponder some of the factors that may have motivated the reversal of rule order. For the present we observe simply that we have here in the history of a single language two stages with rules identical but ordered oppositely.

We might entertain an alternative explanation to rule reordering, one which would fall in the category of RULE ADDITION. Is it not possible that Rule 3.14 (Vowel Lengthening) was added to the grammar before Rule 3.11 (Final Devoicing), similar to the insertion of Lachmann's Law into the grammar of Latin at a point not reflective of its chronological position?

In general it is not always possible to determine whether one is dealing with a case of reordering or of rule insertion at an earlier point in the grammar. In this case we can settle the dispute in favor of reordering. In the first place, there are dialects still spoken in this century that preserve the original order of the rules (Behaghel 1928:276). There are now only a few, it is true, and they are receding, but their indisputable presence is living testimony to earlier grammars in which Terminal Devoicing synchronically preceded Vowel Lengthening.

Second, if Vowel Lengthening had been inserted in the grammar ahead of Terminal Devoicing, then derivations like those that produced:

> lop   lo:bəs   vek   ve:gə   gras   gra:zəs

could never have existed. We would have had from the moment Vowel Lengthening was inserted only the derivations producing the modern forms:

> lo:p   lo:bəs   ve:k   ve:gə   gra:s   gra:zəs

However, relic forms from the earlier derivations exist. One is the adverb *weg* [vɛk] 'away!' Presumably, this form was dissociated from its original noun source *Weg* [ve:k] 'path' at a time when [vɛk] was the only form possible for its source, i.e. at a time when the paradigm had the form *vek ve:gə* instead of the modern *ve:k ve:gə*. Another relic form is *ap* 'from' with short [a] from Middle High German *abe ~ ap* 'off'.

We conclude then that this example is a case of rule reordering and not of rule insertion at a point other than the end of the grammar. We cannot always enjoy such certainty, as the following example illustrates. The grammars of all the early Germanic dialects contained Rules 3.15 and 3.16 in approximately the shapes shown:

$$3.15 \quad \begin{bmatrix} + \text{ obstruent} \\ + \text{ voice} \\ - \text{ strident} \\ \alpha \text{ anterior} \\ \beta \text{ coronal} \end{bmatrix} \rightarrow [- \text{ continuant}] / \left\{ \begin{matrix} \left\{ \begin{matrix} \# \\ [+ \text{ nasal}] \end{matrix} \right\} \text{—} \\ \begin{bmatrix} + \text{ obstruent} \\ + \text{ voice} \\ - \text{ strident} \\ \alpha \text{ anterior} \\ \beta \text{ coronal} \end{bmatrix} \end{matrix} \right\}$$

(The voiced, nonstrident fricatives *ƀ ð g > b d g* word-initially, after nasals, and in gemination. *Stridency* distinguishes *s* from *ƀ ð g*. [+ nasal] is the natural class of nasal consonants /m n/. In stating the third sub-environment of Rule 3.15 a convention proposed by Bach 1968 is used. This convention proposes that the two rules A → B / C____ and A → B / ____ C be collapsed into a single rule written A → B / C with the environment bar deleted. Such a rule effectively says "A becomes B either before or after C." The sequences *ƀƀ ðð gg* become by two successive applications of Rule 3.15 first *ƀƀ ðd gg*, then *ƀƀ dd gg*.)

$$3.16 \quad \begin{bmatrix} + \text{ obstruent} \\ + \text{ continuant} \end{bmatrix} \rightarrow [- \text{ voice}] / \text{\_\_\_\_} \#$$

(Fricatives are devoiced word-finally.)

Rule 3.16 is a less general version of the terminal devoicing rule discussed already as Rule 3.11. It is needed in the synchronic grammars of the Germanic dialects to account for such alternations as Gothic *beidan baiþ bidum bidans* 'to await (principal parts)', where *d* is presumably a fricative, and Old Saxon *hof* : *hoƀos* 'court, courts'. Rule 3.16 also provides for alternations between fricatives and stops of the sort illustrated by OE *hæbbe* OS *habbiu* 'I have' : OE *hæfde* OS *haƀda*, where Old English *f* before *d* was [ƀ]. (Additional motivation for these rules is found in King 1968, where this case of reordering is analyzed in detail.)

The grammars of Gothic, Old Norse, and Old High German contain Rules 3.15 and 3.16 in that order. A derivation of four forms of the Gothic verb 'to bind' in the present indicative, second and third person singular, second and third person plural follows:

Underlying Forms:	ƀinðiz	ƀinðið	ƀinðeð	ƀinðanð
Rule 3.15:	bindiz	bindið	bindeð	bindand
Rule 3.16:	bindis	bindiþ	bindeþ	....
Phonetic Forms:	bindis	bindiþ	bindeþ	bindand

(A later rule would produce correct 2. pl. *bindiþ* from above *bindeþ*.)

In the group of Germanic languages comprised by Old English, Old Saxon, and Old Frisian, however, the opposite order of the two rules is required: Rule 3.16 must apply before Rule 3.15. In these languages we would have the derivations

Underlying Forms:	ƀinðiz	ƀinðið	ƀinðeð	ƀinðanð
Rule 3.16:	ƀinðis	ƀinðiþ	ƀinðeþ	ƀinðanþ
Rule 3.15:	bindis	bindiþ	bindeþ	bindanþ
Phonetic Forms:	bindis	bindiþ	bindeþ	bindanþ

The correct final forms for the individual languages would be produced by rules specific to those grammars. In all of these three languages *n* was regularly lost before voiceless fricatives: 3. pl. *bindanþ > bindaþ*. This form was then extended over the entire plural (syncretism). In Old English unstressed *i* was early reduced to *e*, giving Old English *bindes bindeþ bindaþ bindaþ*.

This example illustrates that the grammars of one group of Germanic languages require these two rules in one order, the grammars of the other group require them in the opposite order. We cannot be sure whether there has been a reordering or whether Rule 3.16 was placed into the grammar of Old English, Old Saxon, and Old Frisian ahead of Rule 3.15. We are relatively certain that Rule 3.15 preceded Rule 3.16 in time as an innovation in Germanic. In view of the fact that the Germanic languages once (perhaps around the birth of Christ) were a close-knit, homogeneous speech community located in southern Scandinavia, we would incline to the view that the grammar of the proto-language once contained the two rules in the chronological order 3.15 followed by 3.16, and that while the grammars of Gothic, Old High German, and Old Norse continue this original order, reordering took place in the grammar of the language from which developed Old English, Old Saxon, and Old Frisian. We shall see in Chapter 4 that there are perhaps independent grounds for assuming that reordering has taken place in this instance, but for the present we only observe that reordering seems likely though we lack definitive evidence. The desired evidence here would be written records before and after the reordering, relic forms, and observable dialects historically descended from Old English, Old Saxon, or Old Frisian that still maintain the original order.

We have postponed until Chapter 4 discussion of possible reasons why reorderings take place. It may be pointed out here, however, that different orderings of rules among neighboring dialects may in some instances be due to a kind of wave effect. That is, rules spread out from prestige core dialects, and different rates of diffusion of the rules lead to different orderings.

Consider hypothetical dialects A and B. Dialect A has a Rule 1 and not a Rule 2 in its grammar, whereas Dialect B has Rule 2 and not Rule 1 in its grammar, and the contiguous dialects C and D have neither rule. This situation may be schematically represented by the following figure:

A Rule 1	D
C .	B Rule 2

Now assume that Rules 1 and 2 diffuse away from their original areas towards Dialects C and D, that speakers of Dialects C and D borrow Rules 1 and 2 into their grammars, adding them on at the end. Further assume that Rule 1 is borrowed immediately from Dialect A into Dialect D but later into Dialect C, and that Rule 2 is transmitted rapidly from Dialect B into Dialect C but later into Dialect D. This could give rise to the situation indicated in the following figure where Dialect C has Rule 2 followed by Rule 1 and Dialect D has the opposite order.

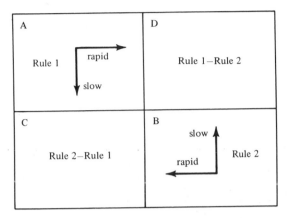

This hypothetical example is intended to suggest ways in which synchronic dialects may come to have rules identical but in different orders. (It is also possible that a rule is borrowed into different grammars at different positions in the grammars.) However, when we are dealing not with synchronic dialects but with different chronological stages of a language, there is no reasonable appeal we can make to some variant of the notion of wave. For concreteness let us take the two rules that were ordered oppositely in two distinct chronological stages of German. Middle High German had only Terminal Devoicing, the intermediate stage Early Modern German had Terminal Devoicing followed by Vowel Lengthening, and Modern Standard German has the two rules in reverse order. In order to develop an explanation in terms of different rates of diffusion of the two rules, similar to our hypothetical example, we would have to posit a hypothetical dialect whose grammar possessed Vowel Lengthening but not Terminal Devoicing. This hypothetical dialect would have to be assumed contemporaneous with Middle High German.

Now the stage is set for a wave explanation. Middle High German had Terminal Devoicing but not Vowel Lengthening; the hypothetical German dialect had Vowel Lengthening but not Terminal Devoicing. We assume different rates of diffusion from these two dialects. In one dialect or group of dialects the result is the order Terminal Devoicing followed by Vowel Lengthening (Early Modern German, some archaic modern dialects); in the other dialect area the result is Vowel Lengthening followed by Terminal Devoicing (Modern Standard German).

The catch in this is, of course, the hypothetical dialect which had only Vowel Lengthening but not Terminal Devoicing. There is not one single hint of evidence that such a dialect ever existed. There is no scribal evidence pointing to such a dialect. Even in those few German dialects or languages (like Yiddish) derived from German that today lack Terminal Devoicing, relic forms point to the earlier existence of a rule devoicing some or all obstruents word-finally. (This was already noted under RULE LOSS.) And bear in mind that each time a case of rule reordering is presented, it will be necessary to assume pro forma the existence of some hypothetical dialect having one but not the other rule.

These exemplify the fatuous lengths to which one is led if rule reordering is to be ascribed to a wave effect. It is obvious that this is quite simply the wrong explanation, and that rule reordering with respect to two chronological stages of a language comes about through some different kind of mechanism. It will be suggested in Chapter 4 that this mechanism is simplification of a particular type, but this proposal will have to be deferred until language acquisition in the child has been discussed. At present we shall continue our enumeration of the categories of primary change.

SIMPLIFICATION.   One of the most common ways in which dialects differ is in the generality of analogous rules in their grammars. Let us consider one rather simple example. As has been pointed out before, most German dialects have a rule that devoices final obstruents (Rule 3.11). In some dialects, however, the rule is less general: in Alsatian, for example, it affects only word-final fricatives (Becker 1967:112–113). This version of the terminal devoicing rule was stated already as Rule 3.16:

3.11 $[+ \text{ obstruent}] \rightarrow [- \text{ voice}] \, / \, \underline{\qquad} \, \#$ (All obstruents affected)

3.16 $\begin{bmatrix} + \text{ obstruent} \\ + \text{ continuant} \end{bmatrix} \rightarrow [- \text{ voice}] \, / \, \underline{\qquad} \, \#$ (Only fricatives affected)

Rule 3.11 is simpler: it has a feature count of three while Rule 3.16 has a feature count of four. (# is arbitrarily assigned here a value of one.) Rule 3.11 is also the more general of the two since it applies to the natural class of all obstruents whether stops or fricatives, and Rule 3.16 applies only to the natural class of fricatives. As regards the terminal devoicing rule, then, the difference between Alsatian and those dialects with Rule 3.11 is that the grammar of Alsatian has a less general, more restricted version of the rule. The lesser generality of Rule 3.16 is reflected formally in its higher number of features.

It seems probable that it is precisely in this way that dialects often differ. In a detailed generative phonological study of three modern German dialects, Becker (1967) found that their grammars differed most often in the increased generality, lessened generality, or presence of a given rule in one grammar but not the other. (In his study only one case of rule reordering was discovered.) We may cite here one of his examples of a typical situation. A given phonological rule whose structural change need not concern us affects /t/ in

Darmstadt Hessian, /p t/ in Alsatian, and /p t k/ in Züritüütsch (the Swiss German dialect spoken in the city of Zürich). The structural analysis of this rule thus contains in the different grammars the segments:

$$
/t/ \qquad\qquad /p\ t/ \qquad\qquad /p\ t\ k/
$$

$$
\begin{bmatrix} + \text{obstruent} \\ - \text{continuant} \\ - \text{voice} \\ + \text{coronal} \\ + \text{anterior} \end{bmatrix}
\qquad
\begin{bmatrix} + \text{obstruent} \\ - \text{continuant} \\ - \text{voice} \\ + \text{anterior} \end{bmatrix}
\qquad
\begin{bmatrix} + \text{obstruent} \\ - \text{continuant} \\ - \text{voice} \end{bmatrix}
$$

The decreasing feature counts of five, four, and three reflect increased generality (Becker 1967:59).

If as a common characteristic of their difference dialects display rules in different degrees of generality, we would expect to find that diachronic stages of the same language similarly differ in the generality of given rules. The earliest records of Old English indicate that the grammar contained a rule like Rule 3.16 affecting only word-final fricatives. Later records show final devoicing applying to all obstruents, not only fricatives; therefore later grammars of Old English contained the simpler (and more general) Rule 3.11.

Before proceeding, let us consider for a moment the relation between simplicity and generality in sound change and dialect borrowing. In the preceding examples a rule was judged more general if it applied to larger natural classes. The later terminal devoicing rule in Old English applies to both stops and spirants, whereas the earlier rule applied only to spirants. The later rule is simpler because it contains fewer features (three against four in the earlier rule): in the structural analysis the feature [+ continuant] is suppressed in passing from Rule 3.16 to Rule 3.11. Frequently, increased generality is expressed in just this way—by suppression of a feature. Yet it is clear that more is involved in assessing the generality of a rule (the naturalness of a rule) than simply the number of features. Consider Rule 3.17, which converts b to d, and Rule 3.17', which changes b to p:

$$
3.17 \quad \begin{bmatrix} + \text{obstruent} \\ + \text{voice} \\ + \text{anterior} \\ - \text{continuant} \end{bmatrix} \rightarrow [+ \text{coronal}]
$$

$$
3.17' \quad \begin{bmatrix} + \text{obstruent} \\ + \text{anterior} \\ - \text{coronal} \\ - \text{continuant} \end{bmatrix} \rightarrow [- \text{voice}]
$$

The two rules have the same feature count, yet intuitively one regards the change $b > d$ as less natural, less expected than $b > p$. Our evaluation procedure is incorrect in that it assigns to each rule the same degree of complexity, and there is no formal aspect of these rules which can be changed on a principled basis so that Rule 3.17′ counts as more natural than Rule 3.17. Chomsky and Halle (1968:400–435) have proposed ways of remedying this serious defect in phonological theory. Here, having pointed out that generality is expressed in ways other than feature suppression, let us consider further cases of rule simplification.

In all examples previously discussed in this context, the environment has been the same in all variants of the rule: only the segment (or natural class of segments) has been different. An example of a different kind can be taken again from Becker (1967:68). All three dialects Alsatian, Darmstadt Hessian, and Züritüütsch have a rule that under certain conditions converts underlying /s/ to [š] within morphemes. One part of the environment can be stated as follows: $s > š$ before [b d g] in Alsatian and Züritüütsch, $s > š$ before [g] in Darmstadt Hessian. We have then two versions of a rule effecting the same change:

$$3.18 \quad \begin{bmatrix} + \text{ obstruent} \\ + \text{ continuant} \\ + \text{ coronal} \end{bmatrix} \rightarrow [- \text{ anterior}] / \underline{\hspace{1cm}} \begin{bmatrix} + \text{ obstruent} \\ - \text{ anterior} \end{bmatrix}$$

$$3.18' \quad \begin{bmatrix} + \text{ obstruent} \\ + \text{ continuant} \\ + \text{ coronal} \end{bmatrix} \rightarrow [- \text{ anterior}] / \underline{\hspace{1cm}} [+ \text{ obstruent}]$$

Rule 3.18 is the rule in Darmstadt Hessian; Rule 3.18′, in Alsatian and Züritüütsch.

The segment acted on by both variants of the rule is the same; only the environments are different. The environment of Rule 3.18 requires two features to state; the environment of Rule 3.18′ requires one feature. Rule 3.18′ hence counts as more general, in agreement with our traditional assessment of generality.

One must not conclude from these examples that generality of rule is necessarily related to the number of segments affected by the rule. We do not consider a rule acting on /p z i r h/ more general than a rule acting on /u o ə/: the latter is a natural class, the former is not. "Generality" in phonology has traditionally been understood to involve "either more members of a natural class or more natural classes." The simplicity metric relates this notion to the number of features in the structural analysis of a rule, as the preceding examples illustrate.

An instance different in kind but not in principle is that of the umlaut rule in Continental West Germanic in contrast to the umlaut rule in Old English. In the grammars of the Continental West Germanic dialects (Old High

German, Old Saxon, and Old Frisian) the umlaut rule has the form of Rule 3.6:

$$3.6 \quad V \rightarrow [-\text{back}] / \underline{\quad\quad} C_1 \begin{bmatrix} -\text{consonantal} \\ +\text{high} \\ -\text{back} \end{bmatrix}$$

This rule, which assimilates a vowel in backness to the [− back] high vowel or glide in the next following syllable, accounts for such alternations in Old High German as *gast* : *gesti* 'guest, guests', the latter from underlying /gast + i/; and *skōno* : *skōni* 'beautifully, beautiful', the latter from underlying /skōn + i/. Old High German orthography gives no indication of fronting in the *ō* of *skōni*, but we are assured of its presence by the later writing *schœne*, which does indicate fronting. In later Middle High German we find OHG *skōno* : *skōni* written *schōne* : *schœne*, and the reflexes in current German are *schon* 'already' (no umlaut) and *schön* 'beautiful' (with umlaut). We thus assume that underlying /skōni/ in Old High German was realized phonetically as [skö:ni], though written without umlaut designation.

Old English, on the other hand, had a more general version of Rule 3.6. Its rule resembles Rule 3.6 in that back vowels were fronted before *i* and *j* in the next syllable (Old English has no long vowels under weak stress, so *ī* does not occur as an umlaut factor): *hlāford* : *hlǣfdiġe* 'master, mistress'; *dōm* : *dōeman* (< *dōmjan*) 'judgment, to judge'; *brūcan* : *brȳċþ* (< *brūċiþ*) 'to need, he needs'; *gold* : *gylden* (< *guldin*) 'gold, golden'. But in addition to palatal umlaut (*i*-umlaut) Old English had in its earliest grammar a rule that backed front vowels before *ŭ* and *w* in the following syllable. Details in the formulation of this rule vary considerably from dialect to dialect (Brunner 1965:80–89, Campbell 1959:85–93); as examples we may cite *clipian* : *cliopode* (< *clipude*) 'call, he called'; *ġeset* : *ġeseoto* (< *ġesetu*) 'dwelling, dwellings'; *hæf* (< *haf*) : *heafu* (< *hafu*) 'sea, seas'. Velar umlaut of *i e a* produced *io eo ea*, which are assumed here to represent back unrounded vowels [ï ë ɑ] in agreement with the views of Stockwell and Barritt (1955) and Hockett (1959). That there are no instances of *u*-umlaut of long vowels is due to various historical changes, one of which caused *u* to be deleted in pre-Old English after a heavy syllable—i.e. a syllable consisting of either (1) a long vowel plus any number of consonants including none, or (2) a short vowel followed by at least two consonants.

Thus, the umlaut rule in Old English—at least in the grammars of some of the earliest dialects—expressed a more general kind of assimilation than did Rule 3.6. The Old English rule not only assimilated back vowels to the frontness of following high vowels and semivowels, but also assimilated front vowels to the backness of following back high vowels and semivowels. For this we assume a rule:

$$3.19 \quad V \rightarrow [\alpha \text{ back}] / \underline{} C_1 \begin{bmatrix} - \text{ consonantal} \\ + \text{ high} \\ \alpha \text{ back} \end{bmatrix}$$

($\breve{u}$ $\breve{o}$ $\breve{a}$ > $\breve{u}$ $\breve{o}$ $\breve{a}$ before at least one consonant followed by $\breve{\imath}$ or j; $i\,e\,a$ >$\bar{\imath}\bar{e}$ a before at least one consonant followed by $\breve{u}$ or w. The backing rule did not apply to long vowels $\bar{\imath}$ $\bar{e}$ $\bar{a}$ since these did not stand in the requisite environment. As mentioned before, the exact form of Rule 3.19 varied according to time and dialect, and no account of such differences is taken in its formulation here.)

Note that Rule 3.19 is a generalization of Rule 3.6 provided we observe the well-motivated convention that in the simplicity metric variables (such as alpha) count less than specified pluses or minuses. Rule 3.19 is clearly a generalization of Rule 3.6 since it effects not only the alternations given by Rule 3.6 but also the parallel set of changes involving the natural class of front vowels. The feature counts of both rules directly reflect this greater generality: they differ only in that Rule 3.19 has [α back] in place of a specified [$-$ back] in the environment, and α counts less than a specified minus.

All examples offered so far have to do with the simplification (generalization) of grammar rules. Other kinds of simplification are relevant to linguistic change, some more trivial than rule simplification, some more subtle. Typically, in the history of a language, a lexical entry is simplified in ways that reduce the number of idiosyncratic features it carries. The change in the verb 'to help' between Middle English and Modern English is characteristic. In Middle English it was conjugated strong with the principal parts *helpe(n) halp hulpen holpen*; today it is weak *help helped helped*. What seems to have changed here is the set of features that determine this verb's morphological behavior. In Middle English it had schematically the lexical entry:

(help+ [+ Verb, + Strong, + Class III, ...])

which characterizes it as a strong verb of the third ablaut class plus whatever else (...) is required to determine its grammatical behavior completely. In Modern English it has the lexical entry:

(help+ [+ Verb, − Strong, ...])

which represents a simplification in that the single feature [− Strong] has replaced the two features [+ Strong, + Class III].

Instances of this kind are common, and the reason for describing them with the term "simplification" is obvious. It is perhaps less obvious that some of the types of primary change discussed earlier also represent an aspect of simplification. This is not in general true of rule addition in any obvious sense, but it is true of rule loss and rule reordering. The simplification in the latter cases amounts to a reduction of allomorphic variation in certain morphemes at the surface level. Before the terminal devoicing rule was lost in Yiddish, a morpheme such as *veg* 'path' would have had two allomorphs: /vek/ and /veg/. The loss of the terminal devoicing rule in effect collapses these two allomorphs into one /veg/; so too for all the forms that display this type of biallomorphy.

In Standard German, before the terminal devoicing and vowel lengthening rules were reversed in order, a noun such as *Rad* 'wheel' would have had the two allomorphs /rat/ and /ra:d/, which differ both in the length of the root vowel and in the voicing value of the final obstruent. Upon reordering, *Rad* would have the allomorphs /ra:t/ and /ra:d/, which are different only in the voicing value of the obstruent.

The Monachi example presented in Section 3.2 as an instance of rule addition can be interpreted as a case of simplification. Recall that the Bishop dialect had nasalized [w̃] corresponding to non-nasalized [w] in the North Fork dialect. Nasalized glides are somewhat unusual in the world's languages; Chomsky and Halle (1968:407), in their marking conventions for glides, state that glides are specified non-nasal. Thus, a grammar that violates this constraint is more complex than one that obeys it. In the Monachi example we seem to have a transition from a grammar that violates a universal constraint on nasality in glides to a simpler grammar that obeys this constraint. Bishop represents the older, more complex stage; North Fork, the newer, simpler stage of grammar.

It is not altogether accidental that types of primary change turn out to be instances of simplification in disguise. Why this should be so is the problem to which we shall devote our attention in the following chapter.

SUPPLEMENTARY READING

Becker, Donald A. 1967. *Generative Phonology and Dialect Study: An Investigation of Three Modern German Dialects.* Unpublished doctoral dissertation, University of Texas at Austin.

Keyser, Samuel J. 1963. Review of Hans Kurath and Raven I. McDavid, Jr., *The Pronunciation of English in the Atlantic States. Language* 39.303–316.

Kiparsky, Paul. 1968. "Linguistic Universals and Linguistic Change," in *Universals in Linguistic Theory*, eds. Emmon Bach and Robert T. Harms. New York: Holt, Rinehart & Winston, Inc.

Saporta, Sol. 1965. "Ordered Rules, Dialect Differences, and Historical Processes." *Language* 41.218–224.

Weinreich, Uriel. 1954. "Is a Structural Dialectology Possible?" *Word* 10.388–400.

4

GRAMMAR SIMPLIFICATION

In the preceding chapter we were primarily concerned with determining types of linguistic change in languages both living and dead. Four individual categories of change were isolated: rule addition, rule loss, rule reordering, and simplification. There do not seem to be other major kinds of change that cannot be reduced to one of these four, and indeed two of the four—rule loss and reordering—can be understood as belonging to simplification in its broadest sense. We shall find later that other types of apparently unrelated changes such as analogy often reduce to special cases of simplification.

It is possible that further investigation will turn up other types of change that do not belong in any natural way to any of the four primary types posited. If this happens, it will affect what has been said only in that we must ascertain its implications for our conception of change as change in the speaker's competence—in the system of rules underlying his ability to speak his native language.

The presentation in Chapter 3 must not be wrongly construed. Although primary change is ultimately reducible to one of four types, one should not conclude that each of the four is equally probable given a particular grammar. Such does not seem to be the case. Rule addition seems characteristically to occur in the adult's grammar, whereas rule loss and reordering seem primarily to occur in the child's grammar. Simplification, rule loss, and rule reordering seem typically to occur in the transmission of language from generation to generation, not within the speaker's adult life span.

This chapter deals primarily with the processes of linguistic change between generations. We shall probe into the mysteries of change more deeply than in the preceding chapter, where we were merely moving about on the surface of linguistic change.

We shall develop here a unified picture of linguistic change as it is at present comprehended within the theory of language and grammar sketched in Chapter 2. Implicit in any theory construction is the setting up of hypotheses, and in this chapter we shall, for example, hypothesize that young children, and not adults, have the ability to construct an optimal (simplest) grammar from exposure to a finite set of speech performances. We shall hypothesize that the grammars of adult speakers change, if at all, by minor alterations relatively "late" in the set of ordered rules comprising a given component of the grammar. Adults, that is to say, are capable of incorporating innovations in their grammar, but not in general capable of redoing their grammar in ways open to children constructing their grammar from scratch. We shall hypothesize that the transmission of a grammar, whether through time or geographic space, is in general accompanied by equal or increased simplicity, and not by complication (reduction in generality).

It must be emphasized that all such statements are hypotheses about linguistic change; that is, they are statements that can be disproved. If a "counter-example" is found, which unequivocally demonstrates the incorrectness or implausibility of an hypothesis, then that hypothesis must be discarded or refined so as to be compatible with the data furnished by the counter-example. We cannot *prove* the hypothesis presented here (or any other hypotheses, for that matter). We can disprove them by finding a counter-example. We can support the hypothesis by showing that it is compatible with an ever widening field of data. We can show that an hypothesis in our theory is neutral with respect to a datum that is a counter-example to an hypothesis in a different theory of language change. But we cannot prove hypotheses in the way we prove, say, certain theorems in geometry given a set of undefined entities (point, line) and a set of axioms which state relations among these undefined entities.

4.1 CHANGES IN THE ADULT'S GRAMMAR

An hypothesis in our theory of language change is that changes in adult grammars are typically limited to minor alterations: addition of items to the lexicon, minor modifications in the formulation of a rule, addition of at most a few rules to a component of the grammar.

Note that "addition of a rule" does not mean that the adult looks around for a rule, finds one, and tacks it on to the end of his grammar in the way that a computer programmer might add to a previously written program an instruction to carry out an additional operation. The statement "Changes in adult grammars are typically limited to . . . addition of at most a few rules" is shorthand for the more complicated formulation: "Of the few ways a speaker's competence in his language changes once he has reached linguistic adulthood, one of the more common is most simply accounted for *in the linguist's model of this competence* as the addition of one or at most a few rules to the set of rules comprising a given component of the grammar. This rule acts on the previously produced output of the grammar and may modify it." Such a statement is neutral with respect to the internal makeup of the speaker's competence—the mass of brain cells, nerves, and so on, that account for speech in neural and physiological senses. In other words, what has happened to the inside of the adult speaker's head is something we at present haven't the faintest notion of. What we do know is that the grammar—that is, here, our account of the speaker's competence—registers such a change by having an extra rule added to it at some point.

What supports the hypothesis that adult grammars are rather severely limited in what can be done to them? One piece of the supporting data is the fact that people past a certain age find it next to impossible to learn a foreign language with native-speaker perfection. A child has no trouble learning his language, and he learns it perfectly unless physiological or emotional factors hinder him in some way. Children can even learn with native or near-native mastery two or more completely different languages if they are exposed in a natural way to speakers of these languages during their early years, say, before the age of thirteen or so (the exact age is subject to individual variation, but is likely near puberty). But adults do have all kinds of difficulty in learning a new language. The percentage of speakers handling two languages with native fluency, one of which they learned as an adult, must be vanishingly small in any culture.

The simplest explanation of this datum is that adults simply cannot do one of the things that children do without even being told: construct a complete grammar on the basis of exposure to a finite number of utterances in a language. Yet adults do exhibit changes in their speech performance. Even nonlinguists know that, and our theory of change must be compatible with the existence of adult change.

What are the typical changes that take place in adult grammar? One of the easiest things an adult can learn, and one of the most trivial, is a new word. Before adulthood the number of new words a speaker learns each year must be in the neighborhood of a thousand or more, and up to complete senility and regression any adult in any language can learn a new word. Whether he habitually uses the word or not is irrelevant: as adults we can and do learn new words that we *can* use as long as we are in any measure open to experience. From the point of view of generative grammar, the learning of a new word is the addition of a new item to the lexicon—an utterly trivial alteration of the grammar. None of the existing output is affected unless the new word happens to displace an old one. No new grammatical rules must be learned to accomodate the addition. In short, addition of items to the lexicon—a typically adult thing to do—involves no major overhauling of the grammar; it is simply an addition to the lexicon, the formally most static component of the grammar.

A second characteristic kind of adult grammar change is the adoption, for some reason or other, of a prestige pronunciation. Such change can be very subtle and even independent of conscious effort by the speaker. Typically it occurs when the speaker wants to bring his speech more into line with the accepted standard or, and this amounts to the same thing, when he wants to be linguistically less striking in a particular social or geographic milieu. Consider, for example, the speaker from the South who goes to college in the North. In most cases, such a person would grow up saying [aˤ·ə̣] 'I', [aˤ·ə̣m] 'I'm', [kraˤ·ə̣m] 'crime', and so on. This is part of his "Southern drawl," and most speakers not from the South readily identify such a pronunciation as typically Southern. Our college student, if he is sensitive about such matters, might very well begin to pronounce the foregoing words closer to the norm of his new environment: [aị̯], [aị̯m], [kraị̯m].

How do we account for a change like this in the grammar of the college student? Whatever the exact way we do this, it should be clear that no major redoing of the grammar is necessitated. The principal phonological rules remain the same, not to mention the syntactic rules. In particular, the rules in the grammar of English which account for such alternations as *crime : criminal, finite : infinite, pronounce : pronunciation, profound : profundity* remain the same. Whether one says [kraị̯m] : [krɪmɪnəl] or [kraˤ·ə̣m] : [krɪmɪnəl], the simplest description in either case would have base forms with tense /ī/ in /krīm/ : /krīminæl/ and include in the grammar phonological rules laxing tense vowels such as /ī/ in certain environments, giving *criminal* with [i], and diphthongizing them in other environments giving *crime* with [ay]. The difference in the grammars of speakers of American English who say [aị̯] and those who say [aˤ·ə̣] is then the difference in a rule in the final, nonbinary section of the phonological component that prescribes the detailed phonetic description of [ay] from underlying /ī/. In the case at hand, probably the simplest way of accounting for the speech behavior of the transplanted Southerner is to assume that in his native grammar there is a low-level rule

$$[ay] > [a˂ ˑ ə̣]$$

and that he has added a rule which is ordered after this rule and gives

$$[a˂ ˑ ə̣] > [ai̯]$$

Whether or not this is the most desirable way of describing the present case, it is clear that no sweeping changes in the original grammar are needed. Almost all his previous rules remain intact after the Southerner learns his new pronunciation.

The claim that adults add late rules to their grammars is not devoid of empirical content. It implies that identical surface forms, even those deriving from distinct underlying sources, will be treated exactly alike by the rule added at the end of the grammar. This produces in certain cases the phenomenon known as "hypercorrection," which will be discussed further on in some detail. Thus, the claim that adults add late rules entails the prediction that adults, not children, tend typically toward hypercorrection, and this prediction is in fact borne out by the data on hypercorrection that are available.

Further cases of adult rule addition are those in which a rule spreads throughout an area. Such instances have been studied in depth by Labov (1963, 1965). We conclude from these studies that sound changes spreading within a few decades throughout large segments of the (adult) population represent instances of rule addition at a point relatively late in the grammar. One of the case studies concerns the variants found in New York City urban speech of the ingliding diphthongs [æə̣] and [ɔə̣]: cf. *bad dog* [bæə̣d dɔə̣g] : [bɛə̣d doə̣g] : [bɪə̣d dʊə̣g]. The occurrence of these variants shows definite age and ethnic correlations, and we assume that they represent in part at least the spread of a rule or rules throughout an adult population. In other words, they involve changes in the grammars of adults. In line with the hypothesis proposed earlier, we would expect that these vowel shifts in New York City are best described as instances of late rule addition that leaves intact underlying phonemic representations and the body of phonological rules that account for the considerable morphophonemic alternation in English. And, indeed, Labov states, "The far-reaching shifts and mergers observed in the long and ingliding vowel system of New York City . . . do not affect the morphophonemic system" (1965:102, n. 20).

A third kind of change often found in the language of adults, and not generally among young children, is hypercorrection. We shall see that hypercorrection is best understood as a sort of overlay of rules added to an already formed grammar, and not as a wholesale restructuring of the grammar.

The general sociological background of the phenomenon of hypercorrection is well known. It requires a situation in which certain items and casts of speech are recognized as prestige-bestowing. The speaker who hypercorrects desires to acquire the prestige conveyed by this sort of speech, has learned a certain number of rules that bring his speech closer to the prestige norm, but applies these rules incorrectly, thus producing a hypercorrect form. A case in point is hypercorrect *whom* for *who*: *There you see the man whom we believe is the murderer*; *Whom do you think will be the next President? Who* is correct in such contexts, and the hypercorrect use of *whom* obviously has something to do with the fact that the vast majority of speakers of English "incorrectly" use *who* for *whom* in, for example, *Who do you see?*; *Is he the man who you wanted to talk to?* The hypercorrecting speaker adds a transformational rule that replaces *who* → *whom* in certain surface syntactic contexts. When applied to the output that his grammar has already produced, this rule will give correct results in *Whom do you see?* but hypercorrection in *Whom do you think will be the next President?* This particular instance of hypercorrection has been thoroughly discussed by Klima (1965), where it is shown that the grammar of the hypercorrect *whom* speaker has an extra transformational rule added at the end of a group of related transformations. There has not been any major change in the grammar; in fact, to use *who* and *whom* in the way sanctioned by Miss Fidditch the speaker would have to reorder two transformations in his grammar, and this the hypercorrect speaker has not done.

A case of phonological hypercorrection from Low German further illustrates the superficiality of the change undergone by the grammar of a speaker who produces something hypercorrect. Low German, originally widely spoken in Northern Germany, has little prestige nowadays. No one speaks "pure Low German" except possibly in rural areas far removed from the inroads of modernity. For any number of historical reasons Low German has retreated before Standard High German, so that today one can hardly rise socially in Germany without High German. Low German and High German are closely related, sharing a large number of cognate lexical items such as Low German *ik* : High German *ich* 'I'. The chief identifying parameters of Low German are phonological ones such as Low German stops corresponding to High German affricates or fricatives, as in *ik* [ɪk] versus *ich* [ɪç]. The major correspondences are: Low German [d] = High German [t]; Low German [p t] = High German [pf ts] in certain environments and [p t k] = [f s x] in others; Low German [iː üː uː] = High German [aị ɔị aụ]. Details vary from dialect to dialect; the following examples are from a dialect of Low German spoken along the lower Elbe (Keller 1961:339–379):

Low German	High German	Gloss
dɔxtər	tɔxtər	daughter
pɛpər	pfɛfər	pepper
tiːt	tsaịt	time
makən	maxən	to make
bɛtər	bɛsər	better
bliːbən	blaịbən	to stay
füːst	fɔịstə	fists
buːk	baụx	stomach

Knowing that Low German has little prestige, that it is similar to High German in many ways, we expect and find a good deal of hypercorrection in the speech of native Low German speakers striving to improve their position and chances in a High German society. We find, for example, the hypercorrect form *[baxən] 'to bake' alongside correct Low and High German [bakən]. The explanation is clear. The native Low German speaker, accustomed to hearing High German [x] or [ç] (after front vowels) in place of his [k] in many items such as [makən] : [maxən] 'to make' and [ɪk] : [ɪç] 'I', adds to his grammar a rule shifting $k > x$ (and $p > f$, $t > s$) in the appropriate environment (primarily post-vocalic). In instances like those of 'to make' and 'I', the result is fine: our Low German speaker trying to speak High German comes up with a form not appreciably different from that of prestigious High German.

The catch leading to hypercorrection is that Low German [k] does not always correspond to High German [x] in the requisite environments; some postvocalic [k]'s in Low German correspond to High German [k]'s: compare Low German and High German [bakən] 'to bake', Low German [ki:kən] versus High German [kʊkən] 'to look'. The correct form produced in the Low German grammar is [bakən], and the correction rule $k > x$ is erroneously applied, yielding *[baxən].

Similar statements could be made about other sets of correspondences. For example, Low German [u:] corresponds to High German [aʊ] in, say, the word for 'stomach', but there are also cases of Low German [u:] = High German [u:]. We have this in Low German [ju:d(ə)] : High German [ju:də] 'Jew', which moreover is a case of Low German [d] = High German [d] as against the also occurring correspondence [d] : [t]. The added rules of hypercorrection when applied to correct Low German [ju:d(ə)] produce hypercorrect High German *[jaʊtə].

Hermann (1931:37) quotes an amusing story as an example of hypercorrection: The story was told by the prominent Low German writer Rudolf Kinau concerning his first day in school, where naturally it was expected of him that he should speak only High German in class. Kinau's nickname was *Rudel*, so that in his native Low German he would have pronounced his name [ru:dəl ki:naʊ]. This is also a perfectly acceptable High German name, and in High German it would also be [ru:dəl ki:naʊ]. When asked on that first day to give his name, in High German of course, Kinau promptly replied *Rautzel Keinau* *[raʊtsəl kaɪnaʊ].

Part of this is readily understandable in view of what has already been said about German hypercorrection by native Low Germans. The rule [i: ü: u:] > [aɪ ɔɪ aʊ] has been added on the Low German grammar at a low level, and it is erroneously applied to the [i:] and [u:] in [ru:dəl ki:naʊ] to give *[raʊtsəl kaɪnaʊ]. The [ts] in *[raʊtsəl] is a sort of hyper-hypercorrection, reflected in the grammar by a reversal in the order of application of two rules. It was earlier pointed out that Low German [d] corresponds in many cases to High

German [t] (*Dach* versus *Tag* 'day'), and that Low German [t] corresponds to High German [ts] (*to* versus *zu* [tsu:] 'to'). To get from Low German to High German in the simplest way, two rules must be added to the Low German grammar:

A. $t > ts$

B. $d > t$

The order of application of the two rules must be A followed by B. These rules, applying to what has already been produced in Low German, will give the right High German forms:

Low German Forms:	fadǝr 'father'	taįn 'ten'
Rule A:	....	tsaįn
Rule B:	fatǝr	....

We get [fatǝr] and [tsaįn], which differ only in relatively minor details of vocalism from the correct High German forms [fa:tǝr] and [tse:n].

What Rudolf Kinau did on his first day of school, in trying under pressure to render his name in High German, was to reverse the order of application of the two rules, at least for the one time in question: the [d] in *Rudel* was changed by Rule B to [t], which then qualifies as input to Rule A and undergoes [t] > [ts]. The net result is hypercorrect *[rautsǝl kaįnau] from correct [ru:dǝl ki:nau]. One cannot assume that Kinau consistently applied the rules in the order B followed by A, which is the opposite of correct, for no German speaker could go around for long saying *[fatsǝr] for correct [fa:tǝr] 'father' and *[tsax] for correct [ta:k] 'day' without having his mistake firmly brought home to him in some way or other.

The point of the example is that rules of hypercorrection do not seem to be firmly embedded in a natively acquired grammar. In hypercorrection there is no perfect mastery of the correct grammar and sequence of rules, no restructuring of the kind that would proceed from native internalization of the grammar. Rules of hypercorrection seem rather to be an inorganic and somewhat ephemeral superstructure built onto the firmer foundation of a grammar acquired through the normal process of language acquisition.

4.2 GRAMMAR CONSTRUCTION IN THE CHILD

When we leave the adult's grammar and turn to the child's grammar and way of acquiring language, we enter a field bristling with question marks. Enough is known, however, to suggest certain hypotheses about language change.

How does a child learn to speak his language? As little as is known about this engrossing and complex subject, certain notions seem definitely wrong. One is the idea that the child, like a parrot learning to talk, repeats what is said to him and in his presence. The older the child becomes, the more he has heard; consequently he is able to say more and his imitations approach the adult model.

The most telling argument against this gross version of the imitative theory is the child's ability to be linguistically creative even at an early age. A normal child of three can say all kinds of things which he could not possibly have heard. He has acquired, in other words, the ability that all native speakers of any language possess: the potential of constant and, in principle, infinite inventiveness. In the course of a single two-hour period a child at age three and a half produced the following monologues while talking to himself at bedtime:

- A. (1) cat (many times)
  - (2) two (many times)
  - (3) bats
  - (4) the cat sees two bats

- B. (1) pig (many times)
  - (2) big
  - (3) sleep
  - (4) big pig sleep now

Repetition drills like these are quite common among children (Weir 1962). What is interesting is that the end results of monologues A and B—*the cat sees two bats* and *big pig sleep now*—were both utterances that the child in question had never heard before either in conversation or in stories read aloud. For him they were new and unique creations.

Whatever the exact nature of the child's competence and whatever characteristics of the human being enable him to arrive at a competence in so short a time, it is certain that a child soon goes beyond the corpus of utterances to which he has been exposed. Following McNeill (1966:19) we propose to explain this by assuming that child speech is not garbled output of a complete adult-type grammar but the product of a first, relatively simple grammar. In this view of child language the "telegraphic speech" (Brown and Fraser 1963) so characteristic of young children (*who you?*; *no more*; *want water*) is not so much a falling short of adult models as the output of a grammar— a system of internalized rules—that is shorter and simpler than that of adults. The progress toward adult speech is a constant process of readjusting and adding to the previous grammar.

The child acquires language roughly as follows. He is provided with a small body of data about his language—the corpus of utterances he has heard. On the basis of this limited corpus he constructs a grammar that produces a set of utterances approximating adult speech. This first grammar is then a sort of hypothesis about the native language from the child's point of view: if I carry out certain rules I will produce my native language, as it were. In general this hypothesis will be at least partially incorrect at first. Its incorrectness will become apparent to the child in various ways: his mother or siblings laugh at his attempts or correct them; he doesn't get what he thought he was asking for; certain internal comparisons, which we know little about, may cause him to reject certain constructions. The child then refines his hypothesis—his grammar—perhaps extending its range in light of the larger number of utterances he has heard, and again produces utterances. By frequent and constant hypothesis testing of this sort the child eventually arrives at a grammar of his language, a competence that underlies speech output close to acceptable adult speech.

Note that we must not take this description of grammar building too literally. What we mean by "a child constructs his grammar" is not that he builds something the same way he builds a house out of Lincoln Logs or a ferris wheel with an erector set. By the process of hypothesizing, testing, evaluating, repeated over and over again, the child develops a competence in his language that we as linguists may represent as a set of components containing ordered rules.

This process of grammar construction in the child is unique—unique as an idiolect, as unique as a personality. Yet like an idiolect or a personality, the grammar a child constructs is not totally different from those of the speakers who cared for him, played with him, and read to him during the years of language formation, just as a child's personality is never completely different from the personalities of the people who move about in his world.

The parallel between grammar and personality is not a bad one. A child developing his personality constructs hypotheses about behavior by observing the social and emotional performance of those around him. He tests these hypotheses in various ways, and they are verified, or rejected in equally various ways. He then discards, corrects, or adds to his previous hypotheses about his place and role in the world, tests these, and so it goes. Unless some severe emotional disturbance is created which disrupts the process of personality building completely (as in autism), the child ends up with a well defined personality—a system of rules determining his image of himself in its social setting—and this basic personality tends to remain with him throughout life. His personality has much in common with those of his overseers and playmates, yet differs from them in various ways both good and bad.

A child's grammar building is to a certain extent analogous to his personality building, yet is typically less of an original product than his personality; for one thing, the child's grammar resembles adult grammars more than is usually the case with personality. If this were not the case, then there would have long since been a pressing need for "linguotherapists" whose relation to their subject's language would parallel a psychotherapist's relation to his patient's psyche. But the instructive point of similarity is that in both cases the child constructs something uniquely his yet not radically different from the models present in his environment. The potentialities of deviation are great in any such original process.

Pressing the analogy one step further, we point out one crucial feature in which grammar construction and personality construction tend to diverge radically. A child rarely, if ever, constructs a grammar more complex than that of his models. He will accept his grammar as it is with perhaps minor deviations, or he will simplify it in various ways and for various reasons; but he will not complicate it. This is not a general rule of personality construction. There are many cases in which the child constructs a more complex, a more maze-like picture of himself and his place in the world than any of his models has constructed for himself.

This sketch of the child's grammar acquisition highlights one of the chief sources of linguistic change: the transmission of language to the new generation, or, to use a less misleading figure of speech, the acquisition of language by each child in a new generation. We saw in Section 4.1 that adult grammars do not seem susceptible to much change once they have "congealed." Yet the histories of languages are replete with examples of radical changes that cannot be reasonably accounted for by rule addition such as might occur in adult grammars. For example, we assume that rule reordering as discussed in Section 3.3 occurs in the child's learning of a language and not within the grammar of an adult, and we attribute such changes to *grammar simplification* (optimization).

The role of grammar simplification is basic to our conception of linguistic change. The underlying idea was originally stated by Halle (1962:64):

> The ability to master a language like a native, which children possess to an extraordinary degree, is almost completely lacking in the adult. I propose to explain this as being due to deterioration or loss in the adult of the ability to construct optimal (simplest) grammars on the basis of a restricted corpus of examples. The language of the adult—and hence also the grammar that he has internalized—need not, however, remain static: it can and does, in fact, change. I conjecture that changes in later life are restricted to the addition of a few rules in the grammar and the elimination of rules and hence a wholesale restructuring of his grammar is beyond the capabilities of the average adult.

Note carefully what this does *not* say. It does not say that change is confined to the child. It does not say that children can speak only with flawless or maximally simple grammars in their heads. It does say that children can and often do construct a grammar formally simpler than adult grammars. It does imply that a child, creating a grammar from the finite and fairly small corpus of examples he has to go on, can come up with a competence—an internalized grammar—that is simpler than an adult grammar yet underlies a speech output either identical with adult speech for all practical purposes or different in relatively minor ways.

Let us examine some of the evidence that supports the notion of child optimization of grammar. That children simplify is well known and obvious to everyone. This is particularly evident at the morphological level: probably every English-speaking child has at some time said something on the order of *I goed*; *two foots*. This simplification is the extension of a pattern of inflection from the regular cases to irregular ones. Ervin (1964) has called our attention to an interesting progression of simplification. The first verb forms which are used in child speech are unmarked for tense: *Where the car go?*; *What he do?*, where the context alone signals which tense is meant. The first past tense forms that emerged in Ervin's observations were irregular ones, such as *went, did, came*, and these at first were formed correctly. This is not surprising since these have a high frequency of occurrence and a child will hear them only in their correct form in a family speaking standard English. Soon, however, the children observed by Ervin went over to regular past tense formations such as *goed, doed, comed* even at a time when the child had control of only a few weak verbs that could serve as a model for the extension. In fact, in Ervin's tape-recorded sample the children produced no weak verbs, though this is attributed to the relative infrequency of weak verbs in the speech normally directed toward a child. In other words, almost as soon as he got the chance the child substituted incorrect but regular past tense forms for his earlier correct but irregular forms. From the point of view of the child's grammar, he has added a rule

$$\text{Verb} + \text{Past} \rightarrow \text{Verb} + /d/$$

which then functions for all verbs irrespective of their idiosyncracies in adult speech.

In the same way, a child's first acquired syntactic rules tend to be simplified versions of similar rules in adult grammars. One of the first rules of syntactic formation internalized by the child has the form (McNeill 1966:23)

$$S \rightarrow (P)\widehat{\ }O$$

where *P* and *O* stand for "pivot class" and "object class" respectively (Braine 1963). This rule produces expansions of *S* as either *O* or $P\widehat{\ }O$, giving a set of one and two word sentences: *allgone milk*; *byebye boat*; *shoe*; *hot*; *baby*; *this baby*. In fact, much of the "telegraphic" nature of child speech results directly from simplified versions of rules like this, and it has even been suggested (McNeill 1966:19) that children produce telegraphic speech for much the same reasons that adults send telegrams saying: BROKE. NEED MONEY instead of I'M BROKE AND I NEED MONEY. The reason is cost—either financial or cognitive. As the adult omits unnecessary words to make his message cheaper, the child economizes on the amount of mental effort needed to express what he wants.

Many cases of simplification in the child's acquisition of language are more subtle than either of these examples from morphology and syntax. The following instance is based on personal observations by the author. Most kinds of American English have a well-known phonological rule that makes *t* into *d* or into a half-voiced (or voiced) alveolar flap ("voiced *t*") after a stressed vowel and before an unstressed vocalic segment. In these dialects *write* : *writer* is [raɪt] : [raɪdɨr], and *latter* differs from *ladder* at most in slight extra vowel length in *ladder*, both being approximately [lædɨr] ([d] here is a cover symbol for the voiced alveolar stop [d] or the half-voiced alveolar flap [ţ]).

A child, closely observed in his linguistic behavior from the age of two and a half on, grew up in a family and in a region (Madison, Wisconsin) where the *t*-voicing rule was operative. Between the ages of five and six, however, he was observed to pronounce, for example, *fight* : *fighting* as [faɪtʰ] : [faɪtʰɪŋ] and also *fighter* [faɪtʰɨr], similarly *sit* : *sitting* [sɪtʰ] : [sɪtʰɪŋ]. Now at that time and earlier no one in his environment or in the television programs he watched said such things: they all had [sɪtʰ] ~ [sɪt] : [sɪdɪŋ], and so on. This is best explained as simplification: his grammar was not appreciably different from that of his adult models, but simpler in that it was a rule shorter, for it lacked the *t*-voicing rule present in the adult grammar. Both the child and the adults had underlying /sit/ : /siting/ for *sit* : *sitting* since the adults have a *t*/*d* alternation. The *t*-voicing rule in the adult grammar would give the biallomorphic forms [sɪtʰ] : [sɪdɪŋ]. The child, having no such rule, would say [sɪtʰ] : [sɪtʰɪŋ] with a single allomorph [sɪtʰ].

Note too that the child said *water* [wadɨr] and *potty* [pʰadiy] as did his elders. The [d]'s in these words were invariant in the speech of the adults; that is, they underwent no phonological alternation with [t]'s elsewhere in the paradigm. Hence the child had no reason to posit base forms with /t/ in such forms. (He had not heard *pot* at this point, only *potty*.) *Water* and *potty* would then have the base forms /wadr/ and /padi/, which give phonetic [wadɨr] and [pʰadiy]. In *sit* : *sitting* and similar alternations, in which the adults around the child presented him only with [sɪtʰ] : [sɪdɪŋ], the child constructed base forms with /t/ giving /sit/ : /siting/ and ignored the [d] in *sitting* by not adding a *t*-voicing rule to his grammar.

We can call this either *imperfect learning* (Kiparsky 1965) or *grammar simplification*. The child has obviously not quite arrived yet at the grammar of the adults around him; that is, he has learned his language imperfectly. His grammar is simpler by a rule than that of his parents and baby-sitters, and this simplification shows up in his speech output as reduction in the amount of allomorphic variation in *fight* : *fighting*, *beat* : *beating*, and so on. At about the age of seven, this child finally added the rule of *t*-voicing to his grammar and started saying [biːt] : [biːdɪŋ], [sɪt] : [sɪdɪŋ], and so on.

This example invites comparison with the case discussed in Section 3.3 of rule loss in Yiddish. There, a rule for devoicing terminal obstruents was lost, producing *veg* : *vege* and *tog* : *teg* from earlier surface forms *vek* : *vege* 'path, paths' and *tak* : *tage* 'day, days'. One of the crucial bits of evidence of rule loss was the presence in contemporary Yiddish of relic forms like *avek* 'away' from original *veg* 'path', indicating the previous existence of a rule of terminal devoicing.

Suppose now that the child discussed in regard to *t*-voicing had retained into adulthood his grammar of age five. Suppose further that other children of the same and following generations also retained a grammar of English that lacked the *t*-voicing rule. This situation is not completely far-fetched because such a grammar is simpler than one containing the *t*-voicing rule and because there are dialects of English (like British English) without the rule. We would then reach a point in several generations where a sizeable portion of the population would be saying [sɪtʰ] : [sɪtʰɪŋ], [raɪtʰ] : [raɪtʰɪŋ] (*write* : *writing*). From the viewpoint of historical linguistics we would know this to be a case of rule loss for the same kind of reason as in Yiddish: the existence of "relic" forms [wadɪr] *water*, [bɪdɪr] *bitter*, [lædɪr] *latter*. If we had sufficient knowledge of the history of English and other dialects of English, we would know that such forms originally had *t* in them, and the fact that they now show [d] would point back to a stage when the *t*-voicing rule was operative.

Note that rule loss might better be termed "rule nonacquisition" to emphasize the likely mechanism by which rules are lost from a grammar. However, the notion of rule loss has been in historical linguistics for a long time, and it is preferable to retain the traditional terminology for this kind of primary change.

Examples such as these, which can be multiplied by close observation of child speech, support the proposal that children simplify (optimize) the grammar that they construct. This does not mean, of course, that they must always simplify or that they can never acquire more difficult grammar rules. The maturation process in child language is precisely characterized by the acquisition of additional rules, the refinement of already acquired rules—in general the construction of a larger and more complex grammar. But in being presented with the data of his language, each child draws his own conclusions about what kind of grammar has produced the data. Each child in each new generation takes a fresh look at the situation, as it were, and the result is often simplification of a sort beyond the capabilities of adults, who have completed the construction of *their* grammars—at the least beyond the capabilities of the average, linguistically unsophisticated adult. The restriction on re-structuring in adult grammars may not be quite so severe for adults who, for one reason or another, have a greater than average concern with language. Anyone who (like the present author) didn't get *who* and *whom* straight until the first year of college has apparently succeeded in reordering a pair of transformational rules. This is what the Klima (1965) analysis would suggest.

At any rate, the assumption is that the average person, as opposed to the linguist or even the linguistically astute educated person, cannot change his grammar in radical ways once linguistic adulthood is reached.

This view, which attributes to the new generation a considerable participation in linguistic change, is by no means novel or revolutionary. It was quite widely held among linguists in the late nineteenth century. Hermann Paul, writing around 1880, stated flatly: "The chief cause of sound change lies in the transmission of sounds to new individuals" (1960:63). Rousselot, in the last decade of the nineteenth century, concluded his immensely detailed study of sound changes in a group of French dialects with the observation: "The principle [of linguistic evolution] resides in the child. . . . Parents set the stage for [linguistic] evolution; but the real impetus for this evolution comes only when the children enter into possession of their language" (1892:412–413). Paul Passy argued cogently that many phonological changes arise in the child's acquisition of speech: "All the major changes in pronunciation that we have been able to investigate originate in child speech" (1891:231). And, most eloquently of all, William Dwight Whitney said of the continuity of language through generations:

> Human institutions in general go down from generation to generation by a process of transmission like that of language, and they are modified as they go. . . . No one has ever yet been able to prevent what passes from mouth to ear from getting altered on the way. . . . Although the child in his first stage of learning is more than satisfied to take what is set before him and use it as best he can, . . . the case does not always continue thus with him; by and by his mind has grown up . . . and begins to exhibit its native and surplus force; . . . it modifies a little of its inherited instrument, in order to adapt this better to its own purposes (1883:34–35).

One must note carefully what the arguments of these last two sections imply, and what they do not imply. The principal point is that the potential for change is more severely constrained in adult grammars than in child grammars. What changes occur in adult grammars seem to be few and minor, mostly limited to addition (and, occasionally perhaps, loss) of late rules. The child, in constructing his grammar, obeys less rigid constraints: he can reorder rules, lose rules, generalize rules—in short, can change his grammar in all sorts of ways.

Such a view, neither denying change in the adult nor confining it to children, seeks to state more precisely what types of changes can occur in child and adult grammars. The hypotheses here and in the preceding section have, a priori, a good deal going for them, as has been pointed out, but it is not claimed that every detail of the arguments presented here will remain unchanged under lengthy investigation. No counter-evidence is known to the present author, but then there have been few empirical studies explicitly of what is possible in adult grammars and what is not. Nor have there been enough investigations of the child's acquisition of grammar to enable us to make much more than reasonable hypotheses about this process. These are serious gaps in the data of linguistics; and further research into linguistic change will depend greatly on how well and how completely these gaps are filled.

In particular, little is known about the constraints on change in a child's grammar: given a particular grammar, which rules can be lost (not acquired), which pairs of rules are especially suitable candidates for reordering, which rules are likely to be simplified? Probably such changes usually can affect only later rules in the phonology; the *t*-voicing rule, discussed earlier as an instance of rule loss, is a late rule in English phonology whose effect on the phonetic output is relatively minor. It is a little difficult to imagine the loss of an early rule that radically changes the forms it acts on, of rules such as Velar Softening or Main Stress in English phonology (see Chomsky and Halle 1968:239–240).

Finally, the claim that adult change is largely confined to rule addition does not deny innovation (rule addition) in the child. It is probable that rules of assimilation often arise in the child's acquisition of grammar. Since assimilation produces ease of articulation in some sense, we expect children to add just such rules. Doubtless this tendency towards ease of articulation accounts for the widespread occurrence of certain rules in approximately the same form in different languages, for example, in the rule of nasal assimilation (nasals agree with the following consonant in point of articulation) found in so many of the world's languages. Even rules less obviously assimilatory may arise in child grammar construction. The author has observed several cases of English-speaking children, from ages two and a half to four, who incorporated in their grammars an optional rule devoicing word-final obstruents; they said, for example, [muwf] 'move', [dɔk] 'dog', and so on. These children did not keep these rules beyond the age of five.

So children seem to go beyond simplification in the ordinary sense to innovation. Likewise, child innovations probably are often (if not always) assimilatory in nature; that is, they are simplifications in a "local" sense. As certain as it is that child innovation occurs, at present little is known about which phonological rules arise via child innovation.

4.3   A MODEL OF LINGUISTIC CHANGE

Our conception of language transmission from parent to child can be summarized as follows. The parent has a competence, an internalized grammar, underlying his speech output. Though the grammar of the adult cannot undergo a radical transformation, it is susceptible to innovation in the form of rule additions and minor rule changes. The child, developing his grammar from the speech output of his parents and older peers, arrives at a linguistic competence not radically different from that of the adult. The child's competence reflects not only the original grammar of the adult but also those innovations that the adult grammar may have undergone. The child will optimize—simplify—and in the process linguistic change may result.

Let us consider two hypothetical examples. Assume a language with the stops /b d g p t k/, and suppose that adults add a rule merging *b d g > p t k* unconditionally. Children, hearing only [p t k], would have no reason to posit underlying /b d g/; hence they would construct a grammar (the optimal grammar) containing only underlying /p t k/ and no rule devoicing [b d g]. If, however, the context-sensitive rule *b d g > p t k* / ___ # had been added by the adults and if this rule produced morphophonemic alternations such as *haba:hap, sidu:sit, pego:pek*, then no simpler grammar would account for the data. (Compare the case of terminal devoicing in German discussed in Section 2.2.) In this case, the child will incorporate this rule in his grammar.

Let us now consider some actual cases. In many dialects of English initial [hw] has been reduced to [w]: *whip, what, when* are pronounced [wɪp], [wʌt], [wɛn], not [hwɪp], [hwʌt], [hwɛn]. The change *hw > w* has occurred throughout the entire British Isles except for the northernmost counties of England; in an extensive coastal section of the Middle Atlantic States, according to the records of the Linguistic Atlas of New England (Kurath and McDavid 1961:178); and, by informal observation, in other large sections of the United States such as the Middle West. (See Section 5.1 for further discussion of this change and for more detail about its phonetics.)

Let us now imagine ourselves in a time when the [hw] pronunciation by assumption was still universal. How can the sound change have taken place and spread? We assume that someone, for some reason, quit saying [hwɪp], [hwʌt], [hwɛn] and began to say [wɪp], [wʌt], [wɛn]. In our account of this speaker's competence we add a rule to his grammar:

$$4.1 \quad \begin{bmatrix} - \text{vocalic} \\ - \text{consonantal} \end{bmatrix} \rightarrow \emptyset \; / \; \underline{\hspace{1cm}} \; \begin{bmatrix} - \text{vocalic} \\ - \text{consonantal} \\ + \text{back} \end{bmatrix}$$

(A semivowel, e.g. [h], is deleted before the semivowel [w].)

We can, if we like, speculate on *why* this rule was added. Perhaps the speaker thought *w* sounded better than *hw*, perhaps *hw* was harder to pronounce than *w*. Such speculation is interesting but outside our immediate major concern, which is to give an account in our grammar of a change in speech habits. The simplest way to do this is to assume that our speaker has added Rule 4.1 to his grammar. This represents an innovation in the speaker's grammar, something new with him.

As before the rule addition, the speaker will have lexical entries with /hw/: /hwip/, /hwat/, /hwen/. Rule 4.1 operates on these lexical items, deletes the /h/, and gives phonetic output with initial [w]. It is altogether possible and likely, in view of the large amount of British territory in which *hw* > *w*, that Rule 4.1 spread among adult speakers of English. If this is true, then Rule 4.1 was added to the grammars of these speakers too as an innovation, presumably with [wɪp] retaining the underlying form /hwip/.

Now we come to the child learning the language. From speakers who have Rule 4.1 in their grammars, the child will hear only forms with [w]: [wɪp], [wʌt], [wɛn], [wɛðɪr] *whether* identical with *weather*. He has no reason to assume underlying /hw/ in such words, so that the *child* enters in the lexicon of *his* grammar the underlying forms /wip/, /wat/, /wen/, and so on. There are no *hw* : *w* alternations in the language of his parents to motivate the inclusion of Rule 4.1. Thus, the simplest grammar is one containing no Rule 4.1 and no underlying /hw/ forms in the lexicon. The child thus arrives at a grammar which produces (in this one respect) the identical output as the parent grammar and which is simpler. The output of this grammar in turn serves as the primary data for the language acquisition of the next generation, whose grammar will likewise lack underlying /hw/ and Rule 4.1. In this way we conceive of the change as having spread first as an innovation in the grammars of adult speakers and then as a simplification of the next generation's grammar.

In arriving at the lexical entries with /w/ replacing /hw/, the grammar has undergone simple *restructuring*. We define restructuring as any change in underlying representations. Thus, the four types of primary change discussed in Chapter 3, since none of them necessarily requires change in underlying (systematic phonemic) representations, are not restructuring. It should be noted that usage differs concerning the term *restructuring*. Other linguists distinguish two categories of change: innovation and restructuring. In this usage restructuring comprises rule loss and reordering, simplification, and change in underlying representations.

In the preceding two sections it was argued that adult grammar change was confined to rule addition. Rule loss and reordering, simplification, and restructuring originate in the child. This is the puristic picture. It may well be that adults are capable of participating in certain minor grammar changes other than rule addition, e.g. loss or simplification of certain low-level rules. Adults may even be capable of minor restructuring, though we assume subject to disconfirmation that major change in underlying representations is beyond the adult's ability. Optional, stylistic rules in adult grammars support this assumption: adults use them or not at will, and the lexicon continues unchanged throughout.

This example of innovation in the adult grammar followed by restructuring in the child grammar could, it should be pointed out, be explained in a somewhat different way. Since forms in *w* and *hw* do not alternate phonologically, an adult might have restructured his lexicon vis-à-vis these morphemes. The restructuring involved here would be minor, and it might very well be within an adult's capabilities to alter his grammar to this extent.

Innovation does not always lead to restructuring in the subsequent generation. If no simpler grammar produces the same speech output, there will be no restructuring. The Great Vowel Shift in English is a case of this kind (Chomsky and Halle, 1968:249–289).

Middle English (spoken approximately from 1100 to 1500) had the tense vowel system:

ī   ū

ē   ō

æ   ā   ɔ̄

By the Great Vowel Shift we understand the set of changes in which /ī ū/ became diphthongized to [ay aw] by way of [e:y o:w] and /ē ō/ were raised to [i: u:], for example:

Middle English	Modern English
mīn	mine [mayn]
þūsend	thousand [θawzɪnd]
sēk	seek [si:k]
schō	shoe [šu:]

We can represent these changes diagrammatically as follows:

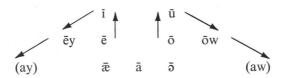

To account for just this part of the data, we assume two innovations in the grammar of Middle English around 1500. (We ignore here changes affecting the low vowels.) The first of these is a diphthongization rule affecting ī and ū:

$$4.2 \quad \emptyset \rightarrow \begin{bmatrix} - \text{vocalic} \\ - \text{consonantal} \\ \alpha \text{ back} \end{bmatrix} / \begin{bmatrix} + \text{vocalic} \\ - \text{consonantal} \\ + \text{tense} \\ + \text{high} \\ \alpha \text{ back} \end{bmatrix} \quad \underline{\quad\quad}$$

(ī > īy and ū > ūw. This rule inserts the glide [y] or [w] depending on whether the preceding vowel is ī or ū.)

The second innovation, added to the grammar after Rule 4.2, is the Vowel Shift rule proper:

4.3 $\begin{bmatrix} \alpha\,\text{high} \\ -\,\text{low} \end{bmatrix} \rightarrow [-\,\alpha\,\text{high}]\ /\ \begin{bmatrix} +\,\text{tense} \\ +\,\text{stress} \end{bmatrix}$

(Tense, stressed, nonlow segments exchange their highness values: $\bar{\imath}y > \bar{e}y$, $\bar{u}w > \bar{o}w$, $\bar{e} > \bar{\imath}$, $\bar{o} > \bar{u}$.)

Derivations then go as follows:

Underlying:	ī	ē	ō	ū
Rule 4.2:	īy	...	...	ūw
Rule 4.3:	ēy	ī	ū	ōw

But this tells only part of the story. Middle English had a rule that laxed vowels before consonant clusters and when followed by two syllables the first of which was unstressed. The approximate form of this rule was:

$$V \rightarrow [-\,\text{tense}]\ /\ \underline{\quad}\ C \left\{ \begin{matrix} C \\ \begin{bmatrix} V \\ -\,\text{stress} \end{bmatrix} CV \end{matrix} \right\}$$

The result of these rules—the laxing rule together with Rules 4.2 and 4.3— was to produce phonological alternations in Early Modern English of the types:

Early Mod. Eng.	British Modern Eng.	Examples
[ey] : [i]	[ay] : [ɪ]	crime : criminal
[ow] : [u]	[aw] : [ʌ]	profound : profundity
[i:] : [e]	[i:] : [ɛ]	keep : kept
[u:] : [o]	[u:] : [ɔ]	goose : gosling

Here, we are ostensibly faced with the same situation as before in regard to the reduction of *hw* > *w* in the adult grammar. Rules have been added to the adult grammar. The underlying forms have remained the same (e.g. the underlying forms of *keep:kept* [ki:p]:[kept] are /kēp/:/kēpt/ as in pre-Vowel Shift Middle English); only the phonetic outputs are different: the speech has changed but the lexicon and its representation have not.

But unlike the case of the child constructing a grammar on the basis of speech produced by his elders with the innovation *hw* > *w*, here there is no simpler grammar that will account for the same output. Because of phonological (morphophonemic) alternations, the simplest grammar still contains underlying tense vowels in *crime, criminal, profound, profundity, keep, kept*, and so on, and it still contains Rules 4.2 and 4.3 (as well as the laxing rule) in essentially the same form. These rules are still present in the grammar of Modern English and have been for the past four centuries or so. This is to say that English has undergone little restructuring among tense vowels during this time. Its underlying phonological representations of forms in tense vowels have changed but little since Middle English, and the synchronic analogues of the Great Vowel Shift as well as other historical innovations have been passed along from generation to generation in approximately the same form.

Thus, there are different modes of simplification in the child generation. The adult may have added a rule giving him a nonoptimal grammar; the child will construct an optimal grammar producing the same output. If there is no simpler grammar that produces the same output as that of the adult grammar plus the innovation, the child's grammar can consist of the adult grammar plus innovation. In these two cases the child's grammar output—his speech—will not differ from that of the adult. On the other hand, if the child goes further and simplifies by losing or generalizing a rule, thus constructing a grammar simpler than the adult optimal one, then his speech will differ correspondingly from adult speech.

Before considering additional cases of diachronic change, perhaps it would be well to examine Figure 4.1, the schematic representation of the process of linguistic change, which is based on Klima (1965:83).

LAD stands for Language Acquisition Device, which is a "black box" construct designed to cover the child's whole complex process of receiving the primary data of his language and developing from it the optimal (descriptively adequate) grammar for his language. Thus, Generation 2 utilizes the Speech Output of Generation 1 to arrive at an Optimal Grammar. In the course of adult life Innovations may be added on to this grammar, giving what we have called the Adult Grammar of Generation 2. The Speech Output B of Generation 2 then serves as input to the LAD for Generation 3, and on it goes.

There are several points in the theory underlying this representation of diachronic change that merit special comment. First, our model does not represent *speech* as changing into *speech* with time. Speech output at one stage is not mapped directly into later speech output: no arrows connect the Speech Output at a given stage with the Speech Output at a different stage. What does change is the grammar vis-à-vis different stages. The grammar of one stage is developed on the basis of speech produced by a grammar at an earlier stage, and the grammar of a speaker may undergo innovations—rule additions. To use the terminology developed in Chapter 2, linguistic change is change in *competence*, not change in *performance*; it is change in the grammar, not originally change in the output of that grammar. This conception of change is all important, as we shall see in Chapter 5, where the nature of phonological change is probed in detail.

A second point is the matter of comparing different stages of the same language. What does it mean to say that Middle English and Modern English are different stages of the same language? What's the same? This is something of a classical antinomy in linguistics, whose synchronic

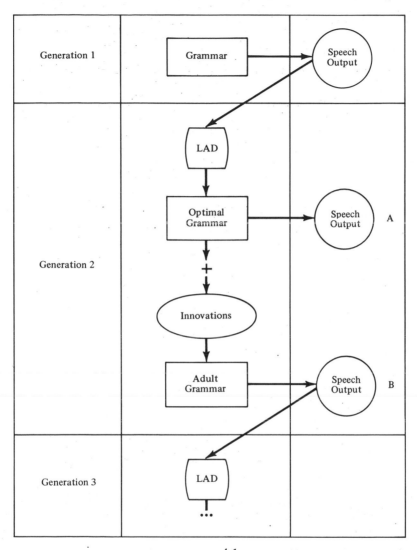

FIGURE 4.1

A MODEL OF LINGUISTIC CHANGE

counterpart was discussed in Section 3.1: what it means to say that linguistic systems A and B are dialects of the same language. If we accept the Saussurean dictum that linguistic elements are defined synchronically by all other elements in the system at that instant in time, then it is not obvious how we can speak of "correspondences" between elements in the language at different times (cf. Hoenigswald 1960:27f). In what sense does Modern English /ay/ correspond to Middle English /ī/?

This dialectal bind dissolves when we shift our notion of change from something happening to the elements of the system (its sounds, phonemes, morphemes) to modifications taking place in a speaker's competence. His grammar changes from one stage to another. We can compare the grammar of Middle English with the grammar of Modern English and posit certain innovations and restructurings that account for the differences. Grammar rules exist not because of any sort of contrast among them. Middle English [iː] "corresponds" to Modern English [ay] in the sense that the optimal grammar at either stage would derive them from underlying /ī/ and they occur in cognate items, but the only significant comparison is between the grammars and not the sounds or morphs.

Finally, nothing in this paradigm of change requires that simplification in the child generation be preceded by innovation in the parent generation. The two processes are independent in that simplification can occur without prior innovation and parents can add rules to their grammars irrespective of whatever kind of grammar their children are constructing. Children seem to simplify spontaneously. They merely build a grammar based on what they hear. They can have no notion of what the adult grammars look like. A child, in other words, couldn't care less how his parents' grammars got the way they are.

Given the tendency towards optimization, one might well wonder why languages don't end up being maximally simple: three vowels or less, a very few phonological rules, a primitive syntax. We shall briefly enumerate here ways that languages become more complex.

One source of increased complexity is innovation in the adult grammar. This needs no further comment here. It was suggested earlier in this section that children too innovate, perhaps most frequently by adding rules of assimilation. It can be argued that such rules contribute to the over-all simplicity of a grammar since assimilation is a "natural" phenomenon, but by present evaluation procedures grammars are more complex if they contain such rules.

A third source of what might appear to be increased complexity is the collapsing of two or more rules. Any extensive set of phonological rules for a language, such as those listed for English in Chomsky and Halle (1968:238–245), contains rules of considerable complexity, and it is not plausible to assume that such rules entered the language as innovations. Rather, it seems more likely that the innovations were, each taken by itself, relatively simple, but that those innovations affecting the same segment(s) were collapsed into a single rule in later grammars. The resulting rule will then appear complex.

Fourth, certain changes may secondarily complicate other parts of the grammar. Consider a hypothetical language with five underlying vowels /i e a o u/ and the underlying stops /p t k b d g/. Suppose there is a rule lengthening vowels before voiced obstruents, and assume that an innovation devoicing every /b d g/ is added at the end of the grammar. From underlying /bat/ and /bad/ the surface forms will be [bat] and [ba:t] from earlier [bat] and [ba:d]. The child exposed to these and like forms will hear only length as the distinguishing feature, and we may hypothesize that the child's grammar will have vowel length in underlying forms but nowhere /b d g/. This is a complication of the underlying vowel system, but it also represents the simplest grammar that can be constructed from the output of the adult grammar.

4.4   THE ROLE OF SIMPLIFICATION

In Section 4.2 rule loss was reduced to a special case of simplification. The grammar resulting from rule loss is formally simpler by the number of features in the deleted rule. The output is simpler: more regular, having less allomorphic variation.

Kiparsky (1968b) has proposed that rule reordering too is an instance of simplification, though of a kind different from that discussed so far. Let us examine the case of German rule reordering discussed in Section 3.3. Originally the two pertinent rules, Final Devoicing and Vowel Lengthening, applied in that order, and we would obtain derivations such as the following for *path:paths*:

	Underlying Forms:	veg	vegə
(I)	*Final Devoicing:*	vek	......
	Vowel Lengthening:	......	ve:gə
	Phonetic Shape:	vek	ve:gə

In the synchronic grammar of German, however, the rules must apply in the opposite order:

	Underlying Forms:	veg	vegə
(II)	*Vowel Lengthening:*	ve:g	ve:gə
	Final Devoicing:	ve:k	......
	Phonetic Shape:	ve:k	ve:gə

In the original grammar each rule applies once at each step of the derivation. In the grammar containing the rules reordered, Vowel Lengthening has shifted into a position where it applies *twice* at its point of application, and Final Devoicing continues to apply once. That is, the rule of vowel lengthening has moved into a position where it acts on a greater number of forms than previously; the grammar gets the maximum mileage out of this rule, so to speak.

Here, since the grammar contains the same number of rules (and features) whatever the order of the two rules, no notation is available at present to convert the greater simplicity of one order into greater brevity of the grammar, though such a notation could easily be devised. Kiparsky (1965) has discussed ways in which this might be done; he further has proposed the use of the terms *marked order* and *unmarked order* respectively for orderings (I) and (II). Unmarked order is the optimal order; marked order, the less optimal ordering. The general criterion of directionality in rule reordering may then be stated as: "Marked order tends to be replaced by unmarked order"; or equivalently: "Rules tend to shift into the order which allows their fullest utilization in the grammar" (Kiparsky 1968b).

Note that in the case discussed moving from marked to unmarked order reduces the extent of allomorphic variation in the output. We found this to be true also of rule loss. In marked order (I) 'path' has two allomorphs /vek ~ ve:g/, which differ in vowel length and voice in the final obstruent; in unmarked order (II) the two allomorphs /ve:k ~ ve:g/ differ only in voice value in the terminal obstruent. Of course, this is also true of the large number of words in German with the parallel allomorphy: *Rad* 'wheel', *Bad* 'bath', *lügen* 'to lie', and so on.

In the German case optimal utilization of rules reordered a later rule to an earlier position, where it now applies to a larger number of forms. Section 3.3 discussed another instance of this type: the order of two rules (3.15 and 3.16) in the predecessor language of Old English, Old Saxon, and Old Frisian differed from their order in the other Germanic dialects. It was suggested there that this was a case of reordering, not insertion of a rule into the grammar elsewhere than at the end, though supporting evidence such as relic forms was not available. If we compare these derivations given in Section 3.3 under RULE REORDERING, we see that the chronologically later Rule 3.16 has shifted into an earlier position where it applies to more forms, specifically *binðanð*. The assumption of reordering here is based primarily on the fact that the direction of the shift is from marked to unmarked order, which is what we find in cases of reordering. (Recall too that all other Germanic languages agreed in having the opposite order.) If the order had shifted the other way— from unmarked to marked, from optimal to less optimal—then we would have a less firm basis for assuming that reordering had occurred. In this case other explanations would merit consideration: either Rule 3.16 was inserted into the grammar elsewhere than at the end of the phonological rules, like Lachmann's Law, or the two rules spread at different rates in a wave-type effect through the Germanic area and reached dialects at different times in the manner discussed in Section 3.3 under RULE REORDERING (cf. King 1968:§3.1).

Cases of rule simplification proper, such as those looked at in Section 3.3 under SIMPLIFICATION, are commonplace in the transmission of language from parent to child. The reason for this is not hard to see; it is as if the child has drawn too much of the right conclusion from the data presented to him. Suppose the parents' grammar has a rule devoicing final fricatives:

4.4 $\begin{bmatrix} + \text{obstruent} \\ + \text{continuant} \end{bmatrix} \rightarrow [-\text{voice}] / \underline{\quad} \#$

In the parents' speech there might then be hypothetical alternations *bif* : *bivo*, *has* : *haza*, *lex* : *lege*. The rule does not apply to stops, so the child would be presented with, for example, *sib* : *sibo*, *wed* : *weda*, *og* : *oge*. Noting alternations such as *bif* : *bivo*, the child correctly intuits that some kind of rule governing the alternation is needed, but his first hypothesis is simpler than that implicit in Rule 4.4. He incorporates into his grammar a rule devoicing all obstruents, whether fricative or stop:

4.4′ $[+\text{obstruent}] \rightarrow [-\text{voice}] / \underline{\quad} \#$

In the child's speech we will then have his best efforts to produce *bif* : *bivo*, and so on, but he will also say *sip* : *sibo*, *wet* : *weda*, *ok* : *oge*. This is wrong from the parents' point of view. They don't pronounce things like that. The child has overridden the data and drawn too general a conclusion from them. That children in fact do what we have assumed in this purely hypothetical example is clear. The Ervin (1964) experiment discussed in Section 4.2 showed how children could first learn the correct forms of past tenses (*went*, *ate*, *drank*) and use them, only later to override not only the data but their own previous successful attempts and generalize a rule giving *goed*, *eated*, *drinked*. And this they did even though the weak verbs furnishing the pattern of inflection were infrequent in the speech directed at them.

At this juncture one of two things is possible. The more likely is that the child will eventually reject Rule 4.4′ in favor of Rule 4.4. Presumably the adults in the child's world have only Rule 4.4, and presumably the majority of his playmates have created their grammars with the correct Rule 4.4. Under this pressure the child will complicate his grammar to the extent that he rejects Rule 4.4′ and internalizes Rule 4.4 in the same way that children eventually give up *goed*, *eated*, *drinked*. If, on the other hand, the simplified version, Rule 4.4′, stays in the grammar to adulthood, we have the possibility of a lasting generalization. Certain circumstances favor Rule 4.4′ becoming a permanent, normal part of the language: numerous members of the new generation acquiring Rule 4.4′ in place of Rule 4.4, or final devoicing of all obstruents becoming marked as a prestige item.

It is important to stress that we do not know at present why one simplification takes place rather than the other. Besides Rule 4.4′, why not have a "simplification" of Rule 4.4 such as:

4.4″ $[+\text{continuant}] \rightarrow [-\text{voice}] / \underline{\quad} \#$

(Any continuant is devoiced word-finally.)

From a purely formal point of view this appears to be as legitimate a simplification of Rule 4.4 as Rule 4.4′. Rule 4.4″ devoices all final continuants, e.g. fricatives and vowels, giving *bif* : *bivǫ*, *has* : *hazǫ*, *sip* : *sibǫ*, and so on, where the subcircle denotes voicelessness in vowels. It is possible that rule simplifications like this exist, but it seems rather unlikely; and in the Germanic languages, all of which at one time had Rule 4.4, the putative simplification Rule 4.4″ is unheard of.

The point of this is that there is more to rule simplification than merely deleting features in the structural analysis of a rule. Distinctive features are more than formal signs; they have intrinsic content, and some account of this intrinsic content must be integrated into an adequate phonological theory. In other words, our theory must have some way of stating what formally possible simplifications (like Rule 4.4″) are in fact excluded because they violate principles governing natural languages. Assuming that Rule 4.4″ is in fact an impossibility, an adequate phonological theory would tell us that [+ continuant] can be deleted in the structural analysis of Rule 4.4 to give a simplification, but that [+ obstruent] cannot be. Current phonological theory does not extensively provide us with such constraints, although important steps in this direction have been taken (cf. Chomsky and Halle 1968:400–435).

Whatever the outcome of these efforts to tighten up phonological theory, the historical evidence suggests that rule simplifications obey some kind of hierarchy of features. Features defining major categories like "vowel," "true consonant," "liquid," and "glide" do not seem to be subject to deletion; that is, we do not usually find features like *obstruent* and *consonantal* being deleted in rules. On the other hand, simplifications are permissible by deleting in the structural analysis of rules features presumably low in the hierarchy like *continuant* and *voice* for consonants and *back* or *round* for vowels. Aside from fairly crude observations such as these, it is not possible at present to say much about why one simplification instead of another took place in the development of a language.

Though the bulk of this discussion has dealt with change from generation to generation, some parts of it apply as well to spatial change, in particular the spread of a rule throughout a geographic (or socially defined) area. Borrowed rules are common in the bilingual situation and in the vicinity of a prestige dialect. Thus, speakers from all over the United States who grew up pronouncing final *r*'s sometimes add a rule dropping them if they spend a long enough time in England. We have noted before that adults often add rules to their grammars (innovations), so that there is nothing surprising in the act of rule addition itself. Often, and perhaps generally, such added rules are at first optional, which is reflected in a variation in performance in one's speech. If they become a permanent part of the speaker's grammar, they provide a possible starting point for restructurings in the grammars of subsequent generations. Often such adult rule additions are stylistic in nature: the speaker uses them to impress his audience or for a raise but normally gets along better without them.

We hypothesize that in borrowing, in general, rules are simplified rather than complicated. That is, a rule is borrowed with the same or greater generality, but not with lessened generality (Harms 1967:172, Bach 1968). Though extensive verification is lacking, this hypothesis has plausibility, and there are some hard data to support it.

Labov (1963) studied the centralization in the first element of the diphthongs /ay/ and /aw/ on Martha's Vineyard and found considerable variation both in the degree of centralization and among social segments of the native population. As Labov (1965:100) concludes, "The centralization of (aw) was part of a more general change which began with the centralization of (ay)." That is, [a] was centralized first in the environment before [y], and as this rule spread over the island of Martha's Vineyard, the environment of centralization was generalized to before [y] and [w]. In terms of the features involved, the environment was simplified from:

$$\underline{\quad} \begin{bmatrix} - \text{ vocalic} \\ - \text{ consonantal} \\ - \text{ back} \end{bmatrix} \quad (\underline{\quad} y)$$

to:

$$\underline{\quad} \begin{bmatrix} - \text{ vocalic} \\ - \text{ consonantal} \end{bmatrix} \quad (\underline{\quad} y, w)$$

Furthermore, there is good evidence (Labov 1963:289–290) that centralization originated in the environment before voiceless obstruents (*right, wife, night, house, out*), but in subsequent generations was present in all phonetic environments (*side, by, I'll, now, down*). This is again a case of a rule simplification (generalization) during transmission.

A similar phenomenon can be observed in the English of certain Canadian provinces, notably Ontario—particularly in and around Toronto. Some speakers centralize the /a/ in /ay/ and /aw/ only before voiceless obstruents. The environment for centralization has been generalized by many speakers to produce centralization in all occurrences of /ay/ and /aw/. There are Canadians whose dogs go [bʌw wʌw].

It seems a priori unlikely in our theory that a rule would become less general as it is transmitted from one dialect to another. Let us consider again the case of the hypothetical language with Rule 4.4, which devoices only final fricatives. Suppose further that this is a prestige dialect. The speaker of a less prestigious dialect, listening to his betters and wanting to sound more like them, is faced with something like the problem of a child learning the language. He cannot directly tap the grammar of his speech models and pick out Rule 4.4; he can only observe the primary data—their speech—and formulate a rule to account for what he hears. What he hears are voiceless final fricatives. It seems highly improbable that he would formulate a *less general* rule than 4.4 to add to his grammar, say:

$$4.4''' \quad \begin{bmatrix} + \text{obstruent} \\ + \text{continuant} \\ + \text{anterior} \end{bmatrix} \rightarrow [- \text{voice}] / \underline{\quad\quad} \#$$

which devoices only labial and dental fricatives, e.g. *v*, *ð*, and *z*. The speaker borrowing the rule will, one may assume, either formulate a rule with equal generality or increased generality (4.4′).

If this hypothesis holds up as more data are amassed, it will give us a useful tool for prying into the linguistic movements of pre-history. If, for example, we know that the living or attested languages A and B share a rule but that this rule is more general in the grammar of A than of B, and if we know that early contact between the two languages existed, then our assumption would be that the rule was transmitted from B (less general) into A (more general) instead of vice-versa.

This assumption runs counter to a widely held view of transmission of rules which holds that rules tend to narrow in generality as they spread farther from the point of origin. The analogy of a stone cast into water insinuates itself here: the ripples are strongest near the center of the disturbance, and they weaken the farther out they go. Our notion of grammar holds no rationale for linguistic behavior like this as a general rule; indeed, the opposite assumption has more inherent credibility within generative grammar. It is as if a stone thrown into water created ripples that grew in strength as they moved away from the center.

A case in point is the High German Consonant Shift, summarized in Section 4.1 with regard to hypercorrection in Low German. This shift—general in South Germany and Switzerland, less general as one travels north, and absent in the native Low German of Northern Germany—has always been regarded as a paradigmatic case of a sound change spreading with decreasing generality (Hockett 1958:480). Our view suggests the opposite direction of transmission: the High German Consonant Shift seems to have begun in the border area between Low and High German (roughly in the area of the "Rhenish Fan"), and to have diffused southward with increased generality. Unfortunately, the dispute cannot be settled because there are too few documents dating from immediately before and after the shift (c. A.D. 500). Cf. Becker (1967:61–64) on this problem.

4.5   A CASE HISTORY: HIGH GERMAN UMLAUT

Let us investigate in detail the progress of a sound change from innovation to restructuring in the development of umlaut—the fronting of back vowels

—in High German from around A.D. 750 to approximately A.D. 1200. The following analysis will provide data for a later inquiry, in Chapter 9, into the relation between scribal practice and phonological representations.

Umlaut was already mentioned in Section 3.3 under SIMPLIFICATION as an example of rule addition and subsequent simplification. All of the surviving Germanic languages show traces of the original process. This is especially true in Standard German, where we still have phonological alternations mirroring the original process: *Kraft* : *kräftig* 'power, powerful', *Lob* : *löblich* 'praise, praiseworthy', *Muße* : *müßig* 'leisure, idle'. Umlaut in the second member of each pair is triggered by the *i* in the suffix. In English, pairs of the type *goose* : *geese, foot* : *feet, blood* : *bleed* are witnesses to an active umlaut process in earlier English.

It is customary to divide the linguistic history of German into three periods: Old High German (to 1100), Middle High German (1100–1350), New High German (1350 to present). (These dates are only approximate and should serve merely as rough attempts to lend chronological perspective.) In the documents of Old High German only the umlaut of short *a* to *e* is customarily indicated, e.g. *gast* : *gesti* 'guest, guests'; there is no scribal indication of the umlaut of the other back vowels ($\ddot{u}$, $\ddot{o}$, $\bar{a}$) during the Old High German period until very late, and then it is sporadic. Thus, corresponding to Modern German *mochte* : *möchte* 'I liked, I would like', we have Old High German *mohta* : *mohti* without umlaut designation in the latter. Nor is orthographic designation of umlaut consistent in the Middle High German period except for short *a*, though we do find in this era increasing scribal inventiveness in orthographic differentiation of the umlaut vowels. In Middle High German we expect to find either *mohte* : *mohte* with no umlaut designation in the latter, or perhaps *mohte* : *mo̊hte*, *mohte* : *möhte*, or some mark to indicate the presence of [ö] in the word for 'I would like'.

The very earliest Old High German documents, those dating from approximately 750 to 800, regularly contain unumlauted short *a*. We reconstruct, therefore, an early stage of Old High German—let us call it pre-Old High German—in which umlaut was not present as a rule in the grammar of the language. At this stage umlaut alternations do not occur at any level, and we have the following derivations:

PRE-OLD HIGH GERMAN

Gloss:	guest	guests	hole	holes	worm	worms
Underlying:	/gast	gasti	lox	loxxir	wurm	wurmi/
Phonetic:	[gast	gasti	lox	loxxir	wurm	wurmi]

We assume that a rule producing umlaut was added to the grammar of pre-Old High German at some time between 750 and 800. We cannot be certain about the precise form of this rule. The most literal interpretation possible from the written evidence is that it originally affected only short *a*, and then was generalized by Middle High German times to all of the back vowels. But we do not accept this interpretation here; rather, in accord with the consensus of modern and traditional scholarly belief, we assume that *all* back vowels were subject to umlaut even during Old High German, and that the absence of overt umlaut designation in *ŭ*, *ŏ*, *ā* was an orthographic lapse rather than a phonetic one. The rule we posit for the earliest stage of attested umlaut in Old High German has the form:

$$4.5 \quad \begin{bmatrix} V \\ \langle - \text{long} \rangle \end{bmatrix} \rightarrow \begin{bmatrix} - \text{back} \\ \langle - \text{low} \rangle \end{bmatrix} / \underline{\quad} C_1 \begin{bmatrix} - \text{consonantal} \\ + \text{high} \\ - \text{back} \end{bmatrix}$$

(All vowels are fronted when followed in the next syllable by *ĭ* or *j*; the short vowels thus fronted become nonlow. Thus, *ŭ ŏ ā a*>*ŭ ŏ ā e*. This rule, and the accompanying discussion, ignores complicating details such as "secondary umlaut," the failure of *u* to umlaut in certain dialects, and the presence of umlaut-inhibiting clusters like *hs* and *ht*. Cf. Kiparsky 1965.)

With this innovation came a change in the surface forms of Old High German. A speaker whose grammar did not contain Rule 4.5 said [gasti] 'guests'; one whose did said [gesti]. There has been, however, no restructuring at this point, no change in underlying representations. Whether a speaker said [gasti] or [gesti], the underlying form in the simplest grammar remains /gasti/, and the difference in surface forms arises from application of Rule 4.5. At this stage of history, which we arbitrarily designate Old High German Stage I, typical derivations are as follows:

OLD HIGH GERMAN STAGE I

Gloss:	power	powerful	hole	holes	worm	worms
Underlying:	/kraft	kraftig	lox	loxxir	wurm	wurmi/
Rule 4.5:	......	kreftig	......	löxxir	......	würmi
Phonetic:	[kraft	kreftig	lox	löxxir	wurm	würmi]
Orthographic:	*kraft*	*kreftig*	*loh*	*lohhir*	*wurm*	*wurmi*

Gloss:	deed	deeds	heard	to hear	skin	skins
Underlying:	/tāt	tāti	hōrta	hōrjan	hūt	hūti/
Rule 4.5:	......	tāti	......	hōrjan	......	hūti
Phonetic:	[tāt	tāti	hōrta	hōrjan	hūt	hūti]
Orthographic:	*tāt*	*tāti*	*hōrta*	*hōrian*	*hūt*	*hūti*

Although there has yet been no restructuring in Old High German as we are presenting the development of umlaut, there was restructuring at this stage in an autonomous phonemic account, namely as regards the umlaut of short *a* (Twaddell 1938). Within autonomous phonemics, at the stage of pre-Old High German, /e/ and /a/ had the single allophones [ɛ] and [a] respectively. After umlaut, /a/ had two allophones: [a] normally, [e] under conditions of (primary) umlaut. It is customarily assumed that the umlaut allophone of /a/ ([e]) was phonetically different from the primary allophone of original /e/ ([ɛ]) on the basis of Middle High German rhyme evidence and testimony from the modern dialects, some of which preserve the two *e*'s distinct: [e] from /a/ under umlaut is higher than [ɛ] from original /e/. Autonomous phonemics requires that the [e] resulting from umlaut of /a/ be assigned to the phoneme /e/ because of phonetic similarity. At Old High German Stage I, /e/ had two allophones: [e] under conditions of umlaut, [ɛ] otherwise. /a/ no longer had its umlaut allophone [e] (though it did have a secondary umlaut allophone [ä], which we have omitted from our discussion). In other words, restructuring has taken place in a part of the data under investigation: the underlying autonomous phonemic form of [gesti] 'guests' has changed from /gasti/ in pre-Old High German to /gesti/ in Old High German Stage I, and similarly in all other cases of the umlaut of short *a*. The other umlaut phones [ŭ ŏ ä], however, retain their allophonic status as in pre-Old High German. At this stage there has been no restructuring in a generative account, but partial restructuring in an autonomous phonemic account.

Next we shall consider developments subsequent to the stage of Old High German Stage I. One of the umlaut-producing factors begins to disappear in the course of the ninth century: *j*. By the end of the ninth century it is in general lost everywhere except after light syllables ending in *r*. This *j* is written *i* or *e* in the early documents, as we see from a comparison of early and later orthographic forms of words containing *j*:

Early Forms	*Later Forms*	*Gloss*
suntiu	suntu	sin (dative singular)
kennian	kennen	to know
hirteo	hirto	of the shepherds
suntea	sunta	sin (nom. singular)

We formulate then, as an innovation in the grammar of Old High German Stage I, the addition of a rule that deletes *j* in these environments:

$$4.6 \quad \begin{bmatrix} -\text{vocalic} \\ -\text{consonantal} \\ -\text{back} \end{bmatrix} \rightarrow \emptyset \; / \; \underline{\quad\quad} \begin{bmatrix} V \\ -\text{stress} \end{bmatrix}$$

(The glide *j* is deleted when it is followed by an unstressed vowel, e.g. *kennian* [kennjan] > *kennen* [kennen] 'to know'. Of course, *j* remains before stressed vowels as in *iār* [jār] 'year'. We leave out of account in Rule 4.6 the retention of *j* after *r* in light syllables.)

We assume further that Rule 4.6 was added to the end of the grammar after Rule 4.5, the umlaut rule. We now can distinguish a second stage, which we designate Old High German Stage II, dating its inception at approximately 800. This stage differs from Old High German Stage I only in the addition of Rule 4.6; hence derivations such as /kraftig/ > [kreftig] 'powerful' remain unchanged. Only forms containing umlaut under the influence of *j* will have changed surface forms; for example, 'to hear' will now have the derivation /hōrjan/ > [hȫrjan] > [hȫren] (*j* generally raised and fronted following unstressed *a* to *e*). Illustrative derivations of forms from paradigms of 'favor', 'back', and 'sin' follow.

OLD HIGH GERMAN STAGE II

Gloss: 'favor'	*Nom. Sg.*	*Dat. Sg.*	*Nom. Pl.*	*Gen. Pl.*
Underlying:	/anst	ansti	ansti	anstjo/
Rule 4.5:	....	ensti	ensti	enstjo
Rule 4.6:	....	....	....	ensto
Phonetic:	[anst	ensti	ensti	ensto]
Orthographic:	*anst*	*ensti*	*ensti*	*ensto*

Gloss: 'back'	*Nom. Sg.*	*Dat. Sg.*	*Nom. Pl.*	*Gen. Pl.*
Underlying:	/hrukki	hrukkje	hrukki	hrukkjo/
Rule 4.5:	hrükki	hrükkje	hrükki	hrükkjo
Rule 4.6:	....	hrükke	....	hrükko
Phonetic:	[hrükki	hrükke	hrükki	hrükko]
Orthographic:	*hrucki*	*hrucke*	*hrucki*	*hrucko*

Gloss: 'sin'	*Nom. Sg.*	*Dat. Sg.*	*Nom. Pl.*	*Gen. Pl.*
Underlying:	/suntja	suntju	suntjā	suntjōno/
Rule 4.5:	süntja	süntju	süntjā	süntjōno
Rule 4.6:	sünta	süntu	süntā	süntōno
Phonetic:	[sünta	süntu	süntā	süntōno]
Orthographic:	*sunta*	*suntu*	*suntā*	*suntōno*

(Note: the "underlying forms" cited in these derivations are in reality several steps removed from the forms we would take as underlying in a more comprehensive grammar of Old High German. *j* is derived from *i* prevocalically, and the geminate *-kk-* in *hrukki* 'back' is predictable. Thus, the correct underlying form of /xrukkje/ 'back (dat. sg.)', as opposed to the form given here for simplicity of illustration, is /xrukie/.)

At this stage an alteration of considerable magnitude is observed in the speech output vis-à-vis that of Old High German Stage I, yet still no restructuring has taken place within the generative grammar accounting for this speech output. As in the grammar of pre-Old High German, as in the grammar of Old High German Stage I, there has been no change in underlying representations. The optimal grammar at this stage still assumes only ten vowels in underlying forms (*ĭ ĕ ă ŏ ŭ*, but not *ŭ ŏ ă*), and rules for umlaut and *j*-deletion are present in that order, so that the speech output is full of forms containing umlaut produced by a *j* which since has disappeared. Thus, even in forms such as *hrucko* [hrükko] 'back (gen. pl.)' and *sunta* [sünta] 'sin (nom. sg.)', where no umlaut factor is phonetically manifested, children learning the language at this point would not construct underlying forms containing /ü/. Phonological alternations of various kinds were still present and even plentiful in the data (speech) from which Rules 4.5 and 4.6 could be posited, hence obviating the need for umlaut vowels in underlying forms: [kraft : kreftig] 'power, powerful'; [wurm : würmi] 'worm, worms'; [anst : ensti : ensto] 'favor (nom. sg., dat. sg., gen. pl.)'; [hrükki, hrükke] 'back (nom. sg., dat. sg.)'.

At Old High German Stage II, then, even though to a phonetician it would *sound* strikingly different from that spoken earlier, differences in the grammars are confined to innovations that do not involve changes in underlying phonological representations. From the point of view of autonomous phonemics, on the other hand, there is additional and considerable restructuring at this point, for a number of umlaut vowels attain autonomous phonemic status with the loss of the first *j*. As soon as the first *j* was deleted, the possibility of a contrast between *umlauted* and *not umlauted* exists, and in fact near-minimal pairs can be found in the data: *sunte : hunte* [sünte : hunte] 'sin (acc. sg.), dog (dat. sg.)' (cf. Modern German *Sünde : Hunde*), *hunte* without umlaut from underlying /hunte/ and *sunte* with umlaut from underlying /suntja/; *māre : wāra* [māre : wāra] 'famous (nom. and acc. pl. masc.), truth', *māre* with umlaut from underlying /mārja/, *wāra* without umlaut from underlying /wāra/.

In other words, the front rounded vowels became autonomous phonemic the instant the first *j* in a word like *suntja* 'sin' dropped. And if we adhere to a strong version of the biuniqueness (invariance) condition in phonemic analysis, according to which a phone once assigned to a phoneme must be regarded as a realization of that phoneme each time the phone occurs, we are forced to reassign the umlaut vowels to /ü/ and /ü/ respectively in, for example, *wurmi* [würmi] 'worms', *hūti* [hüti] 'skins'. That is, if we accept strong biuniqueness, restructuring occurred already in *all* underlying forms containing umlaut vowels in Old High German Stage II, no matter whether an umlaut-producing factor was still present (like *i*) or not (like *j*).

From this point onward it becomes more difficult to make precise statements about what happened next: the documents tell different, often conflicting stories. Fortunately, however, a scribe of uncommon talent and learning, Notker Labeo, was then at the monastery of St. Gall in Switzerland. His translations into Old High German of such works as Boethius' *De Consolatione Philosophiae* stand today as classics of their kind. He was also a keen phonetician and an inventive scribe: he noted and consistently marked long vowels, which was something none of his predecessors had done with Old High German; he recorded in his translations an external sandhi voicing assimilation present in his speech; and he recorded the reduction of unstressed vowels taking place in Old High German during his lifetime. The latter point interests us most at the moment, for umlaut is contingent upon the status of the unstressed vowels *i* and *ī* since the other factor *j* was no longer present in surface phonetic forms. The most apparent vowel reductions in Notker's writings are unstressed *i u > e o*—Notker writes *ubel* 'evil', *fure* 'before', *frido* 'peace', *filo* 'much' instead of the earlier forms *ubil, furi, fridu, filu*. The word *gesti* 'guests' becomes for Notker *geste* with the overt umlaut signal *i* no longer phonetically manifested.

Our question now is: Does this development lead to restructuring? Are we now required to assume underlying front rounded vowels—umlaut vowels— in the underlying phonological representations of Old High German? The answer is again No, and for the following reasons. What was described above as simple unconditioned merger of unstressed *i u > e o* was in reality a case initially of partial merger and subsequently a generalization of the merger rule, not a one-step process. The chronology is fairly clear in Notker's writings, and we may summarize it as follows (see Moulton 1961a:29):

> First, unstressed short *i u > e o* in checked position: *gestim > gesten* 'guest (dat. pl.)', *sibun > sibon* 'seven'.
> Second, unstressed short *i u > e o* in free position: *gesti > geste* 'guests', *fridu > frido* 'peace'.
> Third, unstressed short vowels (now only *e a o*) fell together into [ə].
> Fourth, the unstressed long vowels underwent similar reductions, first lowering of *ī* and *ū*, then total merger into [ə]: *zungūn > zungōn > zungen* 'tongues', *hōhī > hōhē > hōhe* 'height'.

(Note that in Middle High German, and to some extent in the late period of Old High German we have examined here, *e* in unstressed positions spells [ə] or a reduced vowel similar in quality.)

The mergers of *i > e* and *ī > ē* are our primary concern here. With the lowering of *i* to *e* we must consider the possibility that restructuring takes place in subsequent generations. The developments among the unstressed vowels sketched above point to a process of generalization that had the starting point:

$$4.7 \quad \begin{bmatrix} V \\ -\text{stress} \\ -\text{long} \end{bmatrix} \rightarrow [-\text{high}] / \underline{\quad\quad} C_1 \#$$

(The short unstressed vowels *i u* are lowered to *e o* in checked position—that is, when separated from word-boundary by at least one consonantal segment.)

One generalization of Rule 4.7 is caused by an extension of the environment from exclusively checked position to checked and free position:

$$4.7' \quad \begin{bmatrix} V \\ -\text{stress} \\ -\text{long} \end{bmatrix} \rightarrow [-\text{high}] / \underline{\quad\quad} C_0 \#$$

(The short unstressed vowels *i u* are lowered to *e o* in free or checked position —that is, when separated from word-boundary by zero or any number of consonants.)

Rule 4.7' now is generalized by suppressing the feature [− long] in the structural analysis:

$$4.7'' \quad \begin{bmatrix} V \\ -\text{stress} \end{bmatrix} \rightarrow [-\text{high}] / \underline{\quad\quad} C_0 \#$$

(The unstressed vowels *ī ū* are lowered to *ē ō* in checked and free position.)

This then is the scheme of reduction and generalization that emerges from a consideration of Notker's spellings. The fact that even Notker, consistent as he normally was in his practice, fluctuated in his representations of the unstressed vowels would indicate that Rule 4.7 and its generalizations were originally optional rules in his grammar. This is not at all out of the ordinary. It is quite possible that most innovations occur originally as added optional rules that subsequently become obligatory (Klima 1965:95). Such an assumption accounts for many of the inconsistencies, the exceptions to sound laws of the anti-Neogrammarians, so often found in transition and boundary dialects.

We will for simplicity assume that Notker's grammar contained Rule 4.7 at some point. Of this much we can be sure, though some of the details remain unclear. We then have a stage we shall designate as Old High German Stage III, which we date roughly at 950 to 1050 since the documents show the start of the vowel reduction process at the beginning of the tenth century, and Notker died in 1022. This grammar had derivations such as the following, taken from the paradigm of *gast* 'guest':

OLD HIGH GERMAN STAGE III

Gloss: 'guest'	Nom. Sg.	Nom. Pl.	Gen. Pl.	Dat. Pl.
Underlying:	/gast	gasti	gastjo	gastim/
Rule 4.5:	....	gesti	gestjo	gestim
Rule 4.6:	....	....	gesto	....
Rule 4.7:	....	....	....	gestem
Phonetic:	[gast	gesti	gesto	gestem]
Orthographic:	gast	gesti	gesto	gestem

This derivation makes clear the presence of considerable morphophonemic alternation still in the language even after the reduction of unstressed *i* is under way. Furthermore, the umlaut-producing factor is still phonetically present in the paradigms in certain instances, as in *gesti* 'guests (nom. pl.)' above. This would also be true of many other words: *nāmi* [nã̄mi] 'I, he would take', *nāmīs* [nã̄mīs] 'you would take', *nāmi* [nã̄mi] 'you took', all of which have umlaut with *i* or *ī* phonetically present, alternating with *nam* [nam] 'I, he took', *nāmom* [nāmom], 'we took' without umlaut.

From this we conclude that no restructuring of the umlaut vowels had occurred in Notker's grammar nor at this stage in the grammars of his contemporaries in that part of the German-speaking area. Of course, the picture is muddied by the existence of dialects, and here we have made no attempt to present the entire configuration. The point is that the simplest grammar at Stage III has no umlaut vowels in its underlying forms, and the rules 4.5, 4.6, and 4.7 are still present. No restructuring has occurred, though the grammar has become formally more complicated by successive layers of rules since pre-Old High German.

As we have seen, Notker's scribal treatment of the unstressed vowels shows a trend toward generalization of Rule 4.7 which culminates in Rule 4.7″. Subsequently, all vowels under weak stress merge into schwa—the situation in Middle High German. This reduction is carried through with great consistency in the manuscripts from 1100 on. With the generalization to Rule 4.7″ we reach a fourth stage, Old High German Stage IV, and we date its inception at 1050 or slightly earlier. In the earliest form of this grammar we have derivations similar to those given for Old High German Stage III, but Rule 4.7 is replaced by Rule 4.7″. We then have:

OLD HIGH GERMAN STAGE IV

Gloss: 'guest'	Nom. Sg.	Nom. Pl.	Gen. Pl.	Dat. Pl.
Underlying:	/gast	gasti	gastjo	gastim/
Rule 4.5:	....	gesti	gestjo	gestim
Rule 4.6:	....	....	gesto	....
Rule 4.7″:	....	geste	....	gestem
Phonetic:	[gast	geste	gesto	gestem]
Orthographic:	gast	geste	gesto	gestem

At this point the great bulk of phonological alternations between un-umlauted forms and umlauted forms with an overtly marked umlaut have disappeared from Old High German speech. It is true that some umlaut-triggering *i*'s remained, e.g. *mänlich* 'masculine' (base *man* 'man'), *väterlīn* 'daddy' (base *vater* 'father'). That is, a limited number of *i*'s (and *ī*'s) remained when protected by a tertiary stress and under other conditions, and these exist today in Standard German, e.g. *Mann* : *männlich* 'man, masculine', *Hof* : *höfisch* 'court, courtly', but the bulk of umlauting vowels are gone.

Thus, in Modern Standard German—and presumably also in Middle High German and what we have called Old High German Stage IV—there is motivation for regarding some occurrences of umlaut vowels as nonphonemic, that is, derivable by a rule similar to Rule 4.5. Such would be *ä* in *männlich* and *ö* in *höfisch*. There is, however, no compelling motivation for assuming in the optimal grammar of Modern Standard German that *all* umlaut vowels are derivable by phonological rule, in particular those umlaut vowels occurring in monosyllabic, underived words like *schön* 'pretty', *für* 'for', *grün* 'green', and so on. The data from Middle High German point to the same conclusion. (Current phonological theory does not force a clear choice between different treatments of the umlaut vowels in Modern Standard German. Analyses positing no underlying umlaut vowels are possible in the present framework. Here, it is tentatively assumed that some but not all occurrences of umlaut are phonemic.)

We assume, that is to say, that restructuring occurred in the grammars of High German subsequent to Old High German Stage IV and created for Middle High German (roughly from 1100 on) a grammar containing umlaut vowels in underlying forms. The underlying form of [sündə] 'sin' is changed from/ sundja/ to /sünde/, the underlying phonological forms of [gestə] 'guests' and [würmə] 'worms' change from /gasti/ and /wurmi/ to /geste/ and /würme/. Rules 4.6 (*j*-deletion) and 4.7″ (reduction of unstressed vowels) are lost from the grammar, and Rule 4.5 (umlaut) survives as a rule of low "functional load" to account for the forms like *Mann* : *männlich* 'man, masculine'.

Perhaps more than anything else, the foregoing example shows how wide an array of linguistic facts we must appeal to in discussing the diachronic evolution of a language. Literally *everything* in the language is of possible relevance to our analysis—morphophonemic alternation, phonetic changes, morphological processes. All of this affects our decisions at each point in determining what is phonemic, what is predictable by rule, and what the optimal grammar must have been like. We can afford to limit our view to purely phonetic matters, such as phonetic minimal pairs, only at the cost of impoverishing our account of diachronic development.

4.6 SYNCHRONIC GRAMMARS AND HISTORICAL RECAPITULATION

One problem not yet mentioned is the kind of relation that one might suppose to exist between a synchronic grammar and its history. To what extent does a synchronic grammar recapitulate the historical events that have taken place in the historical grammars of the language? Or, more to the point: Are historical facts relevant to the formulation of the synchronic grammar of a language? We might go even further and put the question as follows: Should a grammar recapitulate the historical development of a language?

Note that questions of this sort, as they usually are asked, arise in synchronic analysis; they have to do with the evaluation of grammars. The underlying sentiment seems to be that a grammar correctly recapitulating the history of a language as well as accounting for the synchronic data is higher valued than one accounting only for the synchronic data. It is obvious, therefore, why we have not concerned ourselves here with questions of this general class: they arise in synchrony, not diachrony. They have to do with constraints that might bear on the evaluation of synchronic grammars, but they do not arise in the discussion of historical change proper. Even so, some discussion of the general question is not totally out of place in a book on historical linguistics, if only because of the frequent misunderstandings of the relation between historical development and the synchronic evaluation of grammars.

Let us begin by asking the question: Does historical evidence decide which of two synchronic grammars is higher valued? The answer is a flat No. Given two grammars G_1 and G_2 that correctly account for the same data, and given that G_1 is simpler than G_2 but that G_2 more nearly recapitulates the historical development, then the simpler grammar G_1 is higher valued than G_2. Given two grammars G_1 and G_2 of equal simplicity, and given that G_2 better reflects the historical development of the language, nevertheless both grammars are equally valued in the evaluation measure. There is no reason to prefer G_2 over G_1 (or vice versa, for that matter). What has been said here about the relevance of historical evidence to synchronic evaluation applies *ceteris paribus* to the evidence of neighboring dialects.

Why evidence of these types is not directly relevant to the evaluation of synchronic grammars should be clear. A grammar is an account of a speaker's intrinsic knowledge of his language, his competence—not his father's competence, not any of his ancestors' competences, not the competence of his neighbor whose dialect is slightly different. To admit historical evidence into the evaluation of synchronic grammars would be to claim that the linguistic competence of one's forebears should play a role in evaluating accounts of one's own competence, and there is no reason in fact or theory to entertain such a curious claim.

Note too that if historical information is allowed to enter into the evaluation of synchronic grammars, the whole question of the relationship between a synchronic grammar and its history ceases to be of any interest. As it stands, it is an interesting, *empirical* question whether a particular grammar recapitulates history; for in cases like reordering, where the grammar does not recapitulate history, we can attempt to determine some general criterion (such as greater simplicity) that accounts for this. But if historical recapitulation were a criterion in the evaluation procedure, there would not be any point in asking about the relation of a synchronic grammar to earlier grammars of the language. There would be no empirical issue of the slightest interest since, by definition, history has been accounted for in the grammar.

The historical evidence, however, is indirectly relevant to synchronic formulation in a number of interesting and often subtle ways. One of the best proofs of the naturalness of a rule is to show that such a rule occurred as an innovation in a language. This is cogent evidence for a bona fide phonological rule. Likewise, the plausibility of an analysis proposed on strictly synchronic grounds is bolstered if one can demonstrate parallels in the history of the language. A rule CC→C simplifying geminate consonant clusters in English can be motivated on purely synchronic grounds: the rule is needed to produce, for example, correct *dissimilar* [disimilər] from underlying /dis = similær/, compare *dislike, distasteful* (see Chomsky and Halle 1968:243). It is comforting to know that this rule was added to the grammar of Early Modern English, for this gives us a minimal guarantee that our analysis is not unnatural. But the sole justification for including this as a rule of contemporary English phonology is synchronic.

Very often knowledge of the history of a language is of considerable help in writing its synchronic grammar. Historical knowledge (as well as knowledge of related dialects) often suggests where to look for phonological alternation, what kind of phonological processes to expect, and so on. Historical knowledge might, for example, suggest the setting up of base forms that are at considerable variance with the surface forms in the language. But the ultimate justification for such a choice rests with simplicity, descriptive adequacy, and the synchronic data. Historical development is useful for gaining insights, but it is not a substitute for the synchronic grammar.

The fact is that synchronic grammars do often enough recapitulate a sizeable part of the history of a language. The Great Vowel Shift rule in the synchronic grammar of English is a case in point. Such recapitulation is not surprising since many rules enter a grammar historically as innovations. If an added rule or some variant of it remains in the grammar for a long time, a synchronic grammar recapitulates history since it must contain that rule to achieve descriptive adequacy. But the rule need not remain in the grammar, nor need its position in the grammar bear true testimony to what happened historically. The rule may be lost. It may be switched out of its original order vis-à-vis another rule. It may be added at a point in the grammar that does not correspond to its chronological order. The rule may be simplified. It may lead to restructuring and then be lost.

All these things may make a synchronic grammar bear not the faintest resemblance to some earlier grammar of the language. When a synchronic grammar does recapitulate history, especially in some subtle and superficially disguised way, we have an interesting but hardly remarkable fact since historical change is grammar change. When a synchronic grammar fails utterly to reflect history, we have an interesting but equally unremarkable fact. The point is that grammars sometimes tell us a lot about their history, sometimes next to nothing, and sometimes they tell us one thing and history tells us another.

In light of these considerations the proper historical phonology of a language is clearly much more than a set of rules that derive the sounds of, let us say, West Germanic from proto-Indo-European. Even if these rules are made as simple as possible in terms of the distinctive features involved, there is not the slightest reason to suppose that they correspond meaningfully to historical reality. Historical reality includes restructuring, and a simple enumeration of the innovations in a language need not bear any resemblance to what happened historically if the grammar has been restructured. One cannot expect a priori that any innovation will remain in the language as a rule.

A proper historical phonology is the history of the *grammars* of a language, of the competences of successive generations of speakers. The listing of rules converting the sounds of proto-Indo-European into those of West Germanic may be of interest as an exercise in ingenuity and distinctive feature virtuosity, but historical linguistics it is not.

SUPPLEMENTARY READING

Chomsky, Noam, and Morris Halle. 1968. *The Sound Pattern of English.* New York: Harper & Row, Publishers. Chap. 6.

Halle, Morris. 1962. "Phonology in Generative Grammar." *Word* 18.54–72. Reprinted in *The Structure of Language*, eds. Jerry A. Fodor and Jerrold J. Katz (Englewood Cliffs, N.J.: Prentice-Hall, Inc., 1964).

Harms, Robert T. 1967. "Split, Shift and Merger in the Permic Vowels." *Ural-Altaische Jahrbücher* 39.161–198.

Kiparsky, Paul. 1965. *Phonological Change.* Unpublished doctoral dissertation, Massachusetts Institute of Technology.

5

SOUND CHANGE AND ANALOGY

Of all the topics of conversation and scholarly research in linguistics that have seen the light of day during the last century or so, surely *sound change* ranks high among those accompanied by nonsense and obfuscation. We are all acquainted with some of the better known examples.

Jakob Grimm supposed that the Germanic Consonant Shift and the High German Consonant Shift were provoked by the impetuous nature of the Germanic tribes—a suggestion that at least one twentieth-century linguistic scholar (Prokosch 1939:55) felt "may fundamentally contain a good deal of truth." Other scholars have discovered considerable merit in the view that both those Consonant Shifts were in part brought about by the increase of the force of aspiration resulting from life in mountainous regions such as the Scandinavian highlands (presumably the *Urheimat* of the Germanic peoples) or the Swiss Alps (where it was assumed that the High German Consonant

Shift originated). Race, physiology, national temperament—all have had their day.

Such examples could be multiplied several fold and discussed at great length, though at no gain for the cause of historical linguistics. What most of these explanations have in common is an almost total fancifulness (since the principles invoked have not been shown to have universal or near-universal validity) and a simplistic putative correlation between cause and effect which must appeal greatly to the hidden child in each of us for these beliefs to have maintained themselves with such tenacity. Serious linguistic scholars have, of course, long since abandoned the more notorious "explanations," but the subject of sound change is still studded with question marks even after a century of hard work. Hardly any statement about the precise character, process, or cause of sound change can be made without challenge from at least some quarter of the linguistic world.

Is sound change necessarily gradual? That is, if [a] changes to [ɔ] in some language, does it take place in a single step [a] > [ɔ], or must it occur over a series of small (perhaps infinitesimal) steps of which the following might be a sample:

$$a > a^{\text{ʾ}} > ɑ^{\text{ʿ}} > ɑ > ɑ^{\wedge} > ɔ^{\vee} > ɔ$$

But if the implementation of sound change is gradual, how do we account for such apparent "sudden leaps" as loss, as when initial #kn- in *knight* became #n; epenthesis, as when usual Old English *brōþor* 'brother' is found written *beróþor*; and metathesis, as when pre-Old English *hros* 'horse' became *hors*? Is sound change completely "regular"; is its occurrence determined by phonetic environment and phonetic environment only? Is it really *sounds* that change, or is it grammar?

Like sound change, *analogy* has long held a prominent place in historical linguistics. The process of analogy however, is less mysterious: when some-one (perhaps a child) says *I seed* in place of *I saw*, it seems obvious that he has drawn a false analogy with the regular formations *I kissed, played, dropped,* and so on. Vexed questions of gradualness do not arise. Never-theless, much is still unclear about analogy, in particular about the conditions under which it takes place. Is a "proportion" a necessary or sufficient condition for analogy? That is, before analogy can take place, must a relation of the form *see* : x = *kiss* : *kissed* (yielding *I seed*) be present? Is there any sense in which analogy is regular?

The present chapter will deal with some of the traditional ways of regarding sound change and analogy and will attempt to present a coherent picture within generative grammar.

5.1   THE GRADUALNESS OF SOUND CHANGE

When, for example, Indo-European *b d g* became *p t k* in Germanic, what happened? One view is that gradually during many generations allophones of /b d g/ came to resemble those of original /p t k/, result-ing in a new phonemic series. A change in "habits of articulation" has taken place.

This conception is essentially statistical and may be illustrated by the single change /d/ > /t/. In this view [d], the principal allophone of the phoneme /d/, represents a kind of bull's-eye at which performances of the phoneme /d/ are aimed, much as 50 represents the bull's-eye associated with the number of heads that turn up in a trial of tossing a true coin 100 times. This does not mean that we get 50 heads each time we perform a trial of 100 tosses. Yet in any large number of repetitions of such a trial we expect and find (for a true coin) that the number of heads in each series of 100 tosses tends to cluster around 50, a number we may call (following Hockett 1958:442 and more recently Hockett 1965:194) the "local frequency maximum" associated with the act of tossing a coin 100 times in a row. In this sense the "point" [d] in some abstract articulatory space represents the local frequency maximum, the expected value, associated with performances of the phoneme /d/. The values of performances of /d/ will not necessarily hit the mark exactly, but rather they tend to peak at [d] in accordance with the Law of Large Numbers. We may represent this by the familiar bell-shaped curve:

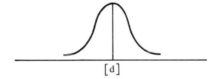

[d]

The sound change /d/ > /t/ consists initially of a random shift of the ex-pected value of /d/ in the direction of [t]. If we assume that [t] lies to the right of [d] in our informal representation, then the initial step in this change would consist of clustering ever so slightly to the right of the previous local fre-quency maximum of /d/. Since the process is gradual and random, occurring over many years or even generations, no speaker is aware that anything has happened. This process of gradual shifting of local frequency maxima con-tinues, always away from the initial position [d], and the final result is a stable clustering around the value [t]. What we have then is a progression from [d] to [t] over a nondenumerable infinity of local frequency maxima. If from this infinity we select [ḓ] (fortis [d]) and [ṯ] (lenis [t]) as two representa-tives, we can represent the process as follows:

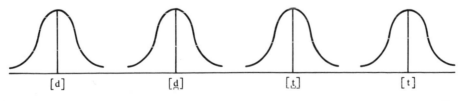

[d]   [ḓ]   [ṯ]   [t]

It is rather as if as one tossed a coin it began to wear on one side so that the probability of getting heads decreased gradually from 0.50 through 0.47 and 0.42 to 0.40, whereupon the coin quit changing its weight and shape and began to turn up heads consistently 40% of the time.

In this way we have arrived at a new phoneme /t/ with the principal allophone [t]. As before with /d/, the random nature of the articulatory process will lead to a normal curve (bell-shaped curve) distribution with its maximum at [t]. Sound change is still going on in the sense that not every performance of /t/ hits the bull's-eye [t] exactly, but the expected value remains relatively constant, at least until some new trend sets in and carries the most likely value of /t/ away from [t] and towards a new frequency maximum, say [tʰ], [tˢ], or [θ].

Several implicit assumptions in this picture of sound change should be emphasized. First, sound change is gradual and imperceptible to a single speaker or perhaps to all the speakers of a single generation. Second, sound change is constantly in progress since performances of a given phoneme differ each time. Third, the speaker's competence—competence in the technical sense, his implicit knowledge of the language—is irrelevant to the process. Sound change is not change in competence but change in performance brought about by external factors that affect and alter renditions of a particular sound type: the amount of moisture in the vocal passages of the speaker, his muscular tone, whether he is drunk or not, and so on (Hockett 1958:443).

Phonological change as it is conceived of in generative grammar differs radically from this. First and foremost, as has been emphasized throughout this book, change is change in competence reflected by alterations in the grammar. The role of performance remains the same, causing the same kinds of fluctuations after the change in competence as before. To be more explicit, in this uncomplicated case of innovation we assume that a rule $d > t$ has been added to the speaker's grammar. Where he previously said d he now says t, and we register this fact in our account by the addition of a rule—a change in competence. Before the innovation, realizations of /d/ doubtless did fluctuate in various ways because of the presence of moisture in the vocal apparatus, the speaker's alertness, and so on; but precisely the same performance factors are active after the innovation as before. Their relation to the change in competence is one of complete neutrality—they neither caused it, contributed to it, abetted it, nor slowed it down. The performance factors simply cause the random fluctuations that always take place in articulating sounds and account for the often heard statement that "each speech act is a unique event: no two pronunciations of the same sound are ever the same, even when pronounced by the same speaker."

Second, nothing in generative grammar requires or supports the assumption that the change was necessarily gradual. We simply assume that the rule changing [d] to [t] was added to the speaker's grammar; this changed [d] to

[t]. Nothing in fact or in the theory of generative phonology suggests that this change, or any other, had to take place as a series of rule additions of the type: [d] → [+ 3 voice], [d] → [+ 2 voice], [d] → [+ 1 voice], and so on.

The statistical model of gradual sound change outlined earlier assumed that change was infinitesimal over a continuum. This strong version of gradualness can be weakened by dropping the requirement of infinitesimal change; rather we posit "small" changes, where "small" is understood as meaning "within the limits set by a given phonetic alphabet and its associated diacritic marks."

Evidence will now be presented that the gradualness assumption, in either of its formulations, is untenable as a necessary condition on sound change. Furthermore, it will be argued that the term "sound change" is an improper concept for the phenomenon to which that designation is customarily applied. Sounds don't change; grammars do. These are substantive issues, not terminological ones, and we must look to the empirical evidence for confirmation.

A number of linguistic facts support the claims that gradualness is not a necessary condition for sound change and that grammars, not sounds, change. First, there is the indisputable existence of cases such as loss, metathesis, and epenthesis in which any kind of gradual process strains the imaginative faculties as well as the set of distinctive features that one assumes to be universal. Let us consider loss. Loss of segments is an almost commonplace kind of historical development: Greek lost its final stops, Germanic lost word-final consonants and vowels under certain conditions. If, say, t is lost word-finally, we account for this simply by assuming that a rule:

$$t \rightarrow \emptyset \; / \; \underline{\hspace{1cm}} \; \#$$

was added to the grammar of one or more speakers as an innovation. Perhaps the rule spread within the speakers of a single generation as a fashionable way of pronouncing things; perhaps subsequent generations of speakers restructured their grammars so that no instances of word-final t were derivable. The eventual result is that no one pronounces word-final t's. It is true that one can postulate some sort of undeniably gradual process, for example:

$$t > \underline{t} > \theta > \underline{\theta} > \emptyset$$

where ‿ denotes laxness of articulation. But in cases of loss like this there is never unambiguous evidence in the form of scribal testimony or dialectal variations that would clinch the argument for a gradual process. What we find is that a consonant was in full force in one stage of the language and gone later.

One might at this point argue that the testimony of historical linguistics is suspect in regard to the gradualness of sound change since no one was around to hear what people were saying and since no scribe would be apt to render a faithful phonetic record of the intermediate stages in sound changes. But there are cases of loss observable in our own day in which no progression of sounds intermediate between the end points can be observed. Some speakers of American English pronounce their final *r*'s, some don't. There is no indication of a gradient of sounds along the progression from [r] to zero or schwa, that is, from [fa:r] > [fa:] or [fa:ə] 'far'. To cite here "*r*-colored vowels" as evidence of gradualness is to beg the question. Even if we assume (and there is no compelling reason to do so) that the loss of *r* in many varieties of English took place through a stage containing an *r*-colored vowel, e.g. *r*-colored schwa [ɚ], then we have the progression:

$$r > ɚ > ə$$

and now the proponent of gradualness must find a progression of sounds intermediate between [r] and [ɚ] and between [ɚ] and [ə].

Another instance in American English of supposedly gradual sound change is the so-called intervocalic "voiced *t*" in *water, latter, sitting, batted*. The phonetic facts concerning this sound summarized by Heffner (1960:129–130) indicate a situation as follows. Some speakers of English have voiceless [t]; some Americans have voiced [d] not distinguishable from the pronunciation of *d* in *ladder, shudder*; and some have "voiced *t*" which differs from voiced *d* in minor phonetic details of tenseness and/or duration of hold. This evidence supports the explanation that some speakers of American English realize intervocalic /t/ as [ṭ], whereas other speakers realize it as [d]. Still other speakers of English, those who do not voice their intervocalic *t*'s at all, realize /t/ intervocalically as [t] or [tʰ].

Data like these are not prima facie evidence for the gradualness of sound change; they merely support the claim denied by no one that speech variation exists in a natural language. To use this in support of gradualness one would have to demonstrate that speakers with [d] earlier had [ṭ], and that speakers with [ṭ] earlier had [t] or [tʰ]. It would even suffice to show that one generation had [t] or [tʰ], a later generation [ṭ], and a still later generation [d]. But no one has tried to show this, and informal observations of the phenomenon of intervocalic /t/ do not suggest a regular gradient by age of the sort envisioned above.

A second, similar case from English involves the pronunciation of initial *wh* in *when, whether, why, what*. This was discussed in Section 4.3 as an instance of innovation and subsequent restructuring, in which a rule deleting *h* before *w* was added to the grammar:

$$5.1 \quad \begin{bmatrix} - \text{vocalic} \\ - \text{consonantal} \end{bmatrix} \rightarrow \emptyset \ / \ \underline{} \begin{bmatrix} - \text{vocalic} \\ - \text{consonantal} \\ + \text{voice} \\ + \text{back} \end{bmatrix}$$

As Heffner (1960:161–162) points out, there are quite a large number of variants of initial *wh*, so that the change expressed by Rule 5.1 is very much an oversimplification. Heffner gives the following variants, where the sub-dot denotes voicelessness in the segment and the sub-omega labialization: [w], [w̥], [hw̥], [h̥], [x̥], [hw]. One might regard these as a "sizeable portion" of a large number of values between [hw] and [w]. But again this begs the question of the progression of intermediate values lying between *these* putative intermediate values: can it be shown that one generation had [hw̥], the next [w̥], the next [w]?

Minor variation in the performance or realization of sounds is simply an aspect of language; there is nothing which requires us to regard such variation as *causing* sound change. The amount of aspiration on initial /p t k/ in English varies from much to very little, both within the speech of a single speaker and between speakers. This has no doubt been true for many centuries; but no sound change has affected initial /p t k/ during this time, nor do current prospects for such change seem auspicious. And similar statements could be made about the majority of sounds in any given language at any particular time. Infinitesimal variations in the realization of sounds are present, always have been, always will be; but it requires empirical confirmation in the form of a generational gradient to show that they are the *mechanism* by which sound change occurs.

Linguistic literature is full of cases of radical change in which no intermediate stages are alluded to. Hermann (1931:15, 33) cites one case in Yaghnobi where children have [i] in place of their parents' [e] and a second case in Frisian dialects where some speakers have [l] and others [d]. In neither case is any intermediate value indicated. Gabelentz (1901:193) cites a study of the Samoan languages in which the spread of a sound change $t > k$ is discussed. In less than forty years, hardly more than a single generation, the sound change had been carried out, and there is no evidence for an intermediate stage or series of intermediate stages.

Even if cases like these were postulated as gradual—if, in other words, the failure to observe the postulated gradient of intermediate sounds were ascribed to insensitivity in the human ear or to crudeness in phonetic and acoustic instruments—there are still certain categories of sound change in which gradualness is even more radically counter-intuitive and unreasonable. Such a category is metathesis (the interchange of two segments). Metathesis is not uncommon as a historical change, and synchronically it is found as a rule in the grammars of currently spoken languages (cf. Chomsky and Halle 1968:360–362). Modern English *third,* Old English *ðirda* comes from earlier *ðridda* via metathesis, as does Modern English *horse* from earlier *hros* (cf. Old High German *hros*, Old Icelandic *hross*). What kind of gradual change by allophones can be imagined here or in any case of metathesis?

What kind of gradualness is reasonably possible in epenthesis? If null becomes the vowel [e] in some environment, is it not simpler to assume the addition of a rule $\emptyset \rightarrow$ [e] rather than some hypothetical and completely implausible gradient of sounds between nothing and [e]?

Similarly, in present-day instances of assimilation there is no evidence of gradualness. When, for example, in Spanish $n > m$ via assimilation as in *San Pedro* [sampeðro], there is no gradual realignment of allophones. Are we to assume that historical sound change was fundamentally different in nature?

A further kind of sound change is even more fundamentally incompatible with the gradualness assumption: the changes effected by the so-called "exchange rules" or "alpha-switching rules" of phonology. One of the best known examples is the Great Vowel Shift in English, briefly discussed in Section 4.3. (On the Great Vowel Shift and exchange rules in general see Chomsky and Halle 1968:254–259. See also Wang 1968.) In this set of changes affecting the tense vowels of fifteenth-century English, high and mid vowels "exchanged" places: $\bar{\imath}$ and $\bar{u}$ were lowered to $\bar{e}$ and $\bar{o}$, original $\bar{e}$ and $\bar{o}$ were raised to $\bar{\imath}$ and $\bar{u}$. The rule for these changes may be stated as:

$$5.2 \quad \begin{bmatrix} \alpha \, \text{high} \\ - \, \text{low} \end{bmatrix} \rightarrow [- \alpha \, \text{high}] \; / \; \begin{bmatrix} \overline{\phantom{+ \text{tense}}} \\ + \, \text{tense} \\ + \, \text{stress} \end{bmatrix}$$

In general, exchange rules have the schematic form:

$$[\alpha F] \rightarrow [- \alpha \, F] \; / \; \ldots$$

where F denotes a feature whose value is switched from $+$ to $-$ and from $-$ to $+$. In Rule 5.2 when α is $+$ the rule applies to high vowels, making them $[-$ high]; when α is $-$ mid vowels are affected, becoming $[+$ high].

Wang (1967:102) has presented several cases in Chinese dialects of exchange rules that involve the switching of tones. One such rule carries out the following changes: high tone becomes low tone, low tone becomes high tone, and mid tone is left unchanged. The rule which makes these changes is an innovation as follows, where the features used are all binary features of tone:

$$5.3 \quad [\alpha \; \text{HIGH}] \rightarrow [- \alpha \; \text{HIGH}] \; / \; \begin{bmatrix} \overline{\phantom{- \text{CENTRAL}}} \\ - \, \text{CENTRAL} \end{bmatrix} \begin{bmatrix} + \text{HIGH} \\ + \text{FALLING} \end{bmatrix}$$

Examples of exchange rules, both synchronic and diachronic, could be given from a variety of other languages. Their existence seems not subject to dispute; and there is no way in generative phonology to exclude them as lawful innovations in the grammar of a language. But if this is so, how can we possibly account for them in a theory of change that requires sound change to be gradual, incremental, and infinitesimal? How could high and low tones switch in a language containing a mid tone without disastrous confusion in the process? The most obvious answer is that such changes are just not gradual: they are phonetic leaps, as it were, and no merger takes place because the sounds or tones being switched never pass through the same point.

It is always possible to assume that two sounds switching places in an exchange rule take different paths, thereby avoiding merger. In explaining how ī and ē did not merge in the Great Vowel Shift, one might postulate intermediate changes as follows, where the numbers denote chronological sequence of change:

$$
\begin{array}{ccc}
 & 4 & \\
\bar{\imath} & \leftarrow & \bar{u} \\
2\downarrow & & \uparrow 3 \\
\bar{e} & \rightarrow & \bar{o} \\
 & 1 &
\end{array}
$$

This way of explaining sound interchanges is always available; but in the absence of confirming data, one must view such explanations as unacceptable. An "alternate route" explanation generally is advanced merely to salvage the gradualness assumption and not because of hard evidence in the form of scribal records or dialect variation (see the remarks on the Great Vowel Shift quoted in Chomsky and Halle 1968:255). This is a high price to pay for retaining an assumption whose appeal is not irresistible to begin with.

That sound change is neither necessarily nor in general gradual is, of course, not a new view, nor is it the exclusive property of generative grammarians. Sommerfelt (1923) wrote in support of abrupt sound change. Hoenigswald (1960:73) suggests that the notion of gradual sound change is a remnant from pre-phonemic days (see also Hoenigswald 1964). Jakobson (1931:249) wrote of the "abrupt character of phonological changes."

The evidence so far presented argues against gradualness as a necessary condition for sound change. In a deeper sense, however, this is a subordinate question; the real question is whether sound change in the traditional sense is a proper concept at all: is it the *sounds* that change, or is it something else? Generative grammar maintains that it is not sounds or phones that change but grammar—a speaker's competence (Postal 1968:269–307). Alteration in competence is reflected by alteration in performance, but not the other way around. Phonological changes result from changes in competence, in the internalized system of rules for linguistic behavior. Such changes are of various kinds; rule additions and losses, reordering, simplification. These changes are not caused by tiny variations in performance that somehow seep osmotically up into competence and change it. To use a concrete example, consider the problem of *wh* in English. Whatever segment underlies this sequence (Chomsky and Halle 1968:223–224 propose /x^w/), speakers of English have rules producing a phonological surface-level sequence [hw]. This sequence is then realized by low-level, possibly n-ary rules in the phonological component. Speakers who habitually say [hw̥] have a late rule devoicing the [w]. Speakers who alternate freely between [hw̥] and [w̥] have an optional phonetic rule deleting the [h].

In other words, variations like these are due to minor differences in late rules in the phonological component of the grammar. We do not at present know very much in detail about performance factors affecting phonetic output, but it is probable that variations such as [hw]∼[h̥] for *wh* are best accounted for not by rules in a particular grammar but within a universal theory of performance. That is, it should turn out that certain kinds of minor phonetic variation are universal or near-universal. If it is true that the sequence [hw] in language can be indifferently realized as [w̥] or [h̥], then this variation is not a part of the grammar at all but is accounted for in the theory of performance associated with the grammar.

Note further that the traditional theory of *sound* change (as opposed to *grammar* change) is indirectly disconfirmed by the existence of nonchronological rule additions like Lachmann's Law in Latin (Section 3.3). The change of *a* to *ā* yielding *āctum* cannot be stated by rules changing the phonetic surface-level sound [a]; Lachmann's Law required the representation [agtum] which never occurs phonetically in Latin. Sound change (i.e. "phone" change) fails to account for this, but there is no problem here for grammar change.

In view of these considerations it would be more preferable to replace the traditional term "sound change" by something more appropriate. The designation "phonological change," which conveys a sense of something more abstract than change by phones, is perhaps the most suitable candidate.

The chief underlying reasons for the assumption of gradual sound change seem to be (a) the sentiment that communication would break down if change were not gradual, and (b) the observation that people are not normally aware of change. There is no empirical confirmation of (a). Languages have an amazing ability to undergo change without impairing communication. Mergers occur, yet communication goes on. Some languages have different varieties of male and female speech (Sapir 1929), yet the sexes communicate. Speakers from the Southeast United States who do not differentiate *i* and *e* before nasals go north and west, but communication does not break down.

Assumption (b), that ongoing phonological change is unnoticed, is doubtless frequently true but, as Chomsky and Halle (1968:250) point out, only because speakers are in general unaware of the contents of their grammar, whether change has occurred or not. The average speaker of a language pays very little attention to pronunciation in the normal course of things; he may notice he's talking to a foreigner or some dialect speaker, but normal speech variation goes mostly unnoticed. Someone who has added a rule to his grammar doesn't feel any different, and he is usually not even aware that he sounds any different. Similarly, a child who has simplified his grammar does not feel he has done something different or naughty.

In short, there is no logical reason why phonological change must be gradual nor empirical confirmation that it is. Subject to counter-evidence yet to be produced, we reject gradualness as a necessary condition for the implementation of any phonological change.

Parenthetically, let it be noted that linguistic change other than phonological is clearly *not* gradual by any stretch of the imagination. If an adult learns to use *whom* in place of *who* in the right places, how could this be anything but sudden and abrupt? When a child says *foots* instead of *feet*, what is gradual about it? In semantic change, as when *in* takes on the additional meaning "fashionable" or "what everyone else is doing," we are not dealing with gradual change. Likewise, it is hard to imagine accentual changes—like shifting place of accent—as occurring gradually.

Some of the puzzling phonological changes in history lose their apparent mystery once we abandon the unsupported notion of gradual phone change. One of these is the change of Latin *ct* [kt] > Rumanian *pt*, e.g. Latin *octo* > Rumanian *opt* 'eight'. This is part of a more general process whereby in addition the velar nasal [ŋ] becomes [m] before dental stops (including here nasals), e.g. Latin *lignum* [liŋnum] > Rumanian *limn* 'wood' (Kiparsky 1965). The problem is not complicated; a rule was added to the grammar of Rumanian of the form:

$$5.4 \quad [-\text{continuant}] \rightarrow [+\text{anterior}] / \underline{\qquad} \begin{bmatrix} -\text{continuant} \\ +\text{coronal} \end{bmatrix}$$

(Stops, including k and the nasal η, become labial before dental stops.)

This change in competence is reflected by a change in performance: the speaker stops saying *kt* and starts saying *pt*. The rule may first have been optional, so that the speaker was inconsistent in its application and fluctuated between *kt* and *pt*, but the Rumanian evidence shows that it eventually became obligatory. The result is a change of *kt* > *pt*, not different in substance from any other less striking change such as Indo-European *b d g* > Germanic *p t k*. This phonological change in Rumanian is puzzling only within a theory of change that requires gradualness, where it is hard to see how k could have become p or η become m without being confused with t and n along the way. One can imagine an "alternate route" gradual process which would avoid this, e.g. $k > k^w$ (with labialization) $> p$, or one may attribute this change to borrowing of various kinds (Naert 1941). But such assumptions result from the assumption of necessary gradualness, and once we have discarded this assumption, they become gratuitous.

Another puzzling change of this sort, which is really no more puzzling than any other phonological change once gradualness is dropped, has already been alluded to in Section 4.5: the umlaut of Old High German *a*. The umlaut of *a* is assumed to have been a higher mid front vowel [e], different from inherited *e* which is assumed to have been [ε]. The poets of Middle High German, as is copiously attested, were careful not to rhyme the two, and we even have a fair number of minimal pairs from Middle High German: *wegen* [wεgən] 'to weigh': *wegen* [wegən] 'to move'; *her* [hεr] 'sir': *her* [her] 'army'. That umlaut-*e* differed in tongue height from inherited *e* is assumed on the basis of testimony of modern German dialects that, unlike Standard German, maintain the two distinct. If the change of [a] to [e] under umlaut conditions was gradual, necessarily at some point in this development the two *e*'s were phonetically indistinguishable and would have merged. One could, of course, propose a route such as [a] > [ö] > [e], which would prevent a "collision" between old [ε] and the umlaut of [a], but neither the written documents nor the modern dialects lend credence to this theory. Instead, it has been tacitly assumed that the path from [a] to [e] via umlaut led over [ε]. How could this have happened without leading to merger of the two sounds? Solutions have been offered (Fourquet 1952). The point is, however, that a problem exists here only if gradualness is assumed. If we do not require gradualness and if we regard this change as the addition of a rule changing [a] to [e] in the umlaut environment (Rule 4.5), then this change is no different from any other such as metathesis, epenthesis, or simply $p > p^h$.

One major point to be made here is that gradualness leads to a fracturing of the picture of diachronic phonological change without conferring any corresponding benefits. If we take gradualness as a necessary condition for at least *some* phonological changes, say simple shifts among single vowels and consonants, then we are forced to establish at least two categories of change: (1) cases of gradual change $x > y$, and (2) cases of nongradual change $x > y$ such as metathesis, epenthesis, and loss. To the latter category we must then assign a mechanism of change that differs in substance from that of the former category, for example, borrowing or perhaps a different kind of analogy.

Considerations such as these have led scholars to regard some sound changes at least as special cases of borrowing (Hoenigswald 1960:55) and to regard even borrowing itself as a special case of analogy (Chafe 1961:117). Within generative grammar there is no formal distinction between borrowing and spontaneous innovation in a single dialect or in the idiolect of a single speaker. In either instance we would be faced with a change in competence—a rule added to the grammar—and any effort to assign the description "borrowed" or "spontaneous" to the rule would not be relevant to the change itself and its subsequent ramifications. The question of whether an innovation was borrowed or sprang up independently is, of course, not devoid of interest, especially in establishing a genetic relationship on the basis of shared features. But there is no reason in generative grammar to distinguish between changes that are regarded as gradual (nonborrowed innovations) and those that are clearly not gradual (borrowed innovations).

Rejecting the gradualness assumption does not force one to exclude a priori the existence of intermediate steps. If, for example, s in an early stage of a language is represented by zero in a later stage, we are not compelled to assume the addition of a rule $s \rightarrow \emptyset$. The sequence $s \rightarrow h \rightarrow \emptyset$ is more likely: $s \rightarrow h$ is a natural change, as is $h \rightarrow \emptyset$. That is, in certain changes increments may be more expected, more natural than great leaps. But intermediate steps are not a necessary condition, and positing h between s and zero is not the same as positing an age gradient of sounds between s and zero.

It should perhaps be stated expressly that in denying the gradualness of phonological change we do not deny the possibility that a phonological change *spreads* gradually throughout a speech community. These are two totally different things, and our stance with one of these questions in no way commits us to a position with the other. In fact, all the evidence agrees that the *spread* of a change is gradual to a greater or lesser extent. Isoglosses usually move about gradually over periods of time: a favored pronunciation spreads out from a prestige focal point, an archaic feature of pronunciation recedes under pressure from increased communication, from schools, from radio and television. Generally in these cases a phonological change takes place—typically a rule is added—and then the rule is gradually acquired in the grammars of an ever-increasing number of contiguous speakers. This process is assuredly gradual, but it has nothing to do with the question of whether phonological change originates in a constant, gradual, imperceptible shifting of allophones.

To make the difference perfectly clear, let us consider an example briefly discussed in Section 4.4: the spread of centralization in the diphthongs /ay/ and /aw/ on Martha's Vineyard (Labov 1963). The facts are clear. Centralization has come to mark its possessor as "belonging" on the island, as being a bona fide Martha's Vineyarder in contrast to the many tourists and summer visitors from the mainland. Careful linguistic interviews from 1933 show some centralization in occurrences of /ay/ and virtually no centralization in occurrences of /aw/, but in 1963 centralization has spread in such a way that the oldest speakers (over 75) have the least amount of centralization, those from 61 to 75 have more, and centralization increases down to the speakers between 31 and 45. "Amount of centralization" is here a measure of two factors: (1) the degree to which the subject centralizes, i.e. whether he says *right* [rə⌄ɪt], [ra⌃ɪt], or [raɪt], and (2) the frequency with which he centralizes at all, i.e. the number of times in the speech sample that he pronounces *right* with centralization of any degree as opposed to *right* with no centralization [raɪt]. The data presented in Labov (1963) bring out several relevant factors: centralization is desirable; there is an age gradient in amount of centralization; certain phonetic environments (before t, s) favor centralization over others (before m, n); the phonological rule expressing centralization is optional with some percentage of the speakers (they can but need not centralize, depending on the situation); even in repeated performances of the same word different degrees of centralization are audible (this seems to depend on stress). (Labov's data show two degrees of centralization between [a] and [ə].)

Note especially that "amount of centralization" has two components. The age gradient showing that amount of centralization varies inversely with age thus does not constitute evidence for a gradual shift in the "habit of articulating" /ay/ and /aw/ through generations. What it does demonstrate is that most older speakers do not centralize at all in pronouncing most instances of /ay/ and /aw/, whereas younger speakers do. Significantly, individual speakers fluctuate between [ai̯], [a˄i̯], and [ə˅i̯] in their own speech performance (Labov 1963:287–289). This is evidence for fluctuation in performance; it is not evidence for a gradual shift over time in the habit of articulating /ay/ and /aw/.

We may interpret this as a case of the spread of a rule in a more general and slightly altered form. We assume that some speakers, presumably older inhabitants whose identity with Martha's Vineyard—its pace of living, its ideals, and so on—was total and unquestioned, had a rule of centralization in their grammars:

$$5.5 \quad \begin{bmatrix} V \\ -\text{round} \\ +\text{back} \end{bmatrix} \rightarrow [-1\text{ low}] / \underline{\quad\quad} \begin{bmatrix} -\text{vocalic} \\ -\text{consonantal} \\ -\text{back} \end{bmatrix} \begin{bmatrix} +\text{obstruent} \\ -\text{voice} \end{bmatrix}$$

(The [a] in the diphthong [ai̯] is slightly centralized when followed by a voiceless obstruent. This is, of course, an idealization in that some speakers doubtless had a slightly less general rule, perhaps centralizing only before *t* and *s* or before *t*, *s*, *p*, and *f*; some speakers a more general rule centralizing [a] in both [ai̯] and [au̯]; and some a rule with greater centralization [− 2 low] in general or depending on environment. Note too that this is a late phonetic rule in which we may freely use n-ary variables.)

On Martha's Vineyard since 1933 Rule 5.5 has been borrowed in all sorts of varying forms. It is a sign of "belonging" to have Rule 5.5 in one's grammar; it is a desirable acquisition. In the grammar of some, and possibly most, it is an optional rule whose application depends on factors such as stress: Labov (1963:290) reports a fisherman using the word *knife* twice in the space of a few seconds, once [nai̯f] and once [na˄i̯f]. The environment of centralization has been generalized to include [au̯], and it is not necessary that the diphthong be followed by a voiceless obstruent. In some grammars the rule has been borrowed with a difference in the structural change; there is greater centralization, which is reflected in the rule by the specification [− 2 low], [− 3 low], or whatever degree of minus lowness a particular speaker uses in a particular environment.

In short we may assume this to be a rather typical paradigm of the spread of a phonological change. An innovation occurs or is present from some source and becomes desirable. The rule expressing the innovation spreads, characteristically in a more general form. At first the added rule is optional but it becomes obligatory if the innovation has "sticking power." Minor variations in the structural change of the rule may occur as it is borrowed among speakers. After a while we have an accomplished fact—a sound change.

But note that nothing in all this forces us to assume that the change was gradual in the sense discussed earlier. Its *spread* is in general gradual, not sudden, and to describe it we should properly reach for statistical tools showing the percentage of speakers in an age group that have the innovation in their grammars, the extent to which the rule is obligatory, and so on. Nothing, however, is gradual or quantitative about the occurrence of the innovation. It is merely one more case of rule addition.

This section has dealt with two aspects of phonological change: its *implementation* and its *spread*. Two positions are possible with regard to each of these aspects of phonological change: they are either *abrupt* or *gradual*. There are thus four logical possibilities in viewing the process of phonological change (Wang 1969).

    (a) abrupt implementation and abrupt spread
    (b) abrupt implementation and gradual spread
    (c) gradual implementation and abrupt spread
    (d) gradual implementation and gradual spread

Both (c) and (d) are rejected because of the considerable amount of evidence against the gradual, incremental view of the implementation of a phonological change. Possibility (a) is rejected for lack of evidence that the spread of a phonological change is particularly rapid. Some changes spread rapidly, some don't; typically it seems to take at least one generation for a rule to become obligatory. This leaves (b), which accurately summarizes the view of phonological change presented here: the act of phonological change, its implementation, is abrupt, but the spread of a phonological change is gradual.

5.2   THE REGULARITY OF PHONETIC CHANGE

One of the great sustained arguments in historical linguistics concerns the "regularity of phonetic change." The term has been variously interpreted, and much discussion could doubtless have been dispensed with if terms had been defined more clearly. Let us take as a point of departure the precise formulation made by Bloomfield (1933:364):

> [Sound change] affects a phoneme or a type of phonemes either universally or under certain strictly phonetic conditions, and is neither favored nor impeded by the semantic character of the forms which happen to contain the phoneme.

There are at least two versions of what has been called the *regularity hypothesis* (Hockett 1965:186). Common to both is the notion of regularity—that is, phonological change applies to a large number of items in the lexicon and not to just a single morpheme. The first hypothesis, which follows from statements like Bloomfield's (see Postal 1968:235–239), amounts to the very strong claim that phonological change can take place only in purely phonetic environments: no environment of a phonological change can contain a reference to "higher-order" information such as morphological or syntactic class; exceptions to phonological changes, if there are any, occur in strictly phonetic environments. This strongest version of the regularity hypothesis, which we shall call H_1 (H standing for hypothesis), may then be stated as follows:

H_1: Phonological change is regular, and its environment can be stated in strictly phonetic terms.

Sound changes in conformity with H_1 are, of course, numerous: for example, Indo-European *b d g* > Germanic *p t k* (the environment here is "everywhere"), and Indo-European *p t k* > Germanic *f þ x* except following obstruents. In each case the change is regular and applies throughout the lexicon, and the environment can be formulated without grammatical categories (Noun, Verb, Accusative, Subjunctive) or syntactic structure (Noun Phrase, Verb Phrase). The environments are strictly phonetic, roughly at the level of representation in a generative grammar after the last binary phonological rule has been applied.

A second, weaker version of the regularity hypothesis can be formulated. The basis for this version is the fact that phonological change is not generally found to be limited to single morphemes. If, in other words, a rule is added changing the segment x to y in a certain diachronic situation, it is not in general the case that $x > y$ in one word or morpheme, $x > w$ in another word, $x > z$ in still another word, and so on with no conditioning factor present. If sound laws, as such changes have been traditionally called, operated like this, there simply could not be a field called comparative linguistics. Rather, we find that in general phonological changes have an across-the-board character, a regularity. They apply across the lexicon, and exceptions to phonological changes fall into three categories: (1) natural subsets of the lexicon (Nouns, Verbs, Adjectives), (2) specific grammatical morphemes and combinations of these morphemes ("first person plural"), and (3) at most a few idiosyncratic lexical items. That is, except for the third category, which accounts for possible isolated and nonsystematic exceptions to phonological changes, even the exceptions to phonological changes tend to be statable in terms of natural phonological, lexical, or grammatical categories. We are not, however, constrained to hold that the change can be stated in strictly phonetic terms. We therefore relax this requirement and formulate a second hypothesis H_2, which expresses the notion that phonological change is regular in the sense just discussed:

H_2: Phonological change is regular, but its environment cannot always be stated in strictly phonetic terms.

Dividing the traditional regularity hypothesis into the two versions H_1 and H_2 makes discussion of the entire question easier. It is possible to cite specific linguistic works, or at the least specific instances in different linguists' work, where the term "regularity hypothesis" or its equivalent has been understood either as H_1 or H_2, and it is perfectly possible to accept H_2 while rejecting the stronger claim of H_1.

Let us begin by observing that the regularity of phonological change (whether H_1 or H_2) is an empirical claim: either phonological change is regular in the sense of one of these hypotheses or it is not, and the only way to settle the question is to examine cases of phonological change. If they turn out to confirm either of the hypotheses, then we may regard that hypothesis as correct. The regularity hypothesis in either formulation is an empirical claim which stands or falls in confrontation with the data. A priori arguments serve us badly here.

When we sift through the data for phonological changes, we find, of course, that H_2 is confirmed—confirmed so well, in fact, that it serves as foundation for the branch of historical linguistics known as comparative linguistics. Phonological changes do indeed apply to large classes of lexical items. Often they are context-free, frequently they occur in purely phonetic environments, and they apply across the board without regard for grammatical category in many cases. When, for example, a rule changing $p\ t\ k > f\ \flat\ x$ everywhere except after obstruents was added to the grammar of the Indo-European dialect that later gave us Germanic, then *every p t k* in the specified environments was affected, and it does not matter whether the word in which $p\ t\ k$ occurred was a noun, verb, or in the dative case.

The verification of the weak version of the regularity hypothesis is, as we see, a trivial matter. The really interesting question is *why* sound change should be regular in the sense that its domain is greater than a single word. It is not, after all, overwhelmingly apparent that this should be the case (see Dyen 1963). By the view discussed in Section 5.1 that at least some sound changes are gradual and random, it does not follow that sound change should in general affect identical sounds in a large number of words. If phonological change is basically random drift of sounds, why shouldn't p in one word drift off in a direction quite different from that of p in another word? Or to push this line of argument to its improbable extreme, why aren't there lots of cases of phonological changes of the following complicated sort?

> $p>f$ in certain words, $p>b$ in others, $p>w$ in still others.
> $t>t^s$ in certain words, $t>t^h$ in others, $t>n$ in still others.
> $k>g$ unconditionally.

Weird cases like this simply do not occur in phonological change (though there are plenty of weird enough phonological changes). If our theory of grammar and language is to account for the facts of historical change, we expect to find in this theory some rationale for the correctness of H_2. The regularity of phonological change in the sense of H_2 does in fact follow from the conception of linguistic change in generative grammar: that speech is the result of an internalized competence, a grammar—a system of rules and a lexicon—and that change consists of alterations in this internalized grammar. In the case of innovation, which is by and large the type of change most commonly referred to as "sound change," a rule is added to this grammar. This rule changes everything that fits its structural analysis. Rules tend to be general—not confined to a single morpheme in the lexicon—so that *every* occurrence of a segment in the designated environment undergoes the structural change of the rule. Phonological changes tend to affect natural classes of sounds (*p t k*, high vowels, voiced stops) because rules that affect natural classes are simpler than rules that apply only to single segments. A rule affecting the natural class /p t k/ is simpler by a feature than the same rule affecting /p t/, and the latter rule in turn is simpler by a feature than the same rule affecting only /p/. That is, a rule applying to:

$$\begin{bmatrix} + \text{ obstruent} \\ - \text{ continuant} \\ - \text{ voice} \end{bmatrix} \qquad \text{/p t k/}$$

is, all else in the rule being the same, simpler than one appyling to:

$$\begin{bmatrix} + \text{ obstruent} \\ - \text{ continuant} \\ - \text{ voice} \\ + \text{ anterior} \end{bmatrix} \qquad \text{/p t/}$$

and this rule is simpler than one applying to:

$$\begin{bmatrix} + \text{ obstruent} \\ - \text{ continuant} \\ - \text{ voice} \\ + \text{ anterior} \\ - \text{ coronal} \end{bmatrix} \qquad \text{/p/}$$

Thus H_2 is adequately confirmed by the data, and generative grammar provides a rationale. It is different with H_1—the strong hypothesis that phonological change occurs only in phonetically defined environments. Nothing in the theory of generative grammar would lend prior logical credence to this claim. In the view advanced here, the class of possible innovations in the grammar of a language is a proper subset of the class of phonological rules. Some phonological rules in natural languages require for their operation grammatical information carried over from the lexicon and the syntactic rules. In English, for example, the rules assigning word stress place stress differently in nouns and verbs, e.g. *cóntent* versus *contént*, *pérmit* versus *permít*. In many languages rules deleting and adding segments apply only to restricted classes such as verbs, nouns, or even subclasses such as strong verbs. Rule 3.13 (discussed in Section 3.3) in the grammars of certain of the Germanic dialects is stated in terms of the grammatical features *Stem-final*, *Past Plural*, and *Past Participle*.

Since this is so, it would be unlikely that every phonological change could be stated in terms of purely phonetic environments. And the empirical evidence bears out this prediction. Cases are not uncommon of changes that occur across the board except in certain morphological environments. In the development of Standard Yiddish from something similar to Middle High German, we find that final unaccented *e*, phonetically [ə], has been lost: *tage > teg* 'days', *erde > erd* 'earth', *gibe > gib* 'I give', *gazze > gas* 'street'. In some cases, however, final [ə] is not lost, principally when the *e* is an adjective inflectional ending: *di groyse shtot* 'the big city', *dos alte land* 'the old country', *a sheyne froy* 'a pretty woman'. A few other final unaccented *e*'s are retained, erratically, but these too are confined to specific morphological environments, e.g. *gésele* 'little street', where *-(e)le* is the diminutive suffix.

The retention of *e* in the adjective endings has nothing to do with a difference in phonetic environment. All schwas were in unstressed position, and there is no phonetic property characteristically associated with adjectives in Middle High German that might somehow account for the loss. We can even find near-minimal pairs containing final unaccented *e*'s that were dropped or retained: *gloyb* 'I believe' : *toybe* 'deaf (inflected adjective)' from Middle High German *gloube* : *toube*; *meyn* 'I think' : *sheyne* 'pretty (inflected adjective)' from Middle High German *meine* : *schœne*.

Nor is there an explanation in analogy. There is nothing to analogize to in these cases. The simplest conclusion is that the environment of this change is not purely phonetic:

$$5.6 \quad \begin{bmatrix} V \\ -\text{stress} \end{bmatrix} \rightarrow \begin{cases} [-\text{next rule}] \,/ + \underline{\quad})_{\text{Adjective}} \\ \emptyset \qquad / \underline{\quad} \# \end{cases}$$

(Unstressed vowels are deleted in word-final position unless that word is an inflected adjective. The rule can be stated as applying to *all* unstressed vowels because only *e* [ə] occurs finally under weak stress.)

This, then, is a case pure and simple of phonological change that cannot be stated in terms of purely phonetic features. It is, in other words, a counter-example to the strong form of the regularity hypothesis H_1. A word sometimes used in attempting to account for morphologically conditioned phonological change like this is *functional* (Sapir 1949:262). The notion (in this case) is that *e*'s serving to mark adjective inflections fulfill a necessary function which requires their maintenance, whereas *e*'s in all the other cases can be dispensed with. This is not an explanation for the dilemma but merely a different term to designate it with, for unless "functional" is defined in some precise, noncircular way it cannot be offered as an explanation.

Another instance of phonological change in nonphonetic environments occurs in Mohawk (Postal 1968:245–254), where the sequence [kw] from proto-Mohawk-Oneida sometimes undergoes epenthesis, cf. the pair Mohawk [kewi'stos] : Oneida [kwi'stos] 'I am cold', parallel to a general process of epenthesis in consonant-resonant sequences that breaks up the clusters [wr, nr, sr, tr, kr, tn, sn, kn, tw, sw, kw, sy] by inserting *e*. Certain [kw] sequences, however, do not undergo epenthesis in Mohawk; one is of the same type as the Yiddish example. When the *k* and the *w* in [kw] are, respectively, the first person marker and the first element of the plural morpheme, no svarabhakti (epenthetic) *e* is inserted: e.g. Mohawk [ya'kwaks] : Oneida [ya'kwaks] 'we several exclusive eat it'. There is nothing irregular or sporadic about this: it happens throughout the language in noun and verb prefixes whenever the sequence [kw] means "first person + plural." Like the Yiddish example, it is regular in the sense of H_2 but not H_1. It applies across the board except that it is impeded in a particular morphological environment. (Notice that the existence of morphologically conditioned phonological rules does not force the conclusion that such rules were added in their synchronic form. It is an interesting but yet unproved claim that all such rules are originally innovated as "purely" phonological rules and later restructured to contain morphological information. In the Yiddish and Mohawk cases there is no reason to suppose that the rules discussed were innovated lacking the morphological conditioning.)

On balance it seems unlikely that such morphologically conditioned phonological changes are rare in the world's languages. They do not figure very prominently in formal accounts of historical linguistic development for a variety of reasons. One reason is that they are counter-examples to H_1. A second reason is a certain dullness which attaches to them. Once we have determined that *x* becomes *y* except in the morphological environment *z*, the story is over, and there is little to do but move on to more interesting things. Speculating *why* [kw] did not undergo epenthesis in a particular morphological environment or *why* final [ə] did not drop in Yiddish in adjective inflectional endings is on a par with speculating why Indo-European $*k^we$ and $*k^wo$ became Indo-Iranian *ča* and *ka*. Usually we simply do not know, though no harm is done by considering possible causes.

One can always devise some ad hoc explanation to save the strong form of the regularity hypothesis when faced with nonphonetic sound changes. Instead of assuming the obvious—that some regular phonological changes take place in environments whose specification requires superficial grammatical structure—one might posit a boundary of some sort (a "plus-juncture") for just these cases. Since many formal boundaries in language do have observable phonetic correlates (word boundary is sometimes realized as pause), one could attribute to the plus-juncture certain purely phonetic characteristics. In this way it is always possible to reduce the original exception to one with a strictly phonetic environment. In the Yiddish example one could assume for Middle High German a plus-juncture ($+$) that precedes all and only adjective endings and then state the rule of schwa-deletion as: schwa disappears word-finally except after plus-juncture. From *toub+e* 'deaf (inflected adjective)' one would obtain Yiddish *toybe*; from *gloube* 'I believe', Yiddish *gloyb*.

It should be obvious that this is a trick, a gimmick. It is no solution to the problem; it merely provides a simple sign ($+$) to designate the troublesome cases with. The reason why this is an illegitimate device is that boundaries in natural languages are hardly ever (probably never) consistently realized in some particular phonetic way. In other words, so far as we know, it is a universal that boundaries, whether morpheme, word, or whatever, are optionally realized as null. All experience with currently spoken languages supports this proposition. To postulate for an historical language a kind of unique boundary *always* phonetically manifested in some defined way violates the cardinal constraint in historical linguistics: descriptions of earlier languages must never violate universals that hold for actually observed languages.

The major reason why morphologically conditioned phonological changes have received relatively little attention is that H_1, the strictly phonetic version of the regularity hypothesis, has been held by the majority of the linguists working in the historical field, certainly by those in the Neogrammarian tradition. If one accepts H_1 as a matter of principle, then the question becomes not whether morphologically conditioned phonological changes exist but what other factor or combination of factors accounts for the aberrancy. The following is a typical example (Bloomfield 1933:362–364). Intervocalic *s* from Indo-European is normally lost in Greek: $*ge\acute{u}s\bar{o} >$ Greek *geúō* 'I give a taste'. However, in a large number of aorist verb forms we find, apparently, a retained intervocalic *s*: *ephílēsa* 'I loved', *emísthōsa* 'I let', *etímēsa* 'I honored'. This is generally attributed to analogy because aorist *s* is preserved when not intervocalic: *égrapsa* 'I wrote', *épleksa* 'I wove'. In this case the explanation is plausible since there is something of a model for the analogical reintroduction of *s* in positions where it would have disappeared by regular sound law. Nevertheless, *ephílēsa*, and so on, are counterexamples to H_1, and to save the hypothesis in its strong version we must look elsewhere for an explanation. In the Yiddish and Mohawk examples, analogy is out of the range of reason. Considerations of this kind rule out the strong form of the regularity hypothesis, H_1, but not the weaker form, H_2.

In other cases phonological change can be stated only in terms of a phonological environment that is not purely phonetic. Generative phonology is insistent for many reasons on the difference between abstract levels of phonological representation and phonetic representation. Roughly speaking, the latter is the level of representation after applying the last binary phonological rule (the n-ary rules that fill out the phonetic detail are irrelevant here). Anything higher is more abstract, "deeper" because further removed from the actual phonetic shape. The most abstract level of phonological representation is the string of formatives present as input to the first rule of the phonological component. The striking difference between deep and surface structure has been evident in many of the examples given here, e.g. the phonetic surface form [dəva·ịn] has a deep structure representation (systematic phonemic, underlying) /divīn/ and intermediate representations such as [divīyn], [divēyn], and [divāyn].

In the light of this hierarchy of phonological representation, the strongest possible form of the regularity hypothesis would be that only surface phonetic structure is permissible to the statement of the environment of a phonological change. This in turn is equivalent to the claim that phonological change consists solely of rule addition at the end of the phonological rules. In this view, every innovation would have to be expressible by adding a rule at the lowest level of phonological representation—the surface level. This is the substance of H_1. In Chapter 3 we examined a number of cases in which this is not true. The only way to express Lachmann's Law in Latin is by assuming that a rule was added *not* at the end of the binary phonological rules but before the rule devoicing obstruents regressively (Rule 3.9). Lachmann's Law thus crucially requires a higher level of representation than the surface phonetic; it requires the representation /agtum/ rather than the surface form [aktum] to give the correct form *āctum* 'having been driven, led'. Without the higher level there would be no way of obtaining the long vowel in *āctum* from surface [aktum] alongside the short vowel in *factum* 'having been made' from surface [faktum].

Notice that it is not claimed here that rules may be added at only two points in the derivation of an utterance—the systematic phonemic and the surface phonetic representations. The claim is not that Lachmann's Law requires the systematic phonemic level of representation for its statement, but only that a rule could not have been added on at the end of the phonological component. We assume rather that the rule was inserted into the grammar of

Latin where it applied to derivations somewhere between the systematic phonemic and surface phonetic.

The problem in Mohawk epenthesis discussed earlier and taken from Postal (1968) offers another case of the same kind. It will be recalled that consonant-resonant clusters normally undergo epenthesis in Mohawk, and that some instances of [kw] do so while others do not. In one of the exceptional cases epenthesis was shown to be impeded in a particular morphological environment. Another case of nonepenthesis must be explained in a different way. An example is Mohawk *ra'kwas* : Oneida *la'kwas* 'he picks it up'. Since this is not in the environment "first person + plural," the non-occurrence of epenthesis must be sought elsewhere. Postal (1968:249) shows that the underlying form of the *kw* in Mohawk *ra'kwas* is /ko/, and that the epenthesis rule applies in the grammar of Mohawk before the rule that converts underlying /ko/ into [kw]. The /ko/ in the underlying form of *ra'kwas* 'he picks it up' is not a consonant-resonant cluster to which the epenthesis rule is applicable; it is a consonant-vowel sequence. Therefore, no epenthesis occurs, and /ko/ later is changed into [kw]. Again, there is nothing irregular or sporadic about this: *every* [kw] from underlying /ko/ comes out [kw], not *[kew]. The explanation is that a rule (epenthesis) is added to the grammar not at the end of the phonological component, where it would operate on surface phonetic forms, but prior to the end so that it operates on more abstract representations (like /ko/ instead of surface level [kw] from /ko/). In this case, the rule converting /ko/ to [kw] belonged to the grammar of proto-Mohawk-Oneida and is several millenia old. The epenthesis rule is only about four hundred or so years old, yet it was inserted into the grammar of proto-Mohawk prior to the /ko/ > [kw] rule. The synchronic ordering of the two rules is (1) epenthesis, (2) /ko/ > [kw]; the chronological ordering is the reverse, (1) /ko/ > [kw], (2) epenthesis.

5.3   ANALOGY

Traditionally, historical linguistics has consisted largely of analysis of the interplay between sound change and analogy. Sound change takes place, pattern irregularities may arise; analogy tends to regularize the results.

Sections 5.1 and 5.2 presented arguments against the traditional views that phonological change is reducible to sound change and that phonological change is regular and phonetic in the sense of H_1, the strong form of the regularity hypothesis. The traditional views have several consequences; one is that phonological change not happening to conform to H_1 is forced into categories of change such as analogy and borrowing. The latter categories, in particular analogy, thereby tend to become terminological receptacles devoid of explanatory power—catchalls for irregularities in the operation of "regular sound laws." This has too often been the demeaning fate of analogy in historical work.

Let us formulate the opposing points of view in this way. Traditional historical linguistics has operated within a framework composed of the concepts of sound change, analogy, borrowing, and grammar. Grammar is the account of language structure; it is central. To account for changes in structure (grammar) one appeals to sound change, analogy, and borrowing. As historical linguistics is treated in generative grammar, grammar is enough: "sound change" is grammar change, "analogy" is grammar change, borrowing is grammar change.

The emphasis in this section is on analyzing traditional cases of analogy as part of a process not different in kind from the other types of linguistic change examined so far. In particular, it will be argued that most kinds of "analogy" too are special cases of simplification, in principle very similar to rule reordering, rule loss, and rule simplification proper. The general premise of this section is that analogy in its traditional sense is not some sort of fifth wheel on the wagon, fundamentally at odds with regular diachronic developments like phonological change. In the discussion that now follows, the term "analogy" is to be understood as a cover designation for those instances of change which traditional historical linguistics would have ascribed to analogy.

Analogy is most palpable and most often appealed to in morphology. A typical, uninteresting because transparent, case is the extension of the *s*-plural throughout the nominal inflection of English. The facts are clear. In Old English each noun was characterized in part by its membership in a stem-class: *dæġ* 'day' was an *a*-stem with the nominative plural *dagas*; *caru* 'care' was an *ō*-stem with the nominative plural *cara*; *dǣd* 'deed' was an *i*-stem with the nominative plural *dǣde*; *tunge* 'tongue' was an *n*-stem with the nominative plural *tungan*. In Modern English, and to a large extent already by Middle English times, the *-(a)s* ending of the masculine *a*-stems has become generalized throughout the nominal system without regard for the original stem class: *cares, deeds, tongues.*

Clearly a simplification has affected at least two components of the grammar: the lexicon and the late transformational rules that attach inflectional endings. In the lexicon of Old English, each noun had, in addition to all the other phonological, grammatical, and semantic information necessary to characterize it, a marker for stem-class. This marker signals the transformational rules for the correct ending. Schematically, then, we would have a set of transformational rules of the following type:

$$dag_{a\text{-stem}} + \text{nominative} + \text{plural} \to dagas$$
$$caru_{\bar{o}\text{-stem}} + \text{nominative} + \text{plural} \to cara$$
$$d\bar{\bar{æ}}d_{i\text{-stem}} + \text{nominative} + \text{plural} \to d\bar{æ}de$$
$$tunge_{n\text{-stem}} + \text{nominative} + \text{plural} \to tungan$$

Some of the divergence in formation might be accounted for by phonological rules and different base forms, but some morphological marker equivalent to stem-class would still be necessary in at least some cases.

The simplification that has taken place here is a twofold one. In the first place, nouns in Modern English do not require a special marker for stem-class. They are all unmarked in this regard; only exceptional plurals (*sheep, children, men*) need a marker to indicate that they do not undergo the regular rule of plural formation. This is simplification in the lexicon. There is also a concomitant simplification in the number of rules of pluralization: all but the first of the above four rules are deleted from the grammar; the synchronic form of the *a*-stem rule remains and attaches -*z*, giving *cats, dogs, houses*, and so on.

No doubt, many cases of analogy—especially analogical leveling—are of this general type whereby lexical entries become simplified and a rule or set of rules are lost from the grammar while others survive. Other instances of analogy are more whimsical in that no apparent simplification is at work, only a realignment. In attested Old English the plural of *ġiest* 'guest', an *i*-stem noun, is *ġiestas*. The original Germanic nominative plural was -*īz*, which would show up in Old English as -*e*, as in *wine* 'friends'. We should expect the nominative plural of *ġiest* to be *ġieste*, but for all practical purposes *ġiest* has become an *a*-stem noun instead of an *i*-stem noun. This is not lexical simplification in any obvious way, but only the change of a marker; and no compensating simplification occurs in the rules of pluralization: the rule attaching *i*-stem plurals must remain in the grammar to give the correct plural in, for example, *wine* 'friends', *dǣde* 'deeds' (though the Early West-Saxon plural *dǣda* shows that *dǣd* had become realigned as an *ō*-stem).

Likewise, if someone says today *bring* : *brang* : *brung* instead of correct *bring* : *brought* : *brought*, the analogy and its source are clear, but superficially the speaker has made no formal simplification in his grammar. *Bring* is changed in its lexical entry from [..., − Strong, − Regular] to [..., + Strong], yet the rule for forming irregular weak past tenses and participles remains (*fight* : *fought* : *fought*; *seek* : *sought* : *sought*). One might well argue that "Strong" is in some way simpler than "Weak Irregular," but this claim does require motivation, though it seems intuitively sound. (Frequency of occurrence may have something to do with this type of realignment and with some other kinds of analogy as well.)

Underlying most cases of morphological analogy is a clear argument for simplification. In this view, then, analogy is not different from what is typical of the child's learning of his language. There is disregard of the data in the interest of a simpler account of one's language; there is generalization of a rule beyond its proper domain in the grammar of the older generation. Most of these incorrect creations will be disposed of during maturation, but some may fit the "cut" of the language so well that they become a part of it, especially if the same type of simplification occurs simultaneously in that or closely following generations. The incorrect learning of one generation is the dominant pattern of the next.

The force of this argument leads us to seek parallels between this kind of simplification and the kinds of simplification found earlier, such as rule loss and reordering. Let us consider the case of Gothic discussed under RULE LOSS in Section 3.3. There it was argued that Gothic once had in its grammar either Verner's Law (Rule 3.12) or its altered synchronic counterpart (Rule 3.13). As long as this rule was present, the surface realizations of verbs in root-final voiceless fricatives included morphs with root-final voiced fricatives: e.g. the principal parts of *kius-* 'to choose' /kiusan kaus kusum kusans/ were phonetically realized as [kiusan kaus kuzum kuzans]. With the loss of the voicing rule, voiced fricatives from underlying voiceless fricatives reverted to their voiceless status: [kiusan kaus kusum kusans]. The crucial bits of evidence were relic forms such as *tigjus* 'decades' (originally from *taihun* 'ten'), *faginon* 'to be happy' ($g <$ original h, cf. *faheþs* 'joy'), and *alds* 'generation' ($d <$ original $þ$, cf. *alþeis* 'old'). These relics, all of which have reflexes of voiced fricatives from original voiceless fricatives via Verner's Law, were disassociated from their sources with voiceless fricatives, hence were restructured in the lexicon with underlying voiced fricatives. There were no synchronic rules linking the pairs cited. The principal parts of verbs, however, were so morphologically cohesive (related by synchronic rules) that they simply reverted to voiceless realizations as in the underlying forms. The few exceptions to the latter statement are all verbs with precarious status and defective distributions, e.g. *aih* 'I possess': *aigum* 'we possess'.

This rule loss introduces a leveling throughout the paradigm of strong verbs. While the rule was still present, some verbs (like *kiusan*) had allomorphs with voiced (z) and voiceless (s) stem-final fricatives, others had throughout no change in the stem-final fricative: *faran for forum farans* 'to wander', *niman nam nemum numans* 'to take', *mitan mat metum mitans* 'to measure'. The rule loss produces uniformity in accord with the latter type, just as Modern English nouns are uniformly inflected with the *s*-plural except for the handful of relic forms (*men*, and so on).

Rule reordering also brings about a regularization of allomorphic variation, as was pointed out in Section 3.3 in the case of German rule reordering. Before the reordering certain nouns had allomorphs with both long and short vowels : *lop* : *lo:bə* 'praise, praises', *gras* : *gra:zəs* 'grass, of the grass'. Others had only one type of vowel throughout: *bet* : *betən* 'bed, beds', *blu:mə* : *blu:mən* 'flower, flowers', *has* : *hasəs* 'hate, of the hate'. The reordering levels out this kind of variation so that throughout the paradigm nouns have only long or short vowels and not some of one and some of the other.

The tenor of the arguments advanced so far is that traditional analogy, rule loss, rule reordering, not to mention rule simplification proper, are all reflections of a universal process of simplification that ultimately goes back to the child's acquisition of grammar. One might propose a different relation among these processes, namely that *analogy* is the central force and is reflected in such things as rule reordering and rule loss. In this view the change of *lop* and *gras* to *lo:p* and *gra:s* would be *caused* by analogical pressure from other forms in the paradigm that have long vowels. Similarly, in Gothic the reintroduction of voiceless stem-final fricatives throughout strong verbs would be caused by analogy, the source being the voiceless stem-final fricatives in certain principal parts. Rule reordering in the one case and rule loss in the other would then be mere descriptions of what has happened rather than the prior events.

Consider carefully these two accounts which, let it be noted, are in no way merely different terms for the same thing. There is more at stake here than terminology. We assume, as was discussed at length in Chapter 4, that simplification of grammars is an option always open to the child and that it derives directly from the transmission of language to the oncoming generation. Simplification is the order of the day in the child's acquisition of language, as was proposed and supported by data in Section 4.2. The formal correlates in the grammar of simplification are many: restructuring, rule loss, rule generalization, rule reordering.

The alternative view—that analogy is basic and the other things follow from it—requires us to be very specific about what analogy is and about the rationale for its occurrence. Even more, we must plausibly demonstrate that it accounts for the changes here attributed to rule loss and rule reordering. An enormous amount has been written about analogy, though typically more as an adjunct to an argument than as the object of investigation by itself. Nevertheless, there are studies of analogy per se (e.g. Hermann 1931, Kuryłowicz 1945–1949, Mańczak 1958), and some recent penetrating studies and collections of studies of historical linguistics could serve as textbooks on the process (Benveniste 1948 and 1962, Kuryłowicz 1958 and 1960, Szémerenyi 1960, Watkins 1962).

The traditional theory of analogy is based on the idea of the *proportion* (Paul 1960: Chapter 5). For example, to explain the occurrence of incorrect *brang* for *brought* one "solves" the proportion *sing : sang = bring : x*. In this way the correct but irregular paradigm *bring/brought* gives way to incorrect but regular *bring/brang*.

There are several grave defects in the proportional theory of analogy. First, it is not clear what conditions must be imposed on the forms in the proportion; it is not even clear that conditions *can* be stated which give the right results for each instance of analogical change. For example, *sing* and *bring* agree with each other phonologically in certain ways—among other things they rhyme, so that it makes some kind of sense to put them in the same proportion. Yet how close must the phonological agreement be before two forms qualify as input to a proportion? Must they rhyme? Is it enough to share the last two, or three, or four phonemes in common and in the same order? It seems highly unlikely that satisfactory agreement conditions can be formulated to account for all analogical changes from the world's languages.

132 / SOUND CHANGE AND ANALOGY

Second, no matter what agreement condition is imposed on the items in a proportion, it will not be possible in general to produce proportions for all the forms undergoing changes that one would like to call analogical. Consider the extension of the *s*-plural in English. To show that *caru* 'care' gave up its plural *cara* for *cares* by proportional analogy, one must produce an *a*-stem noun agreeing with *caru* in some close way. And we must do the same for *dæd* 'deed', *tunge* 'tongue', and the host of nouns that did not originally take a plural in *-s*. This simply cannot be done since, for one thing, *a*-stem nouns ended only in consonants in Old English.

On reflection it should be obvious that defects like these in the proportional theory of analogy cannot be remedied by imposing ad hoc conditions on the proportion. Many just such conditions have been proposed. Vendryes (1925:157) suggested that the formula should be $p : p' = a : x$, where p and p' represent "infinite" quantities. Since no language has an infinite number of lexical items, this condition would make analogical change impossible in every natural language—clearly an unfortunate result for anyone wanting to believe in analogy.

A third, even more serious failure of the proportional theory of analogy is its inability to account for the *regularity* of a very large number of so-called analogical changes. This shows up particularly in cases of rule loss and rule reordering. Given Gothic *kiusan kaus kuzum kuzans* 'to choose' and other strong verbs with a voiceless : voiced alternation, why should *all* of them be analogically realigned with voiceless fricatives? This is not predicted by the proportional theory. Other verbs in the language with no voiceless : voiced alternations present both regular patterns: both voiceless obstruents through-out, e.g. *greipan graip gripum gripans* 'to seize', and voiced obstruents throughout, e.g. *steigan staig stigum stigans* 'to climb'. Both proportions were, therefore, present in Gothic: *voiceless : voiceless = kiusan : x*, from which we obtain correct *kusum kusans*; but also *voiced : voiced = x : kuzum*, from which we would obtain the nonattested form **kiuzan*. The point is that unless it is integrated into a theory of language in a way not hitherto done, the proportion theory of analogy would lead us to expect *both* kinds of leveling for Gothic: leveling sometimes in favor of the voiceless stem-final fricative and other times in favor of the voiced stem-final fricative. But Gothic does not present us with this at all. There is perfect regularity in that voiceless stem-final fricatives alone survive, and only the few relic forms extant in attested Gothic give the slightest hint of the original allomorphic variation. There is nothing sporadic, idiosyncratic about this; it is as regular as the average phonological change.

Note that the complete regularity of this leveling process is explained correctly by rule loss. The rule converting voiceless fricatives into voiced ones was lost, and all forms previously affected by the rule no longer undergo it. Thus, *all* voiced fricatives produced synchronically by this rule revert to their voiceless counterparts.

Similarly, in the case of German reordering by which *lop* 'praise' became *lo:p* and *gras* 'gras' became *gra:s*, why don't we find irregularities in regard to which vowel, the long one or the short one in the allomorphs of such words, survives in the analogical leveling? And if analogy is proportional, affecting one word at a time in the proportion, why aren't there at least a few nouns still around that have not participated in leveling at all? These are the consequences of the proportion theory of analogy, at least in its current formulations. In point of fact, in German *every* vowel before an underlying voiced obstruent (e.g. [lop] < /lob/, [gras] < /graz/) has become lengthened, so that every noun in the class of *lop*, *gras*, and so on, has undergone leveling in favor of the long vowel. Only relic forms like *weg* [vek] 'away' from earlier *Weg* [wek] 'path', underlying /veg/, in which restructuring to /vek/ has taken place *before* reordering, give us any indication of the earlier situation. (Though some dialects preserve the original ordering.)

Analogy in its traditional interpretation as a proportion gives a plausible account of some of the isolated realignments found in virtually all languages. Analogy as a proportion is a kind of one-shot affair duplicated, if at all, only sporadically elsewhere in the language. But the Gothic and German examples are anything but sporadic and irregular. They demonstrate perfect regularity of rule loss and rule reordering respectively. Only when we think of each separate verb and noun form in these languages as solutions to a proportion does the regularity become anything to wonder about. Similarly, as simplification both in the lexicon and in the transformational component, the generalization of the *s*-plural in English is not remarkable. But if it proceeded proportion by proportion, word by word, we would reasonably expect to have more archaic forms like *men* and *brethren* than we actually have.

Consider again the argument tentatively put forth earlier—that analogy should be taken as basic with simplification its consequence. No matter what interpretation we attach to analogy, this relation is bound to be unsatisfactory. In the first place, the proportional theory of analogy seriously fails to account for changes easily explained as simplification. This we have seen. Second, if we accept a much stronger conception of analogy as an irresistible force that *requires* change each time its conditions are met, it is clear that counter-examples can easily be found. If, in other words, we should entertain the claim that each input to an analogical proportion *must* undergo change, we would easily be able to falsify our claim. The noun *foot* still has the plural *feet*, the noun *child* still has the plural *children*; these are counter-examples to analogy as an irresistible force. If we accept the weaker interpretation of analogy as something that merely points the direction of possible change, then analogy becomes superfluous because simplification is enough. This weaker version of analogy would claim that *foot* and *child*, if they give up their old plurals, will become *foots* and *childs*. But since this is already predicted by simplification, analogy is unnecessary. For this reason, as well as for the others advanced in this section, we reject analogy. Grammar and simplification are enough.

In emphasizing the regularity of certain changes customarily attributed to analogy but here attributed to simplification, we should not overlook the fact that simplification in the sense used here sets the stage for queer realignments that dot every language. Latin rhotacism provides us with a simple example. A rule changing $s > r$ intervocalically was added to the grammar of Latin sometime prior to the 4th century B.C., giving rise to alternations such as *amīcus magnus* : *amīcōrum magnōrum* 'a great friend, of great friends'; *genus* : *generis* 'kind, of the kind'; *honōs* : *honōris* 'honor, of honor'. The latter alternation is found in later Latin as *honor* : *honōris*. The forms for 'a great friend, of great friends', and so on, remain, however, with their *s* : *r* alternation. What has happened is that the underlying form of 'honor' has changed from /honos/ to /honor/. This case of restructuring is trivial in that the underlying representation of this one word (and a few others such as *ebur* 'ivory') has changed. The rhotacism rule remains in the language, producing *s* : *r* alternations as before, but restructuring has removed this one word from the domain of the rhotacism rule. Such minor lexical changes are absolutely compatible with the concept of change adhered to in generative grammar, and one need not appeal to analogy.

In the same vein consider an example from German. Middle High German had several patterns of noun pluralization, among them (1) addition of -*e*, e.g. *tac* 'day' with the plural *tage*, and (2) umlaut of the root vowel with addition of -*e*, e.g. *kraft* 'power' with the plural *krefte*. Both rules of pluralization are retained in modern German, cf. *Tag/Tage* and *Kraft/Kräfte*. The noun 'tree' obeyed rule (1) in Middle High German, rule (2) in modern German: *boum/boume* versus *Baum/Bäume*. There is no obvious case for simplification that can be made here; both rules of pluralization are carried along unchanged, the lexical entry for 'tree' is no simpler now in German than it was in Middle High German. There has been an idiosyncratic realignment of this particular noun.

5.4   EXCEPTIONS TO PHONOLOGICAL CHANGES

This general line of consideration can be pursued a bit further. Traditionally, one disadvantage of a strong form of the regularity hypothesis (such as H_1) is the existence of all kinds of exceptions to otherwise regular phonological changes. Included here are not only morphologically conditioned changes like the loss of final schwas in Yiddish, which have excited little interest, but more particularly the bewildering array of exceptions and irregularities that have come to light. Romance linguistics is an especially rich mine of such complex linguistic situations, and it is no wonder that the most convinced and vocal skeptics of the regularity hypothesis traditionally have come from Romance philology (Schuchardt 1885, Hermann 1931).

Examples are rife: paradigmatic resistance to phonological change, the interference of folk etymology in regular change, the avoidance of homonymy. An instance of the latter type occurs in certain French dialects where inter-vocalic *r* has become *z* regularly except for certain words such as *frères* 'brothers' and *oreille* 'ear'. This exception has been attributed (Lerch 1925: 80–82) to a striving to avoid homonymy, to avoid falling together with *fraises* 'strawberries' and *oseille* 'sorrel'. This kind of active participation by the speaker in the processes affecting his language is taken for granted in the work of many Romance linguists, precisely because, one suspects, Romance dialectology has turned up so many exceptions to supposedly regular sound laws. The notions of "therapeutic change" and "lexical pathology" come to mind here, concepts which are exemplified most vividly in the work of the French-Swiss scholar Jules Gilliéron. (Cf. Gilliéron 1915, 1918, also Malkiel 1967.)

Anyone familiar with dialect studies over an extensive language area is not surprised by exceptions to phonological changes that are for the most part regular. Do such irregularities falsify the theory of phonological change proposed here? The answer is No. In this concluding section we shall look into some of the ways that these irregularities may be accounted for in a theory of linguistic change compatible with generative grammar.

Every theory of grammar must be equipped with some way of marking exceptions to general rules. In some languages there is a division between native and nonnative morphemes; typically the latter do not undergo a rule or set of rules affecting the native portion of the lexicon. In Finnish (Harms 1968:120) proper nouns with a single noninitial stop are not subject to a certain rule, which we shall designate as Rule *x*. We account for this in the grammar in the following way. A redundancy rule uses the feature [+ Proper] to state what is special or aberrant about proper noun lexical morphemes. In this instance we would have the redundancy rule:

$$5.7 \quad \begin{bmatrix} + \text{Noun} \\ + \text{Proper} \\ + \text{obstruent} \\ - \text{continuant} \end{bmatrix} \rightarrow [- \text{Rule } x] \, / \, [- \text{obstruent}] \underline{\quad\quad} V$$

This states that any noninitial stop in a lexical item fitting the structural analysis of Rule 5.7 is marked additionally as "minus Rule *x*," which by convention prevents such items from undergoing Rule *x*. Similarly, mor-phemes foreign in a language and therefore exceptions to certain rules will be marked [+ Foreign] in the lexicon, and we will have a redundancy rule of the form:

$$[+ \text{Foreign}] \rightarrow \begin{bmatrix} - \text{Rule } x \\ - \text{Rule } y \\ \cdots \end{bmatrix}$$

indicating that foreign morphemes do not undergo Rule x, Rule y, and any other rules (...) not applicable. (On the treatment of exceptions see Chomsky and Halle 1968:172–176.)

In the cases discussed above exceptional morphemes constituted some small portion of the lexicon. Often, only a single item in the vocabulary is aberrant, usually inexplicably. It just happens not to undergo some rule or rules. English has a laxing rule (Chomsky and Halle 1968:180–181) that laxes the underlying tense vowel in the second syllable of *divinity*, *serenity*, *profanity*, and a large number of other words. An exception is *obese*/*obesity* in most dialects of English: the laxing rule would normally lax the second vowel in *obesity*, yielding *[obɛsətiy], whereas [obiysətiy] is the usual form. This is simply an idiosyncratic property of this morpheme, and to account for it we mark *obese* as [− Rule x], where x is the Laxing Rule in the lexicon. By convention every segment of a formative does not undergo a rule for which the lexical morpheme is marked "minus that rule," hence the tense /ē/ underlying the second vowel of *obesity* will not be laxed to [ɛ].

Similarly, we can use such a marking convention in historical linguistics to account for innovations (rule additions) that sporadically and idio-syncratically pass over individual items. In the case of *frères* and *oreille* mentioned earlier, which would normally have become *frèzes* and *ozeille*, we simply assume that these two items were (for reasons not relevant in the immediate discussion) marked as [− Rule x], where x is the rule converting r to z intervocalically. Hence, these two items do not undergo the rule con-verting intervocalic r into z.

We have not endeavored here to answer the separate question of *why* these two words remained exceptions to a regular phonological change. As a part of sociolinguistics the question would be well worth pursuing: there is no telling what one might find out about ears and brothers, not to mention strawberries and sorrels, in French peasant society. Our concern here, how-ever was rather more astringent: to show that generative grammar has a well-motivated way for dealing with lexical exceptions to rules. Since every language has exceptions to rules, an adequate theory of grammar must be able to cope with them, and one way is the "minus rule feature" as illustrated above. But it is not the role of grammatical theory to explain exceptions to general rules—to explain, in other words, why general rules are not even more general.

A more interesting case of the same kind also comes from Romance linguistics: we might refer to it as a phonological change brought about by morphology (Malkiel 1968). In Old Spanish the behavior of the Latin medial clusters -RG-, -LG-, -NG- before front vowels is aberrant: ǵ, a palatalized g (-RǴ-, -LǴ-, -NǴ-), shifts to z, which was either an affricate [dz] or a fricative [z]. Examples: ARGILLA 'potter's clay' > *arzilla*; GINGĪVA 'gum' > *enzía*; ĒR(I)GERE 'to raise' > *erzer*. This is odd in the general framework of Romance linguistics since the second element of similar medial consonant groups generally remains unchanged: MORDĒRE 'to bite' > *morder*; VENDERE 'to sell' > *vender*. Word-initial Ǵ- never gives *z*- in Old Spanish; cf. GELĀRE 'to freeze' > *elar*, GERMĀNU '(half-) brother' > *ermano*, where G- before front vowels has disappeared.

None of the various attempts to account for this has been widely accepted or even made very plausible. Malkiel (1968) has presented evidence from various sources for the following explanation. A model for the alternation of *g* (before nonfront vowels) and *z* (before front vowels) is provided by the common verb DĪCŌ, -ĒRE 'to say', which has the Spanish reflexes (indicative) *digo*, *dize(s)*, ..., (subjunctive) *diga(s)*, and so on. The pattern of this phonological alternation has spread beyond the original verb. Thus, in the verb FACIŌ, -ERE 'to do', Old Spanish replaces regular **faço, faz(es)*, ..., **faça* by *fago, faz(es)*, ..., *faga*, which has been remodeled along the line of *digo*, *diz(es)*, ..., *diga*. The realignment has spread even further, producing unetymological *g* in other words, for example *oiga* in place of *oya* < AUDIA(M) 'to hear (l. pres. act. subj.)'.

The original rule, accounting for the *g* : *z* alternation in *digo*, had, we assume, the status of a "minor rule" in the language. The environment of the rule was simplified, extending its domain to *fago* and other verbs in the language, especially *-ngo* verbs (FINGŌ, PANGŌ, TANGŌ); and the end result of a progressive series of simplifications in the environment of the rule was a rule *not* restricted morphologically but quite generally applicable to any -NG- before front vowels. This rule, now independent of morphological class, is generalized to affect -RG- and -LG-.

Nothing in this richly varied problem conflicts with our picture of phonological change in generative grammar. It is fundamentally a case of innovation followed by simplification, doubtless made more complex by rule borrowing within Romance and muddied still more by other trends in the language(s). This kind of morphological conditioning of and interference with phonological change is embarrassing only if we insist on the strong version of the regularity hypothesis (H_1). If, as has been argued here, H_1 is not observed, then there is nothing particularly upsetting about this type of change.

It has been proposed that the paradigm of change suggested by Malkiel is even more general than has been realized in the literature of historical change. Let us consider, for a moment, the difference between *major rules* and *minor rules* (cf. Lakoff 1965). Major rules in phonology are exemplified by most of the rules stated throughout this book: they apply automatically to every form unless that form has been marked "minus the rule" by a morpheme feature such as [+ Foreign], [− Rule *x*], and so on, as discussed earlier. A minor rule obeys the convention that no form undergoes it unless specifically marked. (Cf. Lightner 1968 on minor rules in Russian phonology.)

In the case from Old Spanish a minor rule applied only to DĪCŌ, thus making an exception of this tiny part of the lexicon. Subsequently a greater number of morphemes came to be marked as having to undergo this minor rule, e.g. FACIŌ and AUDIA(M), and finally the rule became a major rule applying across a large part of the lexicon.

Wang (1968, 1969) has proposed that in general, phonological change begins in the way indicated by the Old Spanish example. In other words, change starts as a minor rule, making exceptional those items in the lexicon that it affects. The rule extends its domain of application to ever larger portions of the lexicon, eventually becoming a major rule in the grammars of subsequent generations. Exceptions to "sound laws" are then the handful of lexical items not reached by the rule, i.e. those items marked "minus the rule" for the rule in question. (See Wang 1969 for a number of additional conjectures on the cause of irregularities in sound changes.)

However, against the view that phonological changes are initiated as minor rules there is evidence of the following sort. It is possible to show that most minor rules in languages are the synchronic relics of once general phonological rules. There is in modern English a minor rule that accounts for voiceless/voiced alternations as in *leaf/leaves*, *bath/baths*, *house/houses*, and a relatively few other items. To account for this assume that such forms end in underlying voiced fricatives (for example, *house* /hūz/) and that they are marked as having to undergo a minor rule devoicing final fricatives, thus /hūz/ > [hūs] and eventually [haws]. This is clearly a minor rule in English phonology, yet in Old English the rule was completely general: all lexical items were subject to it without exception. Similarly, there was in Gothic a minor rule affecting the *t* of the past tense morpheme (compare *hafts*, *salboþs*, *salboda*, where *t*, *þ*, and *d* are allomorphs of past tense /t/). This was a minor rule of Gothic phonology affecting only *t*'s belonging to certain grammatical morphemes, yet it is the impoverished synchronic residue of part of Grimm's Law—the addition of a completely general rule. This type of data argues against the claim that regular phonological changes originate in the addition of a minor rule. The other way around seems more likely.

In conclusion, let us briefly consider a point often made in the context of these and similar discussions: that the heuristic advantages derived from observation of strict phonetic regularity of phonological change make the strong form of the regularity hypothesis worth retaining even at the expense of its "slight" incorrectness. In other words, we should act *as if* every phonological change were at most phonetically conditioned. The underlying sentiment behind this procedure is that to cease observing H_1 would throw us back to the grim days of Bopp and Rask when no holds were barred in describing phonological change, when one was not constrained to feel that if $p > f$ in one word, it should become f in all phonetically similar words.

However useful this notion may have been at early stages in the development of historical linguistics, it has nothing to do with the truth value of H_1 and should be disposed of once and for all. In discussing as separate entities

H_1, the strictly phonetic version of the regularity hypothesis, and H_2, the weaker claim about phonological change regularity, the main purpose was to demonstrate that a linguist can accept one hypothesis (H_2) while rejecting the other (H_1). This in fact was done here. We have accepted H_2 and even pointed out specific reasons in generative grammar why H_2 should be true. But various kinds of data were produced to falsify H_1, and there is no reason to accept the constraint on change that H_1 embodies.

This does not, however, open the field to wild orgies of unbridled speculation. The more general a rule is, the more highly valued the grammar containing that rule is in the evaluation of grammars. A rule that specifies a change in a purely phonetic environment is higher valued than a rule carrying out the same change in the same environment but now modified by a specification [− Class x], where "Class x" is a nonphonetic specification such as [+ Noun], [+ Adjective], or [+ Plural]. If all else is equal, the first formulation of the rule is to be preferred over the second.

In short, we try to render the simplest account of the facts. If a change has a purely phonetic environment, the simplest account involves writing a rule with a purely phonetic environment. If the change cannot be stated in purely phonetic terms, we still render the simplest account we can. This may require us to write a rule whose structural analysis contains some morphological features (as in the loss of Yiddish final schwa); or to order the rule in the grammar so that it operates on an abstract phonological representation (Lachmann's Law); or to write a minor rule applying to only a small part of the lexicon; or possibly to write a major rule to which several lexical items are marked as exceptional.

This is all merely a complicated way of saying that historical linguists do what they are supposed to do: describe change. A wide array of evidence now shows that phonological change takes place in environments both phonetic and nonphonetic. To describe change we cannot observe a dictum requiring us to make the environment of every phonological change strictly phonetic. This is just the way things are.

SUPPLEMENTARY READING

Bloomfield, Leonard. 1933. *Language*. New York: Holt, Rinehart & Winston, Inc. Chaps. 20–23.

Hermann, Eduard. 1931. *Lautgesetz und Analogie*. Berlin: Weidmannsche Buchhandlung.

Hockett, Charles F. 1958. *A Course in Modern Linguistics*. New York: The Macmillan Company. Chaps. 42–54.

Kiparsky, Paul. 1965. *Phonological Change*. Unpublished doctoral dissertation, Massachusetts Institute of Technology.

Postal, Paul M. 1968. *Aspects of Phonological Theory*. New York: Harper & Row, Publishers. Chaps. 10–15.

Wechssler, Eduard. 1900. *Giebt es Lautgesetze?* Halle: Max Niemeyer.

6

SYNTAX

Syntax has always been something of a stepchild in the family of historical linguistics. A language cannot get along without a syntax, but that it can is exactly the impression one might get from reading the average "handbook" on the historical development of a language. There have been no great "breakthroughs" in historical syntax comparable to the Law of Palatals, Verner's Law, or the discovery of Indo-European laryngeals. We have specific techniques for reconstruction of much of the phonological and morphological structure of proto-languages, but we do not have similarly codified techniques for historical syntax.

Much was done in syntax by nineteenth-century scholars, at least in the syntax of particular languages and proto-languages. The detailed studies of Delbrück, Brugmann, and Wackernagel in Indo-European syntax are unparalleled achievements of their kind, and they, like our predecessors' best work in phonology and morphology, are still rich sources for further research. In this century syntax has not, for the most part, been on the receiving end of the energy devoted to historical linguistics, despite public appeals (Lane 1949) and private lamentations that so little is being done. It is almost a cliché that historical syntax has not been in good health.

Of the many reasons for this neglect the most obvious has been the lack of an adequate theoretical basis for describing syntax. Without a theory, research can only result in the collection and crude organization of data. And for all their erudition and insight, the good traditional works on historical syntax have never gone much beyond the level of observational adequacy (Chapter 2). They are, in other words, at best good accounts of the data: listings of characteristic syntactic constructions, discussions of word order in main and subordinate clauses, often presented in terms of statistical preponderance, and so on.

Moreover, even if syntax had had its proper theory, it is not apparent that all our problems would be over. It is very often as important to know what is *not* a possible syntactic construction as it is to know what *is* one, and no finite corpus of utterances in any language will ever give us enough information to make such decisions with overwhelming confidence. This is less of a problem in phonology, but only in degree, not in kind. Statistically speaking, a corpus of a fixed size will permit statements about phonology at confidence levels significantly higher than the confidence levels associated with syntactic statements based on the same corpus. We would all feel safer drawing phonological conclusions from the Rosetta Stone or the Horn of Gallehus rather than syntactic conclusions.

A major deterrent to the progress of diachronic syntax has been removed with the development of more adequate theories of syntax, particularly transformational theory, which permits us to write grammars that go well beyond the level of observational adequacy. Of course, inadequacies occur in any particular formulation of transformational theory, as is true of every theory that attempts to account for nontrivial phenomena, whether language or the movements of the heavenly bodies. In point of fact, the substantial core of agreement about the form and substance of transformational grammar is certainly enough to support its application to historical problems. This application began in the 1960's and promises to be extremely fruitful. We shall examine some of the results in the remainder of this chapter.

First, let us consider the objection that we cannot make sufficiently correct statements about the syntactic facts of dead languages. This obstacle is not as formidable as people sometimes assume. One must know a great deal about a language to write its transformational grammar and ideally the best person for the job is a native speaker, but numerous languages have been treated successfully within the transformational framework by linguists who do not have a native control of the language. One of the things that make this possible is the universal or near-universal status of many features of syntax. To take a trivial example, no known language lacks transformations. More substantially, most known languages have some means of deriving questions from underlying declarative sentences: *What do you see?* from *You see something.* Most languages have means of coordinating sentences:

$$\left.\begin{array}{l}\text{John likes cigars} \\ \text{Harry likes candy}\end{array}\right\} \Rightarrow \text{John likes cigars and Harry likes candy}$$

Most languages have the equivalent of embedding transformations:

$$\left.\begin{array}{l}\text{John saw the boy} \\ \text{The boy is playing}\end{array}\right\} \Rightarrow \text{John saw the boy who is playing}$$

It would be unreasonable to assume that dead languages and proto-languages lacked similar devices altogether. In other words, our theory of syntax narrows down the possibilities for syntactic structure and gives us clues as to what to look for in the syntax of languages like Latin and Classical Greek for which native speakers are unavailable. If Latin lacks an expected transformation, then it just lacks it and that's all there is to it; but if the records of Latin indicate a particular transformation, then we look through all the written evidence to determine its correct formulation. Similarly, if Old English, Old Norse, Old Saxon, Old Frisian, and Old High German all have, say, the same or nearly the same embedding transformation, then we need not hesitate to posit such a transformation for proto-Germanic.

Similarly, statements about the grammaticality of a sentence in dead languages can be made even without attestation for that sentence. Of the two nonattested sentences in Latin: (a) *Putō Cicerōnem Catilīnam amāre* 'I think that Cicero likes Catiline' and (b) *Putō ut Cicerō Catilīnam amet*, a Latin teacher will know that (b) is ungrammatical and that (a) is grammatical (Lakoff 1969:3–4). If this were not so, if we were powerless to judge grammaticality of nonattested sentences, the teacher would have no basis for correcting pupils' compositions in Latin or Classical Greek.

Thus, though we work under a handicap with the syntax of dead languages, such work is not impossible. The uncertainty is greater than in phonology and there will doubtless always be left over a residue of problems whose definitive solutions elude us for lack of data, but much can be done.

6.1 SYNTACTIC CHANGE

In discussing phonological change in Chapter 3, it was possible to state rather precisely what phonological change was: rule addition, rule reordering, and so on. We do not enjoy such precision in syntax. It is not yet clear just what changes in syntactic change.

The syntax of a language (see Chapter 2) is provided by two components: the base component and the transformational component. Since investigation shows that base rules tend to differ little, if at all, from dialect to dialect or even from language to language, we would not expect syntactic change to result from alterations in the base rules of a language. Rather, the sources of syntactic change are most likely to be sought in the transformations and the rules governing them.

Early investigators of transformational historical syntax (Closs 1965, Klima 1965) assumed that syntactic and phonological change were governed by essentially the same paradigm. In this view syntactic change consists of the addition of a transformation, the reordering of transformations, loss of transformations, and so on. The parallelism with phonological change is attractive, but it is an open question whether or to what degree this parallelism is well motivated.

We shall consider here a sequence of successive syntactic changes that has been analyzed in great depth by Klima (1965). The presentation here is a much simplified account of a problem with many ramifications. Since it is intended only to suggest approaches to syntactic change, alternative analyses are not examined. The problem concerns different styles (following Klima 1964), but each style corresponds to a chronologically definable stage of English grammar.

Table 6.1, on page 144, contains representative sentences from the four styles considered. These are designated as L_1, L_2, L_3, and L_4. The lack of an entry means that the sentence in that style is the same as the one in the column to its immediate left.

The four styles correlate with decreasing degrees of formality or elegance. L_1 is extremely careful cultivated speech which today would tend to be found only in formal writing. L_2 is somewhat less formal, and L_3 is close to "cultivated" colloquial speech. L_4 is vulgar or substandard English.

In regard to the point of salient difference among these styles—*who* for *whom, me* for *I, him* for *he*—we identify each of these styles with specific chronological periods in English (Klima 1965). L_1 is the syntax of English around 1450; L_2, usage in the eighteenth century; L_3, colloquial English by the end of the eighteenth century; and L_4 we may regard simply as later than L_3.

Three transformations in particular are relevant to the problem: Case Marking, *Wh*-attachment, and *Wh*-attraction. Motivation for the inclusion of the transformations in the grammar of English can be found in Klima (1964, 1965). Here they will be assumed necessary, and their effect on underlying strings will be demonstrated.

T6.1 Case Marking

$$\begin{Bmatrix} V_t \\ Prep \end{Bmatrix} \text{Pronoun} \Rightarrow \begin{Bmatrix} V_t \\ Prep \end{Bmatrix} \text{Pronoun}^\frown \text{CASE}$$

(V_t designates a transitive verb, and *Prep* designates preposition.)

TABLE 6.1
STYLISTIC VARIATION IN ENGLISH

L_1	L_2	L_3	L_4
He and I left.			Him and me left.
It was I.		It was me.	
Who could see him?			
Whom could she see?	Who could she see?		
Whom did he speak with?	Who did he speak with?		
Who was it?			
He knew who it was.			
He knew whom he spoke with.	He knew who he spoke with.		
The man who saw him left.			
The man whom I saw left.	The man who I saw left.		
The man whom he spoke with left.	The man who he spoke with left.		
The man with whom he spoke left.			(No counterpart)

From underlying strings such as *I˄see˄he˄Singular* and *I˄sit˄with˄she˄ Singular* (˄ indicates simple concatenation), T6.1 attaches the CASE marker to the object pronoun, giving *I˄see˄he˄CASE˄Singular* and *I˄sit˄with˄ she˄CASE˄Singular*. Later rules replace *he˄CASE˄Singular* by *him* and *she˄CASE˄Singular* by *her*. The final results of the two derivations are *I see him* and *I sit with her*.

T6.2   *Wh*-attachment

     Wh˄X˄Pronoun(CASE)Number˄Y ⇒
     Wh˄Pronoun(CASE)Number˄X˄Y

(*X* and *Y* are cover symbols for strings whose composition is irrelevant to the operation of the transformation.)

The symbol *Wh* is introduced in the base rules. One of its functions is to transform structures underlying declarative sentences into direct questions, e.g. *Can she see?* is derived from *Wh^she^can^see*. Rule T6.2 attaches *Wh* to a *Pronoun(CASE)Number* complex occurring to the right of *Wh* in a string and places this complex immediately to the right of *Wh*, and is applicable in the derivation of sentences such as *Whom could she see?* From underlying *Wh^she^Past^can^see^he^Singular* we get by Case Marking *Wh^she^Past^can^see^he^CASE^Singular*. *Wh*-attachment then operates, producing *Wh^he^CASE^Singular^she^Past^can^see*, which is converted into *Whom could she see?* by other transformations and morphophonemic rules. One of the required transformations is

T6.3   *Wh*-attraction
        Wh(Pronoun^CASE^Number)Subject^Tense(V^m)Verb ⇒
        Wh(Pronoun^CASE^Number)Tense(V^m)Subject^Verb

(V^m stands for modal verb.)

Rule T6.3, which carries out an inversion of subject and auxiliary verb, accounts for the inverted word order of direct questions, e.g. *What are you doing?*, not **What you are doing?* To illustrate the effect of T6.3, let us continue the example developed in the preceding paragraph. After application of Case Marking and *Wh*-attachment, the string which eventually will yield *Whom could she see?* had the shape

Wh^he^CASE^Singular^she^Past^can^see

Past^can is positioned by T6.3 before the subject *she*, thus producing

Wh^he^CASE^Singular^Past^can^she^see

Wh^he^CASE^Singular ⇒ *whom* by a later rule, also *Past^can* ⇒ *could* by later rule, and the outcome is *Whom could she see?*

As we observe from Table 6.1, *Whom could she see?* is proper usage in L_1. This, as well as related facts not presented here, shows that the three transformations are ordered crucially in the grammar of L_1 as follows:

L_1 T6.1   Case Marking

        T6.2   *Wh*-attachment

        T6.3   *Wh*-attraction

In the grammar of L_2, however, a different ordering of transformations is required to account for the facts in the simplest manner possible, and this order is:

L_2 T6.2   *Wh*-attachment

T6.1   Case Marking

T6.3   *Wh*-attraction

The lexicon and base rules may be assumed identical for the two styles, in so far as the present data are concerned. The sole difference is a reordering of two of the transformations. Thus, *Who could she see?*, which is the counterpart in L_2 of *Whom could she see?* in L_1, has the following derivation in the grammar of L_2:

Underlying Form:	Wh^she^Past^can^see^he^Singular
Wh-attachment:	Wh^he^Singular^she^Past^can^see
Case Marking:	(does not apply)
Wh-attraction:	Wh^he^Singular^Past^can^she^see

The pronoun *he* is not marked for case in this derivation, and the string *Wh^he^Singular* ⇒ *who*, not *whom*. The last line of the derivation will then yield the proper surface form of the sentence in L_2, *Who could she see?* Note that, even though the Case Marking transformation does not apply in this particular derivation since its structural analysis is not met, the transformation itself is still required in the grammar of L_2. It is needed to account for the *him* in *Who could see him?* and the *whom* in *The man with whom he spoke left.*

To this derivation we may compare the derivation of the sentence *Whom could she see?* in L_1:

Underlying Form:	Wh^she^Past^can^see^he^Singular
Case Marking:	Wh^she^Past^can^see^he^CASE^Singular
Wh-attachment:	Wh^he^CASE^Singular^she^Past^can^see
Wh-attraction:	Wh^he^CASE^Singular^Past^can^she^see
Surface Structure:	Whom could she see?

The third style, L_3, differs from L_2 only in having *It was me* (*Was it her?*, *That's him*) in place of *It was I* (*Was it she?*, *That's he*). In accounting for this we assume that the grammar of L_3 has the same lexicon and base rules as the grammars of L_2 and L_1 and that the three transformations apply in the same order as in the grammar of L_2. Case Marking, however, is more general in the grammar of L_3, in that V_t (transitive verb) has been replaced by V (any verbal form):

T6.1′   Generalized Case Marking

$$\left\{ \begin{matrix} V \\ Prep \end{matrix} \right\} \text{Pronoun} \Rightarrow \left\{ \begin{matrix} V \\ Prep \end{matrix} \right\} \text{Pronoun}^{\frown}\text{CASE}$$

With the restriction relaxed that the verb in the structural analysis of this transformation be transitive, the way is opened for *It was me*, and so on. This is derived from the underlying string *it^Past^be^I^Singular* from which we get *it^Past^be^I^Singular* in L_1 and L_2 (i.e. no case marking since *be* is not a V_t) and *it^Past^be^I^CASE^Singular* in L_3 (i.e. case marking since *be* is a V). With the application of further rules common to the grammars of all three styles, e.g. *Past^be* ⇒ *was*, *I^Singular* ⇒ *I*, *I^CASE^ Singular* ⇒ *me*, we obtain the final surface forms:

L_1 and L_2:   It was I.

   L_3:   It was me.

The grammar of L_3 thus has the three transformations in the order stated:

L_3 T6.2   *Wh*-attachment

   T6.1′   Generalized Case Marking

   T6.3   *Wh*-attraction

To account for L_4, so-called "vulgar" English, it is necessary to posit several different changes, most of which we ignore here in the interest of brevity. One interesting modification involves a kind of change not previously encountered in our discussion of the four styles, namely change in the lexicon. In the grammars of the three styles hitherto discussed, the pronouns *I, me, he, him, she, her* were assumed to be entered in the lexicon in their "nominative" form: *I, he, she*. It is simplest to assume for the grammar of L_4 that the pronouns are entered in the lexicon in their "objective" forms: *me, him, her*. This accounts directly for the L_4 sentence *Him and me left* and similar ones. Occurrences of *he, she*, and so on that occur in L_4 (*He knew who it was*) are accounted for in the grammar of this style by assuming a Case Marking transformation different from either T6.1, or T6.1′; and we also posit later transformational rules of the sort *me^CASE^ Singular* ⇒ *I; him^CASE^Singular* ⇒ *he*.

As we see from this very brief sketch of a limited problem in historical syntactic change, syntactic change can be analyzed in ways that make it seem similar to phonological change. The analysis just presented includes rule reordering, rule simplification (in that the environment for case marking is generalized), and restructuring (change in the underlying representations of the pronouns). If this analysis is correct, it seems likely too that the fundamental paradigm of change—innovation, simplication by the generation of learners, optimization—carries over to syntax. To see this let us consider the process by which the grammar underlying L_1 changed so as to produce L_2. The grammar of L_1 had the three transformations in the order:

L_1 T6.1 Case Marking

T6.2 *Wh*-attachment

T6.3 *Wh*-attraction

We assume now that an innovation took place in the grammar of the L_1 generation of speakers of English. An added rule changed *whom* to *who* in some, but not all, of its occurrences. To account for this we must assume the addition of a rule that in effect changes clause-initial *whom* to *who* (*Whom could she see?* becomes *Who could she see?*) but makes no change in *whom* when it follows a preposition (*The man with whom he spoke left* is the same in both styles):

T6.4 *Whom*-replacement innovation

Wh^Pronoun^CASE^Number $\Rightarrow$ Wh^Pronoun^Number

The *Whom*-replacement innovation is added after T6.2 (*Wh*-attachment). We cannot assume, however, that the innovation is added at the end of the transformational component since one can demonstrate that it must be added prior to a transformation not discussed here (Preposition Placement) which itself is ordered before T6.3 (*Wh*-attraction) (Klima 1964:13). Evidence from other studies would indicate too that syntactic innovations have no particular propensity for being added at the end of the transformational rules (Closs 1965).

The grammar of L_1 speakers who have innovated will then have the following appearance schematically:

L_1 + Innovation T6.1 Case Marking

T6.2 *Wh*-attachment

T6.4 *Whom*-replacement innovation

T6.3 *Wh*-attraction

. . .

The derivation of *Who could she see?* in this grammar will go as follows:

Underlying Form:	Wh⌢she⌢Past⌢can⌢see⌢he⌢Singular
Case Marking:	Wh⌢she⌢Past⌢can⌢see⌢he⌢CASE⌢ Singular
Wh-*attachment:*	Wh⌢he⌢CASE⌢Singular⌢she⌢Past⌢ can⌢see
Whom-*replacement:*	Wh⌢he⌢Singular⌢she⌢Past⌢can⌢see
Wh-*attraction:*	Wh⌢he⌢Singular⌢Past⌢can⌢she⌢see

Wh⌢he⌢Singular reduces to *who*, not *whom*; hence we get in this grammar *Who could she see?* ultimately from the final line of the above derivation.

However, there is a more economical grammar that will produce the same output. This grammar does not have in it the *Whom-replacement* innovational transformation, and it applies Case Marking and *Wh*-attachment in the reverse order. It is, in other words, the grammar shown earlier to account for L_2. This grammar is simpler because it is one rule shorter: it lacks *Whom*-replacement.

Simplification expressed as the generalization of a transformation seems to be as characteristic of syntactic change as it is of phonological change. Closs (1965), in a study of diachronic English syntax, attributes part of the changes from Old English → Middle English → Modern English to progressive simplifications of a rule that expands the verbal auxiliary. In analyzing a syntactic difference between Northern Mandarin and Southern Mandarin dialects, Wang (1965:463, n. 12) explains the change in the former as regularization (generalization).

The preceding examples would indicate that most syntactic change results from alterations in the transformational rules of the grammar, in a way precisely parallel to the types of primary change discussed in Chapter 3. In comparing certain aspects of Latin and Spanish syntax, however, Lakoff (1969) explains the quite radical changes as due solely to changes in the redundancy rules that govern transformations in particular classes of verbs. The deep structure and transformational rules of Latin and Spanish are alike: all that has changed are the lexical redundancy rules that determine which transformations may apply to which classes of verbs.

It is very much an open question how syntactic change is best accounted for: by changes in the transformations analogous to changes in phonological rules (Klima, Closs), or by changes in lexical redundancy rules (Lakoff). Much further work is needed to get the crucial data that would help decide which analysis is correct. Note, however, that the two analyses are not mutually exclusive, and much of the apparent complexity of syntactic change may derive from the complicated interweaving of two (or more) fundamentally different processes of change.

Diachronic transformational syntax is a science in its infancy. While a great deal is not clear, in transformational syntax generally as well as in diachronic syntax, it is certain that progress in the area of historical syntax cannot be made without a highly structured theory to support and guide one's research. Since so little headway has been made in historical syntax during the last century, almost anything that helps us forward is a welcome gift; and the vistas opened up by the advent of serious and comprehensive theories of syntax offer hope of much future progress. Without a conception of grammar as a structured system of rules, syntactic change and historical syntax must remain no man's lands of linguistic study—the one beyond our comprehension, the other rich and varied but impossible to describe.

6.2   TRANSFORMATIONAL SYNTAX IN HISTORICAL PROBLEMS

We shall examine here an application of transformational grammar to a problem in Indo-European syntax. This example suggests some ways in which transformational grammar may be expected to contribute to the solution of other problems in historical linguistics.

Kiparsky (1968a), who deals with several problems of Indo-European syntax, takes as his point of departure the "historical present." This construction, quite common in Indo-European languages, is essentially semantic (i.e. not governed by a syntactic rule) in those modern Indo-European languages that have it. It gives a sense of immediacy, brings a past event closer to hand. To explain the historical present in a language like English we use semantic means because syntactically the historical present functions like any other present tense.

We might reasonably expect a similarly semantic characterization to carry over to the historical present in early Indo-European languages, and traditional explanations have generally been based in semantics. Kiparsky, however, shows that the situation is quite different in the earlier languages. A purely semantic treatment of the historical present does not do justice to several facts in these languages. For one thing, the historical present in early Indo-European is not attested consecutively in sustained discourse but rather in sentence conjunction after a true past tense, as in this Greek example with a literal but ungrammatical English translation: *háma dè têi hēmérāi têi pólei prosékeito kaì haireî* 'at daybreak he assaulted the town and takes it'. Old Icelandic provides an even more striking example: *þeir hlióþo á hesta sína ok ríþa ofan á Fýresvǫllo, þa sǫ́ þeir, at Aþils konungr reiþ epter þeim . . . ok vill drepa þá* 'they leaped on their horses and ride down to the Fyres-fields; then they saw that King Athils rode after them and wants to kill them'. Other early Indo-European languages, such as Old Irish and Old Latin, have similar constructions in conjoined structures.

The striking feature of the historical present in early Indo-European languages is its failure to occur consecutively in long passages of discourse, unlike its use in modern European languages. In English or German, for example, the historical present is often used in lengthy historical narration to the virtual exclusion of other tenses. This is in contrast to early Indo-European, where the historical present typically occurs in conjoined sequence with a true past tense.

Greek affords a parallel construction involving the future tense. In a sequence of conjoined structures where we expect to find . . . future . . . future . . ., we find . . . . future . . . present . . . In place of the expected future tense in the second occurrence of a verb the present tense is found. An example is: *doulṓsete . . . erēmoûte* 'you will enslave . . . you lay waste (pres.)'. The corresponding construction in English would be a hypothetical *He will see the President and talks to him* in place of *He will see the President and will talk to him.*

A related fact is that the same kind of alternation of past (aorist) and present occurs in conjoined modal structures in Greek. In other words, one finds . . .aorist subjunctive. . .present subjunctive. . . in place of . . .aorist subjunctive. . .aorist subjunctive. . ., and similarly for optative and imperative constructions.

This, together with evidence from other Indo-European languages, suggests a regularity syntactic, not semantic, in origin. It would be hard to argue that the present tenses in the examples cited were semantically different from ordinary past or future tenses. They may well have imported a kind of drama, but the regularity of their occurrence suggests strongly that they are governed by some sort of syntactic rule, a transformation that optionally reduces repeated occurrences of the same tense to the present. Reduction transformations affecting conjoined structures are known from modern languages; for example, the second *he* in *He went to town and he bought bread* can be optionally deleted to give *He went to town and bought bread.* Similarly, *He will do his job and he will arrest the burglar* can be (and usually is) reduced to *He will do his job and arrest the burglar.*

Kiparsky argues that early Indo-European had a similar kind of transformation that reduced the second tense in a sequence of tenses to the present. Schematically, the sequence . . .past. . .and. . .past. . . $\Rightarrow$ . . .past. . .and. . .present. . ., giving rise to an instance of the historical present. Repeated future tenses and subjunctive moods reduce the same way.

Kiparsky proposes that more generally conjunction reduction of this type yields a zero or unmarked form in the sense of Prague School linguistic theory. A number of independent facts indicate that the present is the unmarked tense and the indicative the unmarked mood. In Vedic Sanskrit the so-called injunctive fulfilled the function of the verb form unmarked for tense and mood, and a large proportion of injunctives in Vedic are conjoined to noninjunctive forms.

All of these facts taken together suggest that the older Indo-European languages had an optional transformation of a type that we may represent schematically as:

$$\ldots \begin{bmatrix} \text{Past} \\ \text{Future} \\ \text{Subj.} \end{bmatrix} \ldots \text{and} \ldots \begin{bmatrix} \text{Past} \\ \text{Future} \\ \text{Subj.} \end{bmatrix} \ldots \Rightarrow$$

$$\ldots \begin{bmatrix} \text{Past} \\ \text{Future} \\ \text{Subj.} \end{bmatrix} \ldots \text{and} \ldots \text{unmarked}$$

The oldest form of this transformation is found in Vedic Sanskrit, in which conjunction reduction of tense and mood yielded injunctive forms. This system can also be reconstructed from Celtic and Homeric Greek. In a second stage the injunctive has been lost and its function taken over by the present and the indicative as the unmarked realizations of tense and mood. This is the stage, attested in Greek, Old Irish, early Latin, and Old Icelandic, in which we find occurrences of the historical present.

Kiparsky shows moreover that this solution accounts for other unexplained problems in Indo-European. It is not, in other words, merely an ad hoc device invented to handle the cases discussed above. What from a modern perspective seemed at first glance to be a semantic problem turns out on deeper investigation to be a syntactic one with important implications for other problems in Indo-European syntax.

Another way transformational syntax has potentially great usefulness is in establishing genetic relationships among languages. This possibility has been little explored in the past. Usually when we are dealing with the problem of genetic relationship, we tend to establish cognate sets by searching for items of shared vocabulary with semantic and phonological linking characteristics. There is no reason why we cannot equally well appeal to syntax in establishing or confirming genetic relationships, and much recommends this procedure.

Harms (1966) pursues the implications of morpho-syntactic resemblances for the genetic relationship between Yukaghir and the Uralic languages. The great time-depth involved makes it very difficult to obtain compelling evidence from shared items of vocabulary. Harms, however, shows striking points of resemblance in certain morpho-syntactic features of these languages. He concludes (1966:12):

> The great similarities found between Baltic-Finnish and Yukaghir in the complex system of focus markers—once we examine the basic underlying structures rather than their superficial realizations—can hardly be the result of chance or borrowing. Taken as an unordered list of grammatical forms, they have little weight. It is only in considering their complex structure of morpho-syntactic interrelationships that they justify a claim for the genetic relationship of Uralic and Yukaghir.

The intriguing possibility of supporting a claim for genetic relationship on the basis of shared transformations of a suitably specific type (such as focus) requires extensive research into the underlying syntactic structure of languages and not simply a search for cognates. But we stand to reap worthwhile benefits.

Transformational syntax offers other possibilities for assessing the value of syntactic similarities in determining genetic relationships. Bach (1967), for example, proposes an analysis of English syntax in which the forms *have* and *be* in their use as main verbs are eliminated from the base (lexicon) and introduced by transformational rules. Moreover, Bach argues that in languages generally copula forms (like *have, be,* and so on) are always introduced by a transformation essentially identical to the one he posits for English.

Using this analysis as a basis, Bach proposes a mechanism to account for the widespread "empty" (auxiliary) use of verbs like *have, be, do,* and *go.* This mechanism is a variant of simplification and is, therefore, an option available to speakers of all languages. Given that Bach's analysis of copula forms is valid for all languages, it follows that unrelated languages may be expected to develop usages equivalent to the auxiliary uses of *have* and *be* in English, French, German, and so on. Bach concludes that "similarities in the use of such verbs as auxiliaries in various languages have absolutely no value as evidence for genetic relationship" (1967:484). Additional research may yield similar limitations on the value of syntactic evidence in judging genetic relationship.

SUPPLEMENTARY READING

Kiparsky, Paul. 1968. "Tense and Mood in Indo-European Syntax." *Foundations of Language* 4.30–57.

Klima, Edward S. 1965. *Studies in Diachronic Transformational Syntax.* Unpublished doctoral dissertation, Harvard University.

Lakoff, Robin T. 1969. *Abstract Syntax and Latin Complementation.* Cambridge, Mass.: The M.I.T. Press.

7

RECONSTRUCTION

Reconstruction is a—perhaps the—central theoretical concern of historical linguistics. True, historical linguistics traditionally comprises a great deal more, such as language typology, genetic relationships, and the use of written records, and none of these areas can be studied sensibly without an associated theory. They are all theoretical concerns. But in reconstruction the questions of method and theory have often sounded most like the parallel questions asked in synchronic practice, and in reconstruction step-by-step procedures are laid down to lead to the recovery of prior linguistic structure (Hoengiswald 1950, 1960 and Pike 1951).

It is possible to regard such great concern with reconstruction per se as a trifle absurd. What could rival in pointlessness the mere reconstruction of a word or even a text? What can you do with a reconstructed text but look at it? Hence our chuckling about people who reconstruct fables in proto-

Indo-European. In short, the end result of reconstruction is vastly less interesting for most of us than the assumptions and procedures that advance us toward that reconstruction. Linguistically speaking, a reconstructed word is far less valuable than our method of reconstructing it.

One might well believe that linguists who sit around reconstructing, like lexicographers, are harmless drudges. But linguistic reconstruction is rescued from the ultimate fate of harmless drudgery—inanity—because reconstruction is not possible without concrete assumptions about language, without commitments to a specific theory of diachronic change, without painstaking evaluation of the linguistic processes that must be assumed in passing from one stage of a language to the next. One cannot reconstruct in a vacuum, without asking most of the questions relevant to any theory of diachronic change: What changes when language changes? What constitutes a plausible step in going from language L to the later language L'?

From this perspective it does not seem nearly so curious to place reconstruction very close to the heart of historical linguistics. Reconstruction carries us into a realm of inquiry coterminous at most points with the study of language change in general, a realm in many features not very different from that of synchrony. It forces us to examine our assumptions and, on occasion, to reformulate our goals; and it forces us to be very cautious about what is or is not a reasonable account of language change.

What interests us here, in a book on historical linguistics and generative grammar, is whether, or rather to what extent, generative grammar can contribute to reconstruction. Its major contribution derives from the fact that generative grammar is concerned with the entire grammar of a language: lexicon, syntax, phonology. For reconstruction this systematic aspect of generative grammar has the consequence that more of the structure of a language is amenable to recovery, not just the lexicon, which traditionally has been the main province of reconstruction (Kiparsky 1967:82–83). Furthermore, in its rich and tightly structured view of linguistic change, generative grammar will advance better, more precise, and more realistic techniques of recapturing lost structure. The historical linguist faced with a problem in reconstruction gains advantages of several kinds from generative grammar. First, generative grammar furnishes him with a well motivated account of what the grammar of a language is like, and this account in turn provides the linguist with a sound basis for probing into the past. Second, the concept of linguistic change that emerges from generative grammar opens up new ranges of perception and possibility. And third, the precision of this concept constrains reconstruction in principled ways: it sets limits to our recovery of lost structure and forces us to a sober reassessment of what is and what is not possible in reconstruction.

The general constraint on reconstruction is that nothing unknown or unlikely in synchronic linguistic structure can be assumed for historical linguistic structure. We are not at liberty to posit something for dead languages that is unattested in the living ones. This seems like an obvious truth but neither its obviousness nor its truth has always been taken for granted. Nineteenth-century syntactic investigations are full of fatuous and synchronically unparalleled assumptions about the syntax of Indo-European. The sentiment that processes in historical languages were essentially different from processes in living ones is part of what underlies Bloomfield's statement that "The process of linguistic change has never been directly observed; we shall see that such observation, with our present facilities, is inconceivable" (1933:347).

The claim that historical and living languages are subject to identical constraints has obvious consequences for reconstruction. A grammar violating universal properties of synchronic grammars cannot be assumed for an historical language. A highly marked phonological system in an historical language is suspect. Transformations or syntactic constituencies unknown in living languages require special motivation if one wishes to assume them for dead languages. Conversely, any universal property of synchronic grammars should, one expects, be valid for the grammars of dead languages and may, subject to possible disconfirmation, be assumed as a legitimate reconstruction.

For convenience reconstruction has traditionally been divided into *internal reconstruction* and *comparative reconstruction*. Internal reconstruction takes its data from a single stage of a single language and draws conclusions about what that language looked like earlier, whereas from data of two or more related languages comparative reconstruction infers what it can about the common ancestor of these several languages. The application of internal reconstruction precedes in general the application of comparative reconstruction, though this is not logically necessary and hardly anyone would insist on such puristic separation of the two in practice. In the ideal case, given say three languages L_1, L_2, L_3, we search through each language independently for evidence permitting sound guesses about earlier stages of each language. That is, we engage in internal reconstruction for each language, and when we have pushed things back as far as we safely can, we have three languages L_1', L_2', L_3', which represent the earliest recoverable stages of the three languages L_1, L_2, L_3. At this point the comparative method takes over. We compare L_1', L_2', L_3' and deduce what we can of the common language L, which has diverged to give ultimately L_1, L_2, L_3. In parlance now widely accepted, we assign to L_1', L_2', L_3' the designations "pre-L_1," "pre-L_2," "pre-L_3," and to L the designation "proto-L_1-L_2-L_3." Given the languages Fox, Cree, Menomini, and Ojibwa, by internal reconstruction we get back to the earliest recoverable stages, which we call pre-Fox, pre-Cree, pre-Menomini, and pre-Ojibwa. In general there are no attested versions of pre-languages. By comparison of these four hypothetical languages with each other, we obtain the common ancestor proto-Fox-Cree-Menomini-Ojibwa, which for convenience is called proto-Algonquian.

We may conceptualize the two kinds of reconstruction as follows. In comparative reconstruction we have data for several languages. We write synchronic grammars for the languages separately, and on the assumption that the languages are related we determine the simplest and most plausible way the grammars of the daughter languages could have developed from the grammar of the proto-language. Internal reconstruction is, in a sense, the limiting case of comparative reconstruction when the linguist looks at a single language. He writes the synchronic grammar of this one language and then makes plausible assumptions about the grammar that must have preceded it.

Though it should be obvious, our goal in internal and comparative reconstruction is the reconstruction of a sequence of *grammars* and the changes relating them. Given, say, the attested language Old English, we want to reconstruct the complete grammar of pre-Old English: lexicon, transformations, phonological rules; and we want to state explicitly the changes between the grammars of pre-Old English and Old English. In practice we are usually happy to recapture a few lexical items and rules. But it is grammar and changes between grammars we are reconstructing.

Let it again be noted that internal reconstruction does not have a necessary logical priority vis-à-vis comparative reconstruction. For pedagogical convenience we discuss them in that order, but this bears little resemblance to what a linguist actually does. In practice, he freely mixes the two kinds of reconstruction at all points, using whichever of the two seems more appropriate at any given point in the analysis.

7.1   INTERNAL RECONSTRUCTION

The problem is to determine, from the evidence available in a language and from this evidence alone, which types of linguistic change leave behind traces that permit inference of earlier stages of the language. By definition we rule out comparative data; we rule out anything not part of the grammar of the language.

In Chapter 3 we isolated four types of change, called there "primary change" to distinguish them from restructuring: rule addition, rule loss, rule reordering, and rule simplification. Here we shall look at these processes in reverse, as it were: given a language at time t, how can we determine from its grammar which (if any) of these types of change have taken place to time t? What features of a grammar constitute residues of earlier grammars?

Note that one cannot easily state a general condition that indicates when internal reconstruction is possible and when not. There is no infallible methodology, no discovery procedure. Here as elsewhere, the goal of an explicit discovery procedure is too high; the most one can do is describe the approaches experience has shown to be useful. Certain changes simply cannot be recaptured via internal reconstruction. Other changes may leave an imprint on the grammar, as it were, and this imprint may suggest a plausible antecedent grammar, but traces of the change need not remain in the grammar. Changes that can in general be reflected in later grammars are said to be "potentially reconstructible."

RULE ADDITION. The addition of a rule is potentially reconstructible from internal evidence. We shall begin by distinguishing between the addition of a context-sensitive rule and the addition of a context-free rule. The reasons for discussing them separately are heuristic and will be stated later.

Most of the literature on internal reconstruction is devoted to the recovery of the addition of context-sensitive rules (Chafe 1959, Hoenigswald 1944 and 1946, Marchand 1956; see also Bonfante 1945 and Kuryłowicz 1964). Context-sensitive rules may produce phonological alternations, which may or may not be fully preserved in later stages of the language; but if they are retained at all we can make a good guess concerning the form of the rule that originally produced them. Once we have done this, once we have arrived at a grammar of the language at a stage containing a particular rule, we may usually assume that an earlier grammar did not include the rule.

An often cited example of this is terminal devoicing in German. Synchronic evidence in contemporary German motivates the inclusion of this rule in the grammar of German (the supporting data were given in Section 3.3 under RULE REORDERING):

$$[+ \text{ obstruent}] \rightarrow [- \text{ voice}] / \underline{\qquad} \#$$

(Obstruents are devoiced word-finally.) Thus, the evidence of such voiceless: voiced alternations as *Tag* [tʰaːk]: *Tage* [tʰaːgə] 'day, days' justifies our assuming that the rule is present in the grammar of Modern Standard German, indicated schematically as:

G + Terminal Devoicing Rule

Since rule addition is one of the commoner kinds of primary change, the simplest assumption is that this state of affairs arose through rule addition. We feel justified in assuming that earlier stages of German had G alone— essentially the same grammar as modern German but with the Terminal Devoicing Rule not included. In the output of this grammar we assume no terminal devoicing alternations, and the nominative form of 'day' would be something like [tʰaːg], not [tʰaːk]. In this particular instance we luckily have documentary confirmation of our assumption: the earliest Old High German scribes spelled the word *tag*, also *gab* 'he gave', *lamb* 'lamb', *rad* 'wheel', and so on, and it is generally assumed that *b d g* here spelled voiced sounds. This is an unusual stroke of good fortune; rarely can we enjoy the satisfaction of seeing our guesses in prehistory so nicely borne out.

Note that the mere presence of a rule in the grammar does not necessarily imply that the rule was added: it could have always been in the grammar. Consider the nasal point-of-assimilation rule found in very many languages: nasals agree with the following consonant in point of articulation. If a grammar has this rule, then one would not immediately assume it had been added. A grammar with a rule as natural as this could well have had it forever. And a similar observation applies to other natural rules. It follows, therefore, that German could always have had its terminal devoicing rule, although it is plausible to assume that this rule, which though common enough is not as universal as the nasal point-of-assimilation rule, was added to an earlier grammar of German not containing the rule.

In short, the assumption of rule addition based on internal evidence is a reasonable guess, not a certainty. To clinch the argument one has to go to the comparative evidence: if related languages lack the rule, we assume that it was an innovation. As we will see, given certain purely internal forms of evidence we can positively assert prior occurrence of rule loss and certain kinds of rule reordering. In arguing for rule addition we are at best stating a plausible assumption.

To say that the addition of a context-sensitive rule can be inferred does not mean that we are necessarily in a position to recover the exact form of the rule. Often the rule is lost at some point leaving behind only the flotsam of archaic residues. The alternation of $s:r$ in English *was:were* is hardly enough to justify a synchronic rule that recapitulates Verner's Law, yet such an alternation together with more extensive parallel alternations from other Germanic languages enables us to go part way back toward the reconstruction of the Germanic strong verb system. In the case of German final devoicing, we can reconstruct very nearly the original state of affairs only because the rule added around a millenium ago has remained in the grammar in approximately its original shape. Nothing requires this to be the case, however, and in general we should expect the synchronic reflexes of earlier added rules to have undergone considerable change. A case in point is the Grimm's Law rule $p\ t\ k > f\ \flat\ x$ except after obstruents.

Since this is a context-restricted rule, it could have produced phonological alternations which allow us to reconstruct it. And Gothic, the earliest attested Germanic dialect, does permit something of a foothold toward this end. The past tense marker for weak verbs in Gothic shows up as d, t, or $\flat$, illustrated in the following data:

Infinitive	Past Singular	Past Part.	Gloss
salbon	salboda	salboþs	'to anoint'
haban	habaida	habaiþs	'to have'
bugjan	bauhta	bauhts	'to buy'
waurkjan	waurhta	waurhts	'to effect'
þaurban	þaurfta	þaurfts	'to need'

We are immediately faced with a problem in interpreting these spellings: What were the phonetic values of orthographic *b d g*? There is fairly general scholarly agreement that they represented voiced stops [b d g] after nasals, *r*, *l*, and *z*, and many scholars believe they represented voiced stops initially as well. Here, in analyzing the past tense morpheme for weak verbs, the crucial question is what *b d g* represented intervocalically, as in *salboda* and *habaida*. Krause (1953:63) states flatly that it cannot be decided whether they represented voiced fricatives or voiced stops. Spelling alternations such as *hlaifs:hlaiba* and *staps:stada* suggest that intervocalic *b d g* had the phonetic values [b ð g], at least in early Gothic, but comparative evidence makes it probable that they later were voiced stops.

For the sake of illustration we will assume provisionally that *b d g* represented voiced stops [b d g] in all positions in Gothic, and we will analyze the data on that basis. (Later we will consider the implications for reconstruction of making the other and more plausible assumption that *b d g* represented fricatives [b ð g] at least intervocalically.) Given this assumption, the best way of accounting for the *d/t/þ* alternation in weak verbs is to posit underlying *-t-* as the marker of the past tense of weak verbs. Intervocalic *t* normally remains *t* in Gothic, cf. *inweitan* 'to show reverence' and *gamotan* 'to find room'. Thus, we need a minor rule limited to the weak verbs that changes *t* > *d* in *salboda*, *habaida*, and so on. The underlying forms of the *Past Singular* and *Past Participle* in this analysis will then be:

salbota	salbots
habaita	habaits
baugta	baugts
waurkta	waurkts
þaurbta	þaurbts

To account for the surface forms we need three rules (in addition to the minor rule *t* > *d*). One of these assimilates contiguous obstruents in regard to voice:

$$7.1 \quad [+ \text{ obstruent}] \rightarrow [\alpha \text{ voice}] / \underline{\hspace{2em}} \begin{bmatrix} + \text{ obstruent} \\ \alpha \text{ voice} \end{bmatrix}$$

(In an obstruent cluster $O_1 O_2$, O_1 must agree in the feature of voice with O_2.)

Rule 7.1 is also motivated by the alternation of *z:s* in the comparative and superlative adjectival suffixes; e.g. *managiza:managists* 'more, most'; *batiza:batists* 'better, best'. In the data at hand Rule 7.1 produces /baugta/ >[baukta], /baugts/>[baukts], /þaurbta/>[þaurpta], /þaurbts/>[þaurpts].

After application of the minor rule converting $t > d$ and Rule 7.1 the *Past Singular* and *Past Participle* forms listed above will become:

salboda	salbots
habaida	habaits
baukta	baukts
waurkta	waurkts
þaurpta	þaurpts

Another rule is needed changing /p/ and /k/ to f [f] and h [x] before t. Thus, [baukta] > *bauhta*, [waurkta] > *waurhta*, [þaurpta] > *þaurfta*; and in the participles we obtain correct *bauhts*, *waurhts*, and *þaurfts*. This rule is more general in Gothic than our forms indicate, and we formulate it as Rule 7.2, which converts $p\ t\ k$ to $f\ þ\ h$ when followed by a nonstrident obstruent:

$$7.2 \quad \begin{bmatrix} + \text{obstruent} \\ - \text{voice} \end{bmatrix} \rightarrow [+ \text{continuant}] / \underline{\hspace{1cm}} \begin{bmatrix} + \text{obstruent} \\ - \text{strident} \end{bmatrix}$$

(There are a few exceptions, e.g. *atta* 'father', to this otherwise general rule of Gothic phonology. These are marked as exceptions in the lexicon.)

At this point only *salboþs* and *habaiþs* are unaccounted for. Their underlying forms are /salbots/ and /habaits/, so that we need a rule in the phonology that converts $t > þ$ in the correct environments. We must have a rule spirantizing t as the past tense marker of weak verbs, and in the phonetic environment appropriate to *salboþs*, *habaiþs*, and the other weak verbs like these. This shift must also take place after n, for we have *kunþs* 'known' from underlying /kunts/. Thus, we arrive at the rule:

$$7.3 \quad \begin{bmatrix} + \text{obstruent} \\ + \text{coronal} \\ - \text{voice} \\ + \text{Verb} \\ - \text{Strong} \\ + \text{Past} \end{bmatrix} \rightarrow [+ \text{continuant}] / [- \text{obstruent}] \underline{\hspace{1cm}} +$$

($t > þ$ following nonobstruents when that t is the past tense marker of weak verbs. Thus, t will shift to $þ$ after vowels and nasals, giving *salboþs*, *kunþs*, and so on. t in other morphological environments remains: *kant* 'thou canst', *hairto* 'heart'.)

At this point we have written a fragment of the synchronic grammar of Gothic. As a problem in internal reconstruction our job is to make plausible guesses about how the grammar of Gothic could have gotten this way. What, if anything, can we infer about the earlier history of Gothic from the presence of Rule 7.2 and Rule 7.3 in the grammar of attested Gothic? The least daring inference would be that Gothic at some point in its history innovated by adding the two rules. This is, of course, not very interesting, and it explains nothing. In particular, it does not capitalize on the rather obvious similarities between Rule 7.2 and Rule 7.3: the former turns voiceless stops into continuants in one environment, the latter turns a voiceless stop into a continuant in a different, morphologically restricted environment.

Less conservatively we could assume that $t > \flat$ in general after non-obstruents in pre-Gothic, and that attested Gothic limits this change to weak verbs we might attribute to some quirk of the language by which only t's in the past tenses and past participles of weak verbs still show the effects of the original innovation. This account is closer to what really happened but still a long way from recovering in its entirety the Grimm's Law change $p\,t\,k > f\,\flat\,x.$

To use internal reconstruction to pry into the earlier history of Gothic grammars and determine what happened, we must make reasonable assumptions about the earlier form of Rule 7.3. Let us assume that the change of $t > \flat$ in Rule 7.3 was originally not confined to the past tenses of weak verbs; that is, let us assume the very general rule that t became $\flat$ except after obstruents:

$$7.3' \quad \begin{bmatrix} +\text{ obstruent} \\ +\text{ coronal} \\ -\text{ voice} \end{bmatrix} \rightarrow \begin{cases} [-\text{ next rule}] \,/\, [+\text{ obstruent}] \underline{\hspace{1.5cm}} \\ [+\text{ continuant}] \end{cases}$$

($t > \flat$ except after obstruents. This general form of the synchronic rule happens to be close to what actually was added. The restriction of $t/\flat$ residual alternations in Gothic to the past tense forms of weak verbs is an accident, as it were, resulting from the fact that only t from among $p\,t\,k$ could, as the marker of the past tense in Germanic, stand before both obstruents and nonobstruents in related forms of the same word. Rule 7.3, in Gothic a minor rule in the technical sense, is the impoverished synchronic reflex of a once completely general rule. The absence of $t/\flat$ alternations in other morphological classes is an historical quirk.)

Symmetry considerations, that is to say considerations of the universal character of phonological systems, and simplicity considerations make it probable that the original change was not restricted only to t, as suggested by Rule 7.3'. If we assume that all occurrences of $\flat$ are derived from underlying /t/ by Rule 7.3', we have the following relations between underlying segments and surface segments:

Underlying:	/b	d	g	p	t	k	f	s	x/
Surface:	[b	d	g	p	þ	t	k	f	s	x]

There is nothing that necessarily excludes:

```
p  t    k
b  d    g
f     s  x
```

as a possible system of underlying phonological segments in a language. But we obtain at once greater rule simplicity and a more symmetric system for pre-Gothic by assuming a more general version of Rule 7.3', namely:

$$7.3'' \quad \begin{bmatrix} + \text{obstruent} \\ - \text{voice} \end{bmatrix} \rightarrow \begin{Bmatrix} [- \text{next rule}] / [+ \text{obstruent}] \underline{\quad} \\ [+ \text{continuant}] \end{Bmatrix}$$

($p\ t\ k > f\ \beta\ x$ except after obstruents.)

Note that, aside from being a natural antecedent of Rule 7.3, Rule 7.3″ also serves as the predecessor of Rule 7.2 in the synchronic grammar of Gothic. We obtain a single historical rule source for two synchronic rules in Gothic, and we have the following relations between underlying and surface segments:

Underlying: /b d g   p   t   k   s/

Surface: [b d g   f   p þ   t x   k   s]

Under this analysis $f\ \beta\ x$ do not occur at the underlying phonological level: they are derived from /p t k/ by Rule 7.3″. We also obtain a system of underlying phonemic segments from which the continuants /f/ and /x/ are absent (though /s/ is present, as it is almost universally in the world's languages, cf. Chomsky and Halle 1968:413). This yields the more symmetric phonemic system:

```
p  t  k
b  d  g
   s
```

In this way we have succeeded in recovering completely the original form of the Grimm's Law shift $p\ t\ k > f\ \beta\ x$ except after obstruents. We did so by pondering how such a funny rule as Rule 7.3 could have arisen. We were led to reconstruct a general rule in pre-Gothic and an obstruent system that is simpler, less highly marked, more natural. (On *markedness* and *naturalness* see Chomsky and Halle 1968:400–435 and Postal 1968:53–77, 153–198.)

This procedure is not guaranteed to lead infallibly to the correct form of an innovation. But progress in historical reconstruction has always come from making guesses—not wild and unsupported guesses but those credible by considerations of simplicity and naturalness. In any case, the historical linguist usually has very little to lose and much to gain from pressing his reconstruction to the utmost in the directions of simplicity and naturalness.

Recall that the preceding analysis was based on the assumption that orthographic *b d g* in Gothic represented phonetic [b d g]. This assumption was made in order to illustrate the possibilities for internal reconstruction given the synchronic grammar of a language. The other assumption, that orthographic *b d g* represented the fricatives [ƀ ð g] at least intervocalically, would lead us to take the segment /þ/ as underlying the *d/þ/t* alternation in weak verbs. We would then have rules converting /þ/ to *d* [ð] in certain cases and to *t* [t] in others—a kind of anti-Grimm's Law. On this analysis the synchronic grammar of Gothic would provide us with little material for proceeding back into history; in particular, we would not be led to reconstruct Grimm's Law in anything like its correct form.

Thus, the addition of a context-sensitive rule is potentially reconstructible. Such rules can produce phonological alternations that remain in the language, often (as in Gothic) as fossilized and minor remnants of a once general change. In principle, the same is true of the addition of a context-free rule. This kind of change too is potentially reconstructible, but the heuristics of inferring the addition of a context-free rule are different. Context-sensitive rules produce what we might call "syntagmatic" phonological alternations: alternations conditioned by phonetic environment. Context-free rules cannot produce syntagmatic phonological alternations in this sense, but they can produce what we might call "paradigmatic" phonological alternations: alternations that show up in patterns of inflections. Alternations of this kind will be illustrated later, and their usefulness for reconstruction will be demonstrated. Let us first note, however, two examples of the addition of a context-free rule that *cannot* be reconstructed.

Grimm's Law consists of the following three changes:

(1) p t k $>$ f þ x except after obstruents

(2) bʰ dʰ gʰ $>$ ƀ ð g context-free

(3) b d g $>$ p t k context-free

Change (1) can be reconstructed to some extent from the Gothic evidence, as we saw, but changes (2) and (3) cannot be deduced by internal reconstruction. No evidence—no relic alternation, for example—permits us to reconstruct variants of (2) and (3) from any single Germanic language. There is no reason, looking backward from any one of the Germanic grammars, to assume an earlier grammar *not* containing rules corresponding to changes (2) and (3). When the innovations corresponding to (2) and (3) took place in the grammars of Germanic, immediate restructuring took place in all forms containing /bʰ dʰ gʰ b d g/, in effect removing any possibility of internal reconstruction. This confirms something known all along anyway: that Grimm's Law cannot be inferred in its entirety from the Germanic evidence alone but requires knowledge of Indo-European.

In some cases context-free rule addition can be reconstructed, however, and we shall examine two of these here. Indo-European *ei* > Germanic *ī*, as is known from comparative evidence: Germanic *stīg-* 'to climb, go' is cognate with Greek *steíchō* 'I go'. No phonetic alternation results from unconditioned phonological change (i.e. the addition of a context-free rule). Nevertheless, we can reconstruct this rule by comparing paradigms in the strong verbs of a given Germanic language. In early Old High German, for example, the infinitives of strong verbs are:

Class	Infinitive	Gloss
I	bītan	'to await'
II	beotan	'to bid'
III	helfan	'to help'
IV	beran	'to bear'
V	meȥȥan	'to measure'

Considerable parallelism of formation is apparent here. Most of the infinitive forms have the vowel *e* in the root. Furthermore, in the list given here, the nucleus of each strong verb infinitive with the vowel *e* includes at least one additional segment. This segment is *o* in *beotan*, *l* in *helfan*, *r* in *beran*, *ȥ* in *meȥȥan*, where *-an* is the infinitive ending. Classes II-V all have *e* plus something else in the root, and only Class I strong verbs are aberrant in having *ī*. If we assumed that pre-Old High German had *e* plus something else in place of *ī*, then Class I strong verbs would lose their exceptional status. We shall examine the consequences of this assumption.

Our next problem is to determine what the "something else" was. The past plural form of *beotan* 'to bid' is *butun*; if we assume /beut/ as the underlying form of the root, then the past is formed by deleting the *e*, i.e.:

/beut/ + Past → /butun/

We assume then that orthographic *eo* represents underlying /eu/ (*beotan* = /beutan/), and we assume that the plural is formed by deleting *e* (there is independent motivation in Old High German for assuming that past plurals of most classes of strong verbs are formed in this way).

Symmetry suggests that /ei/ should now be taken as underlying the *ī* in Class I strong verb infinitives. We assume /beitan/ as the underlying form of *bītan* 'to await' parallel to /beutan/ *beotan* 'to bid', and that the rule of *e*-deletion operates on this to give the plast plural *bitun*, the correct form in Old High German.

In short, from a synchronic point of view it is desirable to take /ei/ as the underlying form of surface-level *ī*. This permits us to state a general condition on strong verb stems ("*e* plus something else"), and we preserve the general rule for forming past tenses. (Alternation of this sort—*ī* in one class of verbs alternating with *e* plus something else in other classes—is what previously was designated as a "paradigmatic alternation.") To obtain the correct surface form we need a rule converting *ei* > *ī*—exactly the rule comparative evidence shows was added.

Old High German offers a second example illustrating methods of internal reconstruction of rule addition. Strong verbs in Old High German show in the root-final obstruent characteristic ("paradigmatic") alternations known as *grammatical change*, as the principal parts of the following verbs illustrate:

Inf.	*Past Sg.*	*Past Pl.*	*Past Part.*	*Gloss*
slahan	sluoh	sluogun	gislagan	'to strike'
kiosan	kōs	kurun	gikoran	'to choose'
snīdan	sneid	snitun	gisnitan	'to cut'
heffan	huob	huobun	gihaban	'to lift'

(The form *huob* 'I lifted' is analogical. The expected form would be *huof*.) The alternations between obstruents thus involve the following pairs:

(A)   f : b

        d : t

        h : g

        s : r

The simplest account of this assumes underlying voiceless fricatives in the lexical entries of verbs that have grammatical change. (Note that *h* represents phonetic [x].) The four verbs cited above thus have the following underlying forms (ignoring questions of the underlying forms of vocalic segments):

Inf.	*Past Sg.*	*Past Pl.*	*Past Part.*	*Gloss*
slahan	sluoh	sluohun	gislahan	'to strike'
kiosan	kōs	kusun	gikosan	'to choose'
snīþan	sneiþ	snīþun	gisniþan	'to cut'
heffan	huof	huofun	gihafan	'to lift'

We assume a rule voicing continuants in the past plural and past participle of strong verbs. This rule is the synchronic reflex of Verner's Law, stated as Rule 3.13 in Section 3.3 under RULE LOSS. Application yields the following voiceless/voiced pairs in alternation:

(B)   f : b
       þ : ð
       h : g
       s : z

Comparison of (A) with (B) indicates a need for a number of rules to convert the intermediate-level representations in (B) into the correct surface-level alternations in (A). One such rule, converting z to r, may be stated as:

$$7.4 \quad \begin{bmatrix} + \text{consonantal} \\ + \text{voice} \\ + \text{strident} \end{bmatrix} \rightarrow \begin{bmatrix} + \text{vocalic} \\ - \text{strident} \end{bmatrix}$$

Another required rule makes stops of the continuants b ð g:

$$7.5 \quad \begin{bmatrix} + \text{obstruent} \\ + \text{voice} \\ - \text{strident} \end{bmatrix} \rightarrow [- \text{continuant}]$$

Operation of the rule voicing underlying fricatives in the past plural and participle (Rule 3.13) and of Rules 7.4 and 7.5 yields:

(C)   f : b
       þ : d
       h : g
       s : r

These alternations are correct except in the dental, nonstrident set: þ:d must be converted into surface level d:t, as is clear from a comparison of (A) with (C). The rule that flips these dentals is:

$$7.6 \quad \begin{bmatrix} + \text{obstruent} \\ + \text{coronal} \\ - \text{strident} \\ \alpha \text{ continuant} \end{bmatrix} \rightarrow \begin{bmatrix} - \text{continuant} \\ \alpha \text{ voice} \end{bmatrix}$$

(þ > d and d > t. This type of exchange rule was discussed in Section 5.1.)
     With the operation of Rule 7.6 we obtain the proper grammatical change alternations in Old High German. Note that what we really have done is to conduct a kind of synchronic analysis of Old High German. The simplest way to account for a certain set of facts in the language was to posit

underlying forms in voiceless fricatives and to include Rules 7.4, 7.5, and 7.6 in the grammar of Old High German. In this account we have reconstructed three rules that were added at some earlier time. (Synchronically, certain of these rules must be collapsed.) The three Rules 7.4, 7.5, and 7.6 effect phonological changes well known in the history of Old High German, though they are usually arrived at by comparing Old High German with other languages in the Germanic and Indo-European families. Here, the three phonological changes have been deduced from consideration of evidence found only within Old High German. We were led to them through simplicity of analysis.

Thus, the addition of a rule is potentially reconstructible. Our accuracy of reconstruction hinges upon the ultimate outcome of the rule in successive generations of grammars. If the original rule remains intact or nearly so in later grammars, we can come quite close to reconstructing the original innovation. If, however, the innovation has led to partial restructuring and thus is retained (if at all) only in altered form, we may not be able to recover the original innovation in anything like its correct form. The instance of Grimm's Law $p\ t\ k > f\ þ\ x$ is just such a case. After this occurred, the simplest grammar would have as the underlying form of 'father' /fəþér/ (earliest Germanic), not /pətér/ (Indo-European). Only in the past tense forms of weak verbs, where t could alternate with $þ$ according to phonetic environment, is there no restructuring of t to $þ$; and only from the handful of such residual forms can we recover even part of the original change.

Restructuring after rule addition complicates reconstruction and in some cases effectively sets the limit beyond which we cannot recover lost structure, as is clear in the case of a context-free rule such as Indo-European $*b\ d\ g >$ Germanic $p\ t\ k$: no alternations are produced, the optimal grammar has different underlying forms and lacks the rule, and we are deprived of any chance at reconstruction. Likewise, when a context-sensitive rule does not happen to produce any phonological alternations, restructuring takes place and puts an end to our reconstructing. The change of initial $p\ t\ k > f\ þ\ x$ in Germanic happens not to have produced any morphophonemic alternations. Hence such occurrences of $p\ t\ k$ undergo restructuring and are beyond our reach. The sound t, just happening to be affected, as the marker of the weak preterite could split into t and $þ$ according to environment, permitting us to recover this little piece of the original change. Just these t's were not restructured.

RULE LOSS. The loss of a rule is potentially reconstructible. The process was demonstrated in Chapter 3 (Section 3.3 under RULE LOSS) for two cases: loss of terminal devoicing in Yiddish and loss of Verner's Law in Gothic. In both languages internal evidence consists of forms originally affected by the rule, subsequently restructured out of the domain of the rule, and retained in their phonemically altered forms when the rule becomes lost from the grammar. Let us briefly review the data in Gothic to illustrate the procedure of reconstruction of rule loss.

Strong verbs in Gothic normally have the same root-final obstruent throughout their principal parts:

Inf.	Past Sg.	Past Pl.	Past Part.	Gloss
greipan	graip	gripum	gripans	'to grip'
qiþan	qaþ	qeþum	qiþans	'to say'
hlifan	hlaf	hlefum	hlifans	'to steal'

Gothic has, however, a sprinkling of verbs of defective distribution that show alternations between voiceless and voiced fricatives: *aih*:*aigum* 'I possess, we possess', *þarf*:*þaurbum* 'I need, we need'. This same alternation turns up sporadically as part of the process of causativization. Gothic has a regular way of forming verbs with causative meaning from the past singular allomorph of strong verbs: *-jan* is suffixed and the result is treated as a weak verb. Thus, the past singular of *ligan* 'to lie' is *lag*, from which causative *lagjan* 'to lay'; the past singular of *bi-leiban* 'to remain' is *bi-laif* (with $f < b$ via final devoicing), to which is formed the causative *bi-laibjan* 'to leave behind'. (The causativization process is actually more general than this in that it applies to bases other than verbs.) Some verbs with underlying voiceless fricatives in root-final position form causatives in the usual way, but the result is *voiced* root-final obstruents in the causatives. Examples: *frawardjan* 'to ruin, destroy' is formed from *frawairþan* 'to perish'; the causative *sandjan* 'to send' is formed from *-sinþs* 'path'. Other cases of some kind of voiceless:voiced alternation among the fricatives, none of them immediately identifiable with any well-defined grammatical or phonological process, are also sporadically present: *huhrus* 'hunger':*huggrjan* 'to starve'; *faheþs* 'joy':*faginon* 'to be happy'; *taihun* 'ten':*tigjus* 'decades'.

What all this means is not immediately obvious. It is a clue, however, that a rule voicing fricatives in certain positions was present in earlier grammars of Gothic and has since been deleted, leaving its mark behind only in a handful of archaic residues ("relic forms"). We assume that words like *aigum*, *þaurbum*, *frawardjan*, *sandjan*, and so on, all with voiced obstruents, were morphologically disassociated from their etymological base, changed in their phonemic representations in the lexicon from voiceless fricatives to voiced fricatives, and left in their secondary phonemic representation upon loss of the rule.

This very sketchy and imperfect picture is about the best we can do with the Gothic data alone. Only by recourse to the comparative data, both Germanic and Indo-European, does a full account begin to emerge with clarity. We find that the other Germanic dialects have characteristic and quite regular alternations of voiceless:voiced fricatives in their strong verbs, and we discover (or rather Karl Verner discovered) that such alternations depend upon placement of the Indo-European accent. We find furthermore from Indo-European that causatives are frequently associated with suffix accent whereas most strong verbs had root accent; hence we can see why Gothic has relic causatives with voiced fricatives corresponding to bases in voiceless fricatives. Though we cannot reconstruct all this from Gothic alone, on the basis of the relic forms still in the language we can make a plausible case for loss of the rule corresponding to Verner's Law.

So the reconstructibility of rule loss crucially depends upon relic forms. In contrast to the recovery of rule addition, where restructuring obscures the original situation, the recovery of rule loss is possible only if restructuring has taken place in at least one form. If in Gothic the relic forms had never been morphologically isolated from their historical sources and had not undergone restructuring, they would not have been "relic forms"; they would not be in any way out of the ordinary, and the rule would have been lost without a trace.

Loss of a rule R can thus be reconstructed just in case a lexical form X, yielding two variants y and z of which one undergoes rule R, has been replaced in the lexicon of a later grammar by two lexical forms $Y (< y)$ and $Z (< z)$ *before* loss of rule R. The lexicon of pre-Gothic contained, we assume, the form *frawairþ-* (X). From this were derived the two variants *frawairþan* 'to perish' (y) and the original causative *frawarþján* 'to cause to perish' (z), whence *frawardjan* by Verner's Law. Subsequently the causative *frawardjan* was semantically disconnected from *frawairþan*: the former was no longer synchronically derived from the latter. The causative *frawardjan* remained in the language but required its own lexical entry; thus the lexicon of this later grammar of Gothic contained separate forms *frawairþ-* 'to perish' (Y) and *fraward-* 'to cause to perish', i.e. 'to ruin, destroy' (Z). Upon loss of the rule converting $þ > d$ (Verner's Law), *frawardjan* became a "relic form."

Relic forms are typically created when a morphological process has ceased to be "productive," to use the traditional term. In transformational grammar this means the loss of a low-level syntactic rule. Such a rule was causative formation, which though present in Gothic was in the process of breaking down: the later Germanic languages did not have causative formation as a synchronic transformation. The precarious status of this rule doubtless contributed to the lexical split of pre-Gothic *frawairþ-* into attested Gothic *frawairþ-* and *fraward-*.

All else being equal, loss of a phonological rule leaves no traces. Such loss is usually reconstructible just in those cases where, fortuitously, an independent change (e.g. loss of a low-level transformation) has taken place affecting forms that are input to the phonological rule.

In the general case we may count ourselves fortunate to have so many relic forms around in Gothic. In Standard Yiddish only one form, *avek* 'away' from *veg* 'path' historically, permits us to infer the loss of final devoicing from Yiddish evidence alone. Comparative material clinches the case, however, since Yiddish has many words ending in voiceless obstruents that correspond to underlying voiced obstruents in German: Yiddish *hant*: *hent* versus German *Hand*:*Hände* 'hand, hands'; Yiddish *honik* versus German *Honig* 'honey'. One of the classic papers on reconstruction of rule loss is Sapir (1926), in which a handful of aberrant forms in Chinookan lead to the reconstruction of a previously unnoticed sound law.

RULE REORDERING. Kiparsky (1968b) calls attention to two important kinds of rule reordering. The first of these types, which we shall refer to neutrally as *Type A*, is illustrated by the example of German rule reordering discussed under RULE REORDERING in Chapter 3 (Section 3.3; see also Chapter 4, Section 4.4). In this kind of reordering the (originally) second rule occupies a position where it applies to more forms. Schematically, we may represent this as follows:

Type A	Rule X	xxx	. . .
	Rule Y	. . .	xxx
		⇓	
	Rule Y	xxx	xxx
	Rule X	xxx	. . .

(xxx indicates that the rule applies; . . . indicates that it does not apply.)

The instance of German rule reordering discussed previously in this book is of this type (cf. Section 4.4). Originally in German, the two rules Final Devoicing and Vowel Lengthening applied in the order:

Underlying Forms:	veg	vegə
Final Devoicing:	vek	. . . .
Vowel Lengthening:	. . .	ve:gə
Surface Forms:	vek	ve:gə

Upon reordering in the later grammar of standard German we have:

Underlying Forms:	veg	vegə
Vowel Lengthening:	ve:g	ve:gə
Final Devoicing:	ve:k	. . . .
Surface Forms:	ve:k	ve:gə

Type A reordering, like rule loss, is potentially recoverable by internal reconstruction. It too can leave behind relic forms which could have arisen only as a result of the original ordering. In standard German we thus have the adverb *weg* [vek] 'away' historically from the base *Weg* 'path'; [vek] from underlying /veg/ is impossible in the synchronic ordering of the two rules in German (only [ve:k] is possible). It could arise only as output from a grammar that has the rules in the opposite order, the original order.

The second type of reordering distinguished by Kiparsky, *Type B*, has the schematic representation:

Type B   Rule X   xxx   . . .
               Rule Y   . . .   xxx

$$\Downarrow$$

               Rule Y   xxx   . . .
               Rule X   xxx   xxx

In Type B reordering two rules are reordered so that the (originally) first rule catches more forms than before. In the schematic representation Rule X and Rule Y apply each to a single form in the original order of the two rules. After reordering, Rule Y still applies to a single form but Rule X now acts on two forms.

An example cited by Kiparsky (1968b:197–198) and based on the work of Halle and Lightner is from Slavic (cf. Chomsky and Halle 1968:420–430). By the First Velar Palatalization *k* and *g* became *č* and *ǰ* before front vowels and *y*: **kĭto > čĭto* 'what', **givŭ > ǰivŭ* 'alive':

$$7.7 \quad \begin{bmatrix} + \text{consonantal} \\ - \text{anterior} \end{bmatrix} \rightarrow \begin{bmatrix} + \text{coronal} \\ + \text{strident} \end{bmatrix} / \underline{\quad\quad} \begin{bmatrix} - \text{consonantal} \\ - \text{back} \end{bmatrix}$$

The voiced affricate *ǰ* that resulted from Rule 7.7 has become the continuant *ž* in all Slavic languages by the rule:

$$7.8 \quad \begin{bmatrix} + \text{voice} \\ + \text{coronal} \\ + \text{strident} \end{bmatrix} \rightarrow [+ \text{continuant}]$$

At this point then 'alive' had the derivation **givŭ > ǰivŭ > živŭ*.

At a time later than the addition of Rule 7.8 a new front vowel *ě* was produced by the rule:

7.9 ai $>$ ě

By the Second Velar Palatalization, *k,* and *g,* (palatalized *k* and *g* derived from *k* and *g* by an earlier rule) became dental *tˢ* and *dᶻ* before the new front vowels produced by Rule 7.9: **k,ěna > tˢěna* 'price'; **g,ělo > dᶻělo* 'very'. This was a result of the following rule:

$$7.10 \quad \begin{bmatrix} + \text{obstruent} \\ - \text{anterior} \\ - \text{strident} \end{bmatrix} \rightarrow \begin{bmatrix} + \text{strident} \\ + \text{anterior} \end{bmatrix} / \underline{\quad\quad} \begin{bmatrix} - \text{consonantal} \\ - \text{back} \end{bmatrix}$$

The resulting affricate d^z is retained in Old Church Slavic and modern Polish. The grammars of these languages have Rules 7.7 through 7.10 in the order of their relative chronology. In other Slavic languages, however, d^z has become the continuant z, e.g. $d^z \check{e}lo > z\check{e}lo$. All four rules are retained in these other languages, but Rule 7.10 precedes Rule 7.8. Derivations in the original grammar then take the form given below for 'alive' and 'very':

Underlying Forms:	givŭ	gailo
Rule 7.7:	jivŭ	....
Rule 7.8:	živŭ	....
Rule 7.9:	....	g,člo
Rule 7.10:	....	d²člo
Surface Forms:	živŭ	d²člo

In the grammars of the Slavic languages other than Old Church Slavic and Polish the following order obtains:

Underlying Forms:	givŭ	gailo
Rule 7.7:	jivŭ	....
Rule 7.9:	....	g,člo
Rule 7.10:	....	d²člo
Rule 7.8:	živŭ	zčlo
Surface Forms:	živŭ	zčlo

Rules 7.8 and 7.10 are reordered according to Type B reordering. In the original grammar each of the two rules applies to a single form at its point of application. In the grammar of the nonchronological order of rule addition, Rule 7.8 applies to two forms in the sample derivation given here.

In Type B reordering relic forms that betray the original rule order do not arise. That is, a form like $d^z \check{e}lo$ which is a surface form in the original grammar does not become ineligible as input to rules in the grammar that reorders. In the latter grammar, as we see from the above derivations, $d^z \check{e}lo > z\check{e}lo$. This would be the case whether the base form of the word was gailo or $d^z \check{e}lo$. The latter form would be the base form if we assumed restructuring of /gailo/ to /d²člo/ in the original grammar. In Type A reordering, on the other hand, as in the veg:vegə derivations for German, if [vek] is restructured to /vek/ in the lexicon of original grammar, it will not be acted upon by the rules in the later order. Hence vek survives as a relic form.

In summary, recoverability of a rule reordering depends on what form that reordering takes. Type A reordering can create relic forms which form a basis for internal reconstruction. Type B reordering does not produce relic forms; it can in general be reconstructed only on the basis of comparative evidence such as that provided by the grammars of Old Church Slavic and Polish.

RULE SIMPLIFICATION. Simplification in the structural analysis of a rule cannot be recovered by internal reconstruction. Old English provides an example that illustrates why this is so. The earliest written records of Old English contain clear evidence of a terminal devoicing rule that affects fricatives in word-final position. Thus we have *wrāh*:*wrigon* 'to cover (past singular and plural)'; *hebban*:*hōf* 'to raise (infinitive and past singular)'. (Here *g* and *b* are underlying fricatives.) The rule in the language at this point is:

$$7.11 \quad \begin{bmatrix} + \text{ obstruent} \\ + \text{ continuant} \end{bmatrix} \rightarrow [- \text{ voice}] / \_\_\_ \#$$

(Fricatives are devoiced word finally.)

Later Old English documents indicate that final devoicing has come to apply to stops as well: e.g. *felt* < *feld* 'field', *hēafut* < *hēafod* 'head'. With this much written evidence to go on, we would have no hesitation in assuming that simplification of the structural analysis of Rule 7.11 has taken place, giving:

$$7.12 \quad [+ \text{ obstruent}] \rightarrow [- \text{ voice}] / \_\_\_ \#$$

(All obstruents are devoiced word finally.)

If, however, our vantage point were the language *after* Rule 7.12 has become no longer an optional rule, we would have no basis for reconstructing an earlier grammar containing the restricted version Rule 7.11. All we would know is that Rule 7.12 is included in the grammar—that all obstruents, whether continuants or stops, are devoiced, and nothing in the data shows us that the rule originally applied only to fricatives. If we are examining the language at a point in time when final devoicing obligatorily applies to fricatives and only optionally to stops (as the later doublet spellings of Old English seem to disclose), then we could safely assume that Rule 7.11 is in the process of becoming generalized to Rule 7.12.

This example demonstrates that simplification of the structural analysis of a rule is not in general reconstructible. Since simplification is a characteristic of diachronic development, as we argued in Chapter 4, we are usually safe in hypothesizing simplification as a likely process in any given language. But it is not reconstructible as are addition of a rule, rule loss, and Type A reordering.

Kiparsky (1968b:200–202) has observed an interesting correspondence between types of change: rule loss and Type A reordering on one hand, rule simplification and Type B reordering on the other. Rule loss and Type

A reordering both level out alternations, both can give rise to relic forms, both are reconstructible via internal reconstruction. Rule simplification and Type B reordering extend existing alternations to new instances, neither produces relic forms, neither is in general reconstructible on internal evidence.

Rule loss and Type A reordering both lead to what traditionally has been called *leveling*: alternations, usually allomorphic variations within a paradigm, are leveled out. Rule simplification and Type B reordering correspond to the traditional notions of *extension* or *polarization*: a restricted alternation extends its domain. Because of this parallelism it is desirable to replace the terms "Type A" and "Type B" reorderings by more descriptive terms. Kiparsky (1968b:196–200) has introduced the notions of *bleeding order* and *feeding order* in this context. Two rules A–B are said to be in bleeding order if A "bleeds" B: removes representations to which B could apply. Two rules A–B are in feeding order if A "feeds" B: supplies a new set of cases to B. Reordering is governed by the two principles:

I.   Bleeding order tends to be minimized (Type A Reordering).
II. Feeding order tends to be maximized (Type B Reordering).

or more generally:

III. Rules tend to shift into the order which allows their fullest utilization in the grammar.

It would be heuristically useful to replace "Type A Reordering" and "Type B Reordering" respectively by "Leveling Reordering" and "Extension Reordering" or "Polarization Reordering." The point is that reordering, superficially a rather arcane and nonintuitive sort of change, corresponds to the well established notions of leveling and extension (polarization).

7.2   COMPARATIVE RECONSTRUCTION

In certain ways the comparative method resembles the use of generative phonology to describe dialect differentiation. This can lead to serious misunderstandings. The notion of "rule" is not foreign to comparative linguistics; in a sense a set of phonological changes, say the three parts of Grimm's Law, might be said to "generate" a language or set of daughter languages from a unified proto-language: we get from Indo-European to Germanic by applying the three Grimm's Law "rules" in succession. These points of similarity, however, are far more apparent than real, and the crucial differences between traditional comparative grammar and generative grammar must be kept clear if the latter is to make its legitimate and novel contribution to historical linguistics.

To formalize comparative reconstruction in a way that emphasizes the points of similarity between the comparative method and generative phonology (cf. Becker 1967:8–11), we must first assume a uniform "lexicon" in the proto-language. That is, given say Sanskrit *bhrấtar* and Gothic *broþar* 'brother', we posit a common lexical source in the common parent language of the two, which we shall call as usual "proto-Indo-European." Next, using some version of a "simplicity metric," we would state rules that economically describe the development of each proto-phoneme into the daughter languages. This simplicity metric would count rules and features in a way that penalizes the reconstruction of proto-forms necessitating ad hoc rules peculiar to just one or two dialects and that rewards reconstructions yielding sound laws shared completely or partially in most of the daughter languages.

When the reconstruction is complete, we have a minimal set of proto-phonemes which spell items in the lexicon of the proto-language and a set of maximally general rules which give the outcome of each proto-phoneme in each of the daughter languages. Rules specific to a single language would comprise what is traditionally called the "historical phonology" of that language. Each rule deriving daughter-phonemes from proto-phonemes is a sound change, a chronological event in the development away from the common source. The sum of such rules defines a mapping of the lexicon of the proto-language into the separate lexicons of the daughter languages.

If we may borrow here terms introduced in Chapter 2, reconstruction by the comparative method in the above sense is directed toward "observational adequacy"—a compact, consistent, and unambiguous account of the data. An adequate reconstruction accounts as simply as possible for the historical development from common source to divergence. The "grammar" resulting from comparative reconstruction makes no claim to represent the intrinsic knowledge of a speaker of the proto-language; it is no grammar at all in the sense of generative grammar.

This should make it clear that the concerns of the comparativist and the historical linguist working within generative phonology are essentially different. As the latter sees comparative reconstruction, his job is to reconstruct grammars—formal accounts of competence—for various stages of linguistic development ranging back to the proto-language. He begins with the data of each daughter language taken by itself and constructs a grammar. This kind of analysis, basically the same as synchronic description, is applied to each daughter language in turn. Rules shared by all the grammars are assumed present in the grammar of the proto-language. Using his knowledge of what kinds of change are possible—reordering, loss, and so on—he reconstructs plausible antecedent grammars that go as far back as possible into pre-history.

But there is no assumption of direct linear change in this. In particular, we do not assume that language change reduces to the chronological accretion of phonological and analogical changes, one coming after the other, which carry us step by step from parent to daughter language. The paradigm is change from one grammar to another. The proper account of the historical development of a language is not a history of its sounds or grammatical forms but rather the history of its grammars.

The contribution of generative phonology in comparative reconstruction derives from the manifold possibilities for grammatical change that generative grammar encompasses. If all change were reducible to rule addition, and if the order of rules in synchronic grammars necessarily reflected the chronological order in which they were added, then traditional comparative grammar could not be improved upon. But rule addition is only one kind of primary linguistic change, and synchronic ordering does not necessarily reflect chronological ordering. All of which has immediate implications for comparative reconstruction.

Our first example is based on the problem of reordering in the grammars of early Germanic that was discussed in Section 3.3 under RULE REORDERING. Here we shall regard this as a problem in reconstruction. The second and third person singular and plural present indicative verb endings in Germanic contain the following obstruents (Gth. = Gothic, ON = Old Norse, OHG = Old High German, OE = Old English, OS = Old Saxon, IE = Indo-European):

	IE	Gth.	ON	OHG	OE	OS
2. Sg.:	s	s	r	s	s	s
3. Sg.:	t	þ	r	t	þ	þ
2. Pl.:	t	þ	þ	t	þ	þ
3. Pl.:	t	d	..	t	þ	þ

By internal and comparative reconstruction we can establish an earlier situation in which pre-Gothic, pre-Old Norse, and so on had the following obstruents in these endings:

	IE	Gth.	ON	OHG	OE	OS
2. Sg.:	s	z	z	z	s	s
3. Sg.:	t	ð	ð	ð	þ	þ
2. Pl.:	t	ð	ð	ð	þ	þ
3. Pl.:	t	ð	ð	ð	þ	þ

Disregarding for the moment what we know of the original Indo-European obstruent in these endings, we find in the Germanic data alone the correspondence sets z:s and ð:þ. Since both sets differ in the same feature (voice), one set, here designated as Set I, subsumes both correspondences: Gth.–ON–OHG z, ð:OE–OS s, þ. In another correspondence set, Set II, however, s and þ are shared throughout all five Germanic dialects: Gth, *sunus*, ON *sunr*, OHG *sunu*, OE *sunu*, OS *sunu* 'son'; and Gth. *þeins*, ON *þinn*, OHG *dīn*, OE *þīn*, OS *thīn* 'your'. (The change of **þ* > OHG *d* is regular, and some dialects of Old High German even retain *þ*.) Finally, in a third correspondence set, Set III, *z* and *ð* are reconstructed across the board in all five dialects: Gth. *maiza*, ON *meire*, OHG *mēro*, OE *māra*, OS *mēro* 'greater'; and Gth. (*ga-*)*deþs*, ON *dāþ*, OHG *tāt*, OE *dǣd*, OS *dād* 'deed'. (*z* > *r* regularly in all Germanic dialects except Gothic. Original *ð* is assumed for the second set containing *d* in all dialects except Old High German, in which **ð* > *t*.)

Thus we have three correspondence sets for the Germanic dialects:

	I	II	III
Gth., ON, OHG:	z, ð	s, þ	z, ð
OE, OS:	s, þ	s, þ	z, ð

Sets II and III are no problem, of course, since for them we can reconstruct **s*, **þ* and **z*, **ð* without further ado. The trouble lies with Set I, since somehow we must account for the fact that one group of dialects in this set has voiceless dental continuants, the other voiced dental continuants. Because a phonetic environment for Set I cannot be stated, the correspondences in Set I cannot be derived from the proto-phonemes assumed for Sets II and III. We are forced to posit two additional phonemes (different from **s*, **þ*, **z*, **ð*) for Set I. There is no alternative: if we cannot state the phonetic environment in which split occurs, we must posit additional phonemes. Strict application of the comparative method requires this; and one uses the comparative method strictly or not at all.

We happen to know for certain, however, that Indo-European had only one set of obstruents (*s* and *t*) in these endings which have given the correspondence Set I. This gives us pause to wonder. One might well entertain the idea that some conditioning factor in Indo-European is responsible for the differentiation of *s* into *s* and *z* and *t* into *þ* and *ð* in the two groups of Germanic dialects. Verner's Law does indeed give rise to differentiation of this kind, and most traditional explanations of this problem have assumed that Verner's Law is ultimately responsible for the split. But as King (1968) shows, such an explanation requires an ad hoc analogy unsupported by any other Germanic data, and such an explanation moreover does not explain certain related matters.

If we dismiss the resort to analogy, we must reconstruct two additional proto-phonemes for Set I. Let these be, say, voiceless lenes **/z̥/* and **/ð̥/*. We have:

	*z̥, *ð̥	**s, *þ*	**z, *ð*
	I	II	III
Gth., ON, OHG:	z, ð	s, þ	z, ð
OE, OS:	s, þ	s, þ	z, ð

Assuming */z̦/ and */ð̦/ is unsatisfactory in several respects. First, we have to use an ad hoc feature (lenisness) never needed elsewhere in the proto-Germanic obstruent system. Second, Set I is severely limited in its distribution: Set I occurs only in verb endings, but Sets II and III have few distributional limitations. One would like to have an explanation for this. Positing */z̦/ and */ð̦/ gives no explanation; it merely provides two symbols for marking the puzzle. However, setting up two new phonemes is our only choice: if neither sound laws nor analogy account for Set I, we are required to posit new phonemes.

Once we admit the possibility of rule reordering, however, the correspondences in Set I become readily explicable. We posit the continuants in Set III (z and ð) for the present indicative endings. We posit two rules, both of which can be motivated on very general grounds, for the grammar of proto-Germanic. These rules, discussed in Section 3.3, were: (1) $b\, ð\, g > b\, d\, g$ in certain environments, (2) final fricatives are devoiced. The majority of Germanic dialects (Gothic, Old Norse, and Old High German) have the two rules in an order faithful to their chronological order of addition. In these dialects we obtain z and ð. Old English and Old Saxon, on the other hand, have the two rules in the opposite order, and in these dialects we obtain s and þ.

Thus correspondence Set I is explained as a difference in the ordering of two rules in the grammars of two groups of Germanic dialects. We need not, therefore, reconstruct an additional pair of phonemes to handle Set I, and we have no need to propose an unsupported analogy of doubtful legitimacy. But, of course, this reconstruction is possible only if we admit the possibility of reordering rules in grammars. If our conception of linguistic change does not extend beyond addition of rules in their chronological order, Set I remains problematic.

Note that this conclusion cannot be arrived at by appeal to some formulation of the Wave Theory. King (1968) argues at some length against such an appeal, and these arguments may be summarized here. Gothic, Old Norse, and Old High German have the two rules in the order: first $b\, ð\, g >$ $b\, d\, g$ in certain environments, and second final fricatives become devoiced. Old English and Old Saxon have the opposite order. In this analysis the rules are synchronic in these dialects, and they are posited on the basis of attested morphophonemic alternation. An alternative proposal would be that they are sound changes in the usual sense of that term—rule additions —and that their different order reflects their arising and spreading throughout the Germanic area in different dialects and at different rates. The reverse ordering then is not synchronic; rather it shows that the "waves" of the spread of these changes reached the different dialects at different times. Thus, the rule $b\, ð\, g > b\, d\, g\, / \ldots$ arose in some or all the dialects Gothic, Old Norse, and Old High German and spread to Old English and Old Saxon. Final devoicing of fricatives must, in this view, have been an innovation in

Old English and Old Saxon which spread subsequently to the other dialects, and we must assume that final devoicing arose in Old English and Old Saxon before the rule $b\ \eth\ g > b\ d\ g\ /\ \dots$ reached these languages. This goes beyond the limits of what normally is regarded as probable in Germanic. The rule converting $b\ \eth\ g$ to stops in certain environments has been ascribed by generations of scholars to proto-Germanic—the period before the split-off of the different dialects—and general agreement has placed final devoicing later. There seems to be no basis in fact for attributing this reordering to the wave-like spread of change.

Our second example illustrating the benefits of generative phonology for comparative reconstruction comes from comparative Crow-Hidatsa. (I owe the data and analysis to G. H. Matthews.) The problem is to account in proto-Crow-Hidatsa for certain correspondences between Crow /c/ and /k/ and Hidatsa /c/ and /k/. Disregarding word-final position, there are three such correspondences:

	I	II	III
Crow:	c	c	k
Hidatsa:	c	k	k

Crow /c/ has two allophones: [t] before a low vowel, [c] = [tˢ] elsewhere. Thus, the correspondence Crow *cikátak*:Hidatsa *kikákak* 'when he sewed it' illustrates in the first three obstruents the correspondences II (*c/k*), III (*k/k*), and II (*c/k*). The latter set is realized here as [t]/[k]. (We ignore an apparent correspondence *k/c* in word-final position as not immediately relevant to the reconstruction problem at hand.) Examples phonetically transcribed of the three correspondences in contrastive positions:

SET I $\neq$ SET II

	Crow	*Hidatsa*	*Gloss*
c/c	wŭsācik	wŭtācic	'I nibbled at it'
c/k	cikácik	kikákic	'He sewed it'
c/c	raxcík	raxcíc	'He tied it'
c/k	ihcikék	ihkiké?ec	'He scratched himself'

SET I $\neq$ SET III

	Crow	*Hidatsa*	*Gloss*
c/c	raxták	raxcák	'When he tied it'
k/k	íkak	íkāk	'When he saw it'
c/c	cŭse	cŭta	'half'
k/k	kuráci	kurá?āci	'hold, carry in both hands'

SET II ≠ SET III

	Crow	Hidatsa	Gloss
c/k	cikátak	kikákak	'When he sewed it'
k/k	ihcikák	ihkiká?ak	'When he scratched himself'
c/k	cikátācik	kikákācic	'He sewed it (but just enough to hold it together temporarily)'
k/k	íkācik	íkācic	'He got a look at it'

The correspondence c/c contrasts with each of the other two sets in several different environments, so that we must reconstruct at least two proto-phonemes *c and *k, but Sets II and III contrast only in certain restricted environments, notably before ā (as in the examples cited above). It seems likely, therefore, that only one proto-phoneme need be reconstructed for Sets II and III. The question is: On what basis may we reconstruct only one proto-phoneme for two correspondences that, after all, do contrast in certain environments?

One solution, the most unsatisfactory, is to postulate three phonemes in proto-Crow-Hidatsa:

	*c	*č	*k
	I	II	III
Crow:	c	c	k
Hidatsa:	c	k	k

The most telling objection to this solution is that it is no solution at all but merely a formula giving the distribution of the three sets in the proto-language. It explains nothing; in particular, it does not explain the rather tenuous distributional differences between Sets II and III.

There are other similar solutions logically equivalent and just as or only slightly less unsatisfactory. For example, we might posit a vowel, say *æ, that governs a palatal allophone (č) in a preceding k in Crow but not Hidatsa, and having done this merges with *a in both daughter languages. This will account for the offending c/k correspondence, but this is only another way of marking the special status of Set II. Phonetically speaking, this solution is a bit more phonetically plausible than the first one in that it makes phonetic sense for a front vowel æ to palatalize a velar k. Since *æ is reconstructed merely to solve this one problem, however, it is really nothing more than a sign for an unsolved problem.

A third solution, one that might very well be proposed for this case, would be to appeal to analogy. We might try to argue that Crow c in Set II (c/k) comes not from regular phonological change but from analogy: originally the form was Crow k, making Set II identical with Set III, which became c by analogy. Even if we could find an unambiguous source of this analogical pressure, we would still lack an explanation of why the occurrence of Set II (c/k) is (we shall see) completely predictable—provided we admit the possibility of nonchronological rule addition to a grammar. The main objections to analogy here are those raised in Section 5.3: analogy fails to explain why certain changes that produce irregularities at the surface phonetic level are really completely regular if regarded in the light of more subtle forms of change such as nonchronological rule placement, rule loss, and rule reordering.

Let us dig deeper into the history of comparative Crow-Hidatsa and try to unravel the puzzle surrounding *c and *k. The consonant system of proto-Crow-Hidatsa was:

p   t   k
    c
       š   x   h
w   r

A certain phonological rule occurs in both Crow and Hidatsa and thus, we assume, in the grammar of proto-Crow-Hidatsa:

PCH 1   Within a word an unrounded vowel is deleted before a morpheme-initial low vowel, and this low vowel becomes long if the deleted vowel is long and stressed if the deleted vowel is stressed.

Proto-Crow-Hidatsa has, therefore, derivations such as the following: the suffix -ak is added to verbs in dependent time clauses, -āci is added to verb stems to give a meaning similar to that of the verb but reduced, as it were, and -c is added to the main verb of declarative sentences.

cúhka+c > cúhkac 'It is level'
cúhka+ak > cúhkak 'When it is level'
cúhka+āci+c > cúhkācic 'It is sort of level'

kará+c > karác 'He ran away'
kará+ak > karák 'When he ran away'
kará+āci+c > karácic 'He ran off a little way'

kí+c > kíc 'He came back'
kí+ak > kák 'When he came back'
kí+āci+c > kácic 'He came back (but he hadn't gone far)'

The only major phonological change from proto-Crow-Hidatsa to Hidatsa is that c became š intervocalically when following a stressed front vowel.

A number of changes have occurred in Crow but we shall be concerned with only four. Three of them took place at the phonetic level; they were rules added toward the end of the phonological component. The fourth change, the one that accounts for the correspondence c/k, operated on underlying systematic phonemic representations. It must apply *before* PCH 1, hence must have been added to the grammar of Crow at a position that does not agree with its chronological placement. It was inserted in Crow ahead of a number of rules already present in proto-Crow-Hidatsa and ahead of a number of rules added in the grammar of Crow itself.

The three low-level phonetic rules added to the grammar of Crow were:

C 1 $t > \check{s}$ in all environments.
C 2   Before a low vowel $c > t$, and $\check{s}$ (both original PCH $*\check{s}$ and the $\check{s}$ from Rule C 1) became s.
C 3 $c > k$ in word-final position.

At some point in the evolution of the Crow language the grammar consisted of the rules PCH 1, C 1, C 2, C 3 applied in that order plus all the other rules which do not concern us here. This stage of pre-Crow had the following forms, some of whose Crow and Hidatsa reflexes were cited earlier in giving correspondence Sets I, II, and III in contrastive positions. The morpheme added to the main verb of a declarative sentence is now -k.

ihkikǽ + k > ihkikék   'He scratched himself'
ihkikǽ + ak > ihkikák   'When he scratched himself'
ihkikǽ + āci + k > ihkikácik   'He scratched himself (with the palm of his hand)'

íka + k > íkak   'He saw it'
íka + ak > íkak   'When he saw it'
íka + āci + k > íkācik   'He got a look at it'

kikǽki + k > kikǽkik   'He sewed it'
kikǽki + ak > kikǽkak   'When he sewed it'
kikǽki + āci + k > kikǽkācik   'He sewed it (but just enough to hold it together temporarily)'

wǘši + k > wǘšik   'I ate it'
wǘši + ak > wǘsak   'When I ate it'
wǘši + āci + k > wǘsācik   'I nibbled at it'

raxcí + k > raxcík   'He tied it'
raxcí + ak > raxták   'When he tied it'
raxcí + āci + k > raxtácik   'He tied it (but not very tight)'

cǘta > cǘse   'half'

kurǽ + āci > kuráci   'hold in both hands'

At some time after the preceding stage in Crow a fourth rule was added to the grammar of Crow (but not Hidatsa). This rule was:

C 4   ki > ci

Unlike the preceding three rules which were added at the end of the phonological component, Rule C 4 had to have been added in a position where it applies before Rule PCH 1. In other words, its order in the synchronic grammar of Crow is not the same as its chronological order. This rule affected just those morphemes containing *ki* as they appear to the left of the arrowhead. Of the examples given above this affected only the verb stems meaning 'to scratch' and 'to sew', and their forms are now:

ihciké + k > ihcikék   'He scratched himself'
ihciké + ak > ihcikák   'When he scratched himself'
ihciké + āci + k > ihcikácik   'He scratched himself (with the palm of his hand)'

cikáci + k > cikácik   'He sewed it'
cikáci + ak > cikátak   'When he sewed it'
cikáci + āci + k > cikátācik   'He sewed it (but just enough to hold it together temporarily)'

The Hidatsa cognates of the forms cited are:

ihkikè + c > ihkiké?ec
ihkikè + ak > ihkiká?ak
ihkikè + āci + c > ihkiká?ācic

íkā + c > íkāc
íkā + ak > íkāk
íkā + āci + c > íkācic

kikáki + c > kikákic
kikáki + ak > kikákak
kikáki + āci + c > kikákācic

wúti + c > wútic
wúti + ak > wútak
wúti + āci + c > wútācic

raxcí + c > raxcíc
raxcí + ak > raxcák
raxcí + āci + c > raxcácic

cúta > cúta

kurè + āci > kurá?āci

A comparison of the Crow with the Hidatsa forms shows that the problematic correspondence Set II (*c*/*k*) is completely accounted for. This means that we need to reconstruct only two proto-phonemes *c and *k for the three correspondences. The correspondence *c*/*k* derives from *k in a natural and exceptionless way if (and only if) we assume that Crow added the rule *ki* > *ci* out of chronological order.

These examples from Germanic and Siouan are but two illustrations of the implications that generative phonology has for comparative reconstruction. In a sense the moral to be drawn here is the same as that of Chapter 5: we have a lot to lose by assuming that phonological change is confined to purely phonetic environments. The consequence of this for a theory of diachronic change is that a more adequate and intuitively more satisfactory picture emerges only if we recognize the many possibilities of change admissible in generative phonology. An accurate reconstruction results only from an analysis that goes deeper than the search for correspondences in contrastive environments among daughter languages.

7.3 RELATIVE CHRONOLOGY

The determination of the relative chronology of a series of changes is as integral a part of reconstruction as the postulation of proto-phonemes (cf. Kuryłowicz 1964). Often the former is an impossible task. We know, for example, that Indo-European *b d g* > Germanic *p t k* and that Indo-European *o* > Germanic *a*. The two changes are independent in that the operation of one does not require previous operation of the other. Hence there is no way of deciding which occurred first.

It is possible, however, to recover relative chronology in certain cases, as, for example, when restructuring has taken place. When Indo-European *p t k* > *f þ x* / . . ., partial restructuring occurred. After the addition of the rule the optimal grammar has the word for 'father' entered something like /fəþér/ in its lexicon, not /pətér/ as previously. Similarly, when Indo-European *b d g* > *p t k* in Germanic, there is restructuring, this time complete since there is no longer any reason to set up underlying forms in /b d g/. The Germanic grammar, therefore, has changed all Indo-European forms in /b d g/ to /p t k/. The change *p t k* > *f þ x* had to have preceded *b d g* > *p t k* because otherwise Indo-European forms in /b d g/ would end up in Germanic in at least some cases as /f þ x/, which does not happen.

The second means at our disposal for getting a hold on relative chronology derives from the insight (due to Kiparsky, cf. Section 4.4) that ordered rules stand in marked or unmarked relationship. Unmarked order is the optimal order, marked order is less optimal. The precise way of formulating unmarked versus marked order in the simplicity metric is still open to question (Kiparsky 1965). But a large number of reorderings clearly involve a shift from marked to unmarked order, and we may accept this directionality as we accept any other empirical claim—as valid subject to possible falsification.

Thus, given a grammar with two crucially ordered rules A and B in that order, there are two possibilities: the order A–B is unmarked (optimal, catches more forms) or the order A–B is marked (less optimal, catches fewer forms than the opposite order). The unidirectionality of development toward optimality implies that marked order can give way to unmarked order, but rarely vice-versa. Thus if the order A–B is unmarked, the possibility is open that the original order in earlier grammars was B–A. On the other hand, if the synchronic order A–B is marked, then the likelihood of an earlier order B–A is very small, for in this case the progress would be from unmarked to marked, from optimal to less optimal.

In terms of procedure, then, given a synchronic grammar with rules A–B in unmarked order and an historical problem that can be resolved by assuming the earlier order B–A, we are justified in assuming tentatively that earlier grammars did contain the two rules in marked order B–A. Confirmation of this assumption can potentially be found in relic forms (since rule reordering of the leveling type can give rise to relic forms) or in comparative evidence. The relevant comparative evidence would be the presence in other languages in the family of the rules in marked, therefore presumably original, order.

Note finally that the possibility of rule reordering can erode the basis for even well-established rule chronologies. Halle (1962) discusses the chronology of Grimm's Law and Verner's Law in connection with simplicity. (This example was pointed out to me by Stanley Peters.) The relevant part of Grimm's Law is:

(1) $p\ t\ k > f\ \mathit{þ}\ x$ except after obstruents.

Verner's Law states that:

(2)   Voiceless continuants become voiced in certain environments: $f\ \mathit{þ}\ x > b\ ð\ g$, and $s > z$.

The consensus of scholarly belief places the Grimm's Law change (1) earlier than Verner's Law (2), though there is no external evidence one way or the other. Since *all* voiceless continuants are subject to Verner's Law in the attested Germanic languages and therefore in proto-Germanic, it is simplest to account for the facts by ordered rules (1)–(2); hence, Halle concludes, simplicity motivates the prevailing view that Grimm's Law preceded Verner's Law chronologically.

Observe, however, that the order (1)–(2) is unmarked order, so we are entitled to assume original marked order (2)–(1). In this order only *s* would be voiced to *z* by the Verner's Law rule that "Voiceless continuants become voiced in certain environments" since *s* was the only voiceless continuant in Indo-European. This order is marked; "feeding order" in Kiparsky's sense is maximized by the reordering to (1)–(2); and the traditional relative chronology turns out not to be the original one.

This analysis is not contradicted by available data. Whether it is correct or not is irrelevant. The reordering is possible and plausible from marking considerations and thus cannot be dismissed out of hand.

SUPPLEMENTARY READING

Bonfante, Guliano. 1945. "On Reconstruction and Linguistic Method." *Word* 1.83–94, 1.132–161.
Chafe, Wallace L. 1959. "Internal Reconstruction in Seneca." *Language* 35.477–495.
Hall, Robert A., Jr. 1950. "The Reconstruction of Proto-Romance." *Language* 26.6–27. Reprinted in *Readings in Linguistics I*, ed. Martin Joos, (New York: American Council of Learned Societies, 1958).
Hockett, Charles F. 1958. *A Course in Modern Linguistics.* New York: The Macmillan Company. Chaps. 55–60.
Hoenigswald, Henry M. 1960. *Language Change and Linguistic Reconstruction.* Chicago: University of Chicago Press.
Lehmann, Winfred P. 1962. *Historical Linguistics: An Introduction.* New York: Holt, Rinehart & Winston, Inc. Chaps. 5–6.
Marchand, James W. 1956. "Internal Reconstruction of Phonemic Split." *Language* 32.245–253.
Meillet, Antoine. 1925. *La méthode comparative en linguistique historique.* Oslo: H. Aschehoug & Co. (W. Nygaard).

8

CAUSALITY OF CHANGE

A certain category of questions has been avoided so far in this book: *why* linguistic change occurs in the first place, *why* one change takes place instead of another. Nothing, or very little, has been said about the causes of change. Our concern has been to describe change, to determine what it is rather than why it takes place.

Though we have made no attempt at explanation, we have at times related certain facts of change to certain others more general in nature. This comment applies especially to simplification. It was observed in Chapter 4 and elsewhere that some changes, notably rule loss and rule reordering, are variants of simplification and that grammar simplification frequently accompanies diachronic development. This lends psychological plausibility to loss and reordering as bona fide events of linguistic history, and we can predict how grammars might change on simplification. But we do not thereby explain *why* loss and reordering occur. In losing a rule of terminal devoicing Yiddish has simplified its grammar, but why did Yiddish, along with a few other German dialects, "choose" to simplify in this way? Why do languages innovate rules?

There is a long history of attempts at arriving at the cause or set of causes of phonological change, at a solution of the "actuation riddle" of phonological change (Weinreich *et al* 1968). We know nothing more about this than did Hermann Paul. To use one of the better-known putative causes of phonological change as an illustration, it is all very well to attribute a number of changes to "ease of articulation," e.g. *octo > otto,* but why do so many languages so successfully and so persistently resist ease of articulation? Why have not *all* languages assimilated to the utmost, parallel to *-kt- > -tt-?*

In view of the failure of phonological changes to occur under readily formulated conditions and in view of the notoriously weak principles hitherto invoked to explain the inception of change, many linguists, probably an easy majority, have long since given up inquiring into the why of phonological change. As Leonard Bloomfield bluntly put it: "The causes of sound change are unknown" (1933:385). No one runs any risk in being an utter cynic about the causes of phonological change.

One extreme position, then, holds that the cause of phonological change is not a part of linguistics proper:

> There is no more reason for languages to change than there is for automobiles to add fins one year and remove them the next, for jackets to have three buttons one year and two the next, etc. That is, it seems evident within the framework of sound change as grammar change that the "causes" of sound change without language contact lie in the general tendency of human cultural products to undergo "nonfunctional" stylistic change (Postal 1968:283).

Earlier linguists have held this view or something quite similar to it. Hugo Schuchardt, one of the Neogrammarians' most persistent critics, took a position strikingly similar to Postal's:

> While I am not quite prepared to compare sound laws to the laws of fashion, sound laws do seem to me to be matters of fashion for the most part. They derive from conscious or semi-conscious imitation (Spitzer 1922:55).

Against this position stand a large number of phonological changes in which a phonetic basis such as assimilation is clearly discernible. Simple cases of assimilation are commonplace in the development of languages: $kt > tt$, $ki > č$, $s > z$ between voiced sounds, and so on. An obvious case can be made for assimilation as the underlying cause of Germanic umlaut:

$$8.1 \quad V \rightarrow [-\text{ back}] / \text{——} C_1 \begin{bmatrix} -\text{ consonantal} \\ +\text{ high} \\ -\text{ back} \end{bmatrix}$$

(A vowel is fronted when separated by at least one consonant from a following high front vowel or *j*).

From the phonetic point of view, umlaut involves the assimilation of a vowel in tongue position to a following nonconsonantal segment. The phonetic basis of umlaut has been recognized by generations of scholars and given the appropriate designation of "assimilation at a distance" (*Fernassimilation*). Some of the well-known phonological changes of history are assimilatory: Verner's Law, for example, where voiceless fricatives assimilate to the presence of voice in the surrounding environment depending on the placement of the accent. There is assimilation in changes of the type *ai* > *e* and *au* > *o,* found in a variety of languages (Sanskrit, German, Semitic).

But over against cases like these of phonetic-based phonological changes there are baffling instances of change that do not conform at all to prior notions of phonetic plausibility or naturalness. The Old High German Consonant Shift removed the phonetic segments *p t k* from the language, replacing them by homo-organic affricates or fricatives according to phonetic environment: *pf tz kx* initially, after resonants, and as the second segment in gemination; *ff ʒʒ xx* after short vowel; *f ʒ x* after long vowels, diphthongs, and word-finally. (We assume that *ʒ* was a dorsal sibilant contrasting with apical *s* inherited from Indo-European, cf. Joos 1952.) Note that *p t k* are almost universally present in the world's languages and that affricates like *pf tz kx* are relatively uncommon. In markedness terms *p t k* are among the least marked consonants, fricatives like *f ʒ x* are intermediate in complexity, and the affricates *pf tz kx* are highly marked (Chomsky and Halle 1968:412). In view of all this, how could one argue that there is anything phonetically reasonable at all about the Old High German Consonant Shift? In particular, how could anyone argue for a basis in assimilation? A similar comment applies to the Great Vowel Shift of English. (I exclude here the possibility that these were borrowed innovations; I am not aware of any "substratum" from which Old High German and Early Modern English could have borrowed these rules.)

There is unquestionably something to be said for the phonetic basis of phonological change; it may well turn out that most phonological change at bottom results from assimilation. Each phonological change may not itself be assimilatory but rather secondarily induced by other changes themselves assimilatory in origin. A great deal of research would be needed to validate or falsify this hypothesis, but the results would be extremely rewarding. If there is little risk in being a cynic about the origin of phonological change, there is also little profit. In fact, linguistics has a great deal to lose by the position that the cause of phonological change is beyond principled research.

In previous chapters we have dealt with problems such as: What is linguistic change? What are the constraints on change? Does our theory of grammar permit us an adequate and intuitively sound account of change? Which changes can we reconstruct? But so far little has been said about general and specific principles that might be assumed to govern change. In this chapter we shall discuss briefly a few aspects of this problem.

8.1 PHONOLOGICAL SPACE

One consequence of the conception of language as a system where "tout se tient" is the assumed existence of implicational relationships between changes in different parts of the system. If *e* merges with *i* in a language, it is not surprising that *o* merges with *u*. If a language has a "hole" of some kind in its phonological system, the hole gets filled. To many linguists the explanatory potential of such implicational relationships has promised to be exciting.

The linguist who most readily comes to mind in this context is André Martinet. In various publications (1952, 1955) Martinet has argued at length for a theory of phonological change embedded within the notions of *function, structure,* and *economy.* Here we are concerned not with these ideas in general but only with their implications for what Moulton (1962) has called "phonological space." This term defines the realm of sound structure within which the phenomena described by Martinet are assumed to be effective. Phonological space is the articulatory area, as it were, defined by the set of segmental contrasts of a given language or dialect. Within this space "functional" and "structural" sound changes occur: the filling of holes in the pattern, push chains, drag chains, shifts of phonemic targets in the direction of maximum differentiation, the striving of a system toward symmetry.

The questions to which our inquiry must be addressed are of two kinds. First, is there anything to the idea of functional phonological changes—the filling of holes in a sound pattern, drag chains, movements to symmetry, maximal differentiation? Second, if such phenomena are indeed real, is generative phonology adequate to account for them?

Various tendencies of this general kind do exist. In many cases they seem to result from simplification (optimization) manifested in different ways and thus can be accounted for in a natural way within generative phonology. Frequently simplification takes the form of moving from a highly marked phonological system to one less highly marked, or of simplification in the rule component of the phonology. We shall consider a few cases here that illustrate the general type of problem.

Consider a language with the five-vowel system /i e a o u/, and assume an innovation affecting the vowel /e/. The structural analysis of this rule is:

$$\begin{bmatrix} + \text{ vocalic} \\ - \text{ consonantal} \\ - \text{ high} \\ - \text{ low} \\ - \text{ back} \end{bmatrix}$$

Like all rules this one is subject to simplification in the child generation. We saw in Chapters 3 and 4 that one commonplace form of rule simplification was the loss of a feature in the structural analysis. It would, therefore, not be surprising to lose some feature in the above structural analysis, say [− back], and to obtain a rule with the structural analysis:

$$\begin{bmatrix} + \text{ vocalic} \\ - \text{ consonantal} \\ - \text{ high} \\ - \text{ low} \end{bmatrix}$$

The rule now applies to both /e/ and /o/, producing a common type of "movement towards symmetry."

The principle that sounds tend to be maximally differentiated acoustically in a given language, though not fully understood, seems to be sound. Presumably this derives from the communicative function of language, but whatever its origin the fact is that vowel systems like:

	i	u		i	u	
		a		e	o	
					a	

are common, whereas vowel systems like the following are rare or unknown:

	ɨ	u			ü	ɨ	
e						o	
		æ			a		

This gets us close to the notion of "markedness" (Chomsky and Halle 1968:400–435). In the technical sense of this word phonological systems of a natural type, e.g. /i e a o u/ and /p t k b d g s/, are said to be less highly marked than systems such as /i e æ ö u/ and /p θ č f d z ž/. Markedness seems to play a part, not completely understood at present, in the evolution of sound systems. For example, the original stop system of Indo-European:

p t k
b d g
bʰ dʰ gʰ

was highly marked in that it required both voice and tenseness for its classification (most languages require at most one or the other). The vast majority of Indo-European languages have developed less highly marked obstruent systems; only Sanskrit and the modern Aryan languages have retained the original highly marked system.

An example further illustrating this kind of evolution can be taken from the German dialects of north-eastern Switzerland (Moulton 1960, 1961b). The Middle High German short vowel system, which furnishes a point of departure for the later history of the Swiss German short vowel systems, may be represented as follows:

i ü u

e ö o

ε

æ a

It is not certain how many of these vowels are present in underlying forms (phonemic), but it does seem probable that at least the four-way contrast in the front vowels $i \neq e \neq \varepsilon \neq æ$ is phonemic. However one measures markedness, a system containing the front vowels /i e ε æ/ in underlying forms is highly marked, and one would expect such a system to undergo modifications reducing its degree of markedness (complexity). This in fact does happen in the short vowel systems of northern Switzerland, most of which now have only three degrees of tongue height in the front vowels. Only a tiny pocket of dialects in the eastern cantons of Switzerland retain the original /i e ε æ/ system.

Marking theory has just begun to be formulated and to be integrated into phonological theory. For that reason alone one should be circumspect in citing a markedness consideration as a cause of phonological change. Furthermore, it must be emphasized that markedness is a *systematic* measure: a condition on grammars, not merely a measure of the complexity of phonological segment systems. (It is often forgotten that simplicity too is a systematic measure applied in principle to grammars and not individual rules.) It follows that an appeal to markedness is superficial unless all of the grammar is considered as well, and the statement that "phonological systems become less highly marked" is inadequate unless one can also show that the overall complexity of the grammar is reduced.

Another principle often invoked is that "holes in the pattern tend to get filled." Any claim containing the statistical qualifier "tend" is usually so weak as to be valueless, and this one is not an exception. That systems are more often symmetric than completely asymmetric is one of the bases for the notions of distinctive feature and markedness. But statistical statements are not explanations, not in linguistics, not anywhere. The vague claim that holes in the pattern tend to be filled cannot be taken seriously as a mechanism of linguistic evolution unless something in our theory of grammar and change can be shown to underlie it. A superficial inspection of the world's languages will reveal gaps—systematic phonemic, autonomous phonemic, and phonetic —in many languages. Standard German has no /g/ corresponding to /x/. Russian, with standard Spanish, has no phonemic /ǰ/ though it does have phonemic /č/. Hill Remo, a Munda language spoken in the state of Orissa in central India has neither phonetic, autonomous phonemic, nor systematic phonemic č, though it does have a phonetic [ǰ] that is autonomous phonemic. And Hill Remo lacks [č] even though Oriya, the Aryan prestige language in which it is immersed, has frequent occurrences of [č].

What, then, is the status of the claims that holes get filled and that systems strive towards symmetry? The basis for the latter claim seems to be in part the directionality of movement from highly marked to less highly marked systems. Generally speaking, an asymmetric system has a high markedness value that we would expect to see reduced in a movement toward symmetry. As for the notion that holes in the sound pattern get filled, such a process may be a case of asymmetry giving way to symmetry and would fall in the category of movement toward less markedness. Other cases may be simplification in the grammar, and some instances of this kind will be investigated here.

Holes in patterns are often filled by processes Martinet (1955:59) has called *push chains* and *drag chains*. These metaphors describe (n.b. *not* explain) the covarying shifts often enough encountered in the evolution of phonetic systems. In a *drag chain* segment A moves out of the system, perhaps by merger with a segment C, and another segment B moves into the position previously occupied by A. The exit of A "drags" B into its former slot. Schematically, this drag chain may be represented:

$$
\begin{array}{c}
\quad 1 \\
A \rightarrow C \\
2 \uparrow \\
B
\end{array}
$$

The term *push chain* describes the situation of a segment B moving away gradually from its phonetic norm in the direction of A. As B encroaches on the allophonic range of A, the latter in turn gradually moves away in the direction of C. If one rejects the gradualness of phonological change (cf. Section 5.1) and the notion that language abhors merger, push chains are deprived of their major sources of plausibility. For this reason the notion of push chains is rejected here; a covarying shift of this general type must be a drag chain—that is, a segment moves into a slot vacated by another segment. (King 1969 discusses the question of push chains and drag chains with a larger number of examples.)

Old High German has a pair of changes that illustrates the notion of drag chain. In pre-Old High German the obstruent system was:

p t k
b d g
f þ s x

In the High German Consonant Shift the voiceless stops *p t k* leave the system of simple stops, becoming either affricates *pf tz̧ kx* or fricatives *f(f) z̧(z̧) x(x)* depending on environment as noted earlier. Beginning in the seventh century A.D., *d > t* in many dialects. Somewhat later, and not in all dialects, the written records show that *þ > d*.

This is a typical example of a drag chain. Using the terminology of functional theory, one might explain this sequence of events as follows. The High German Consonant Shift produced two new obstruents in the tongue-tip region: *tz̧* and the dorsal sibilant *z̧*. These were in addition to the dental obstruents already present: *d, þ, s*. With the voiceless stop series empty, *d* was free to move into the hole at the *t*-slot, thus relieving the pressure in the dental region and lessening the danger of impaired communication. In any case *þ* was an unstable member of the system, being relatively rare in the world's languages as well as here being unsupported structurally by a voiced counterpart *ð*. Greater stability was thus achieved by the shift of *þ* into the position formerly held by *d*, and not a single contrast was lost in the entire shuffle.

This argument would be advanced within Martinet's theory of function, structure, and economy. The drag chain character of the set of shifts is made clear by the following diagram.

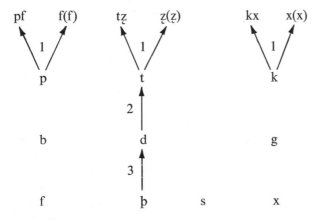

We shall investigate here the relation between *d > t* and *þ > d*. It should first be made clear that neither of these changes affects the underlying set of systematic phonemes. King (1968) shows that underlying þ must be assumed in Old High German in order to account for Verner's Law alternations of the type d/t parallel to f/b, s/r, and h/g (cf. Section 7.1) and that surface [t] comes from /d/. Thus, if a causal relation between the two changes exists, it must be accounted for in terms of the rules of the phonological component, not in terms of symmetry at the underlying level. Both changes remain as rules in the grammar.

This may be explained as a special case of simplification of "alpha-variable generalization" (Harms 1967:190). We assume that Rule 8.2 shifting $d > t$ was first added to the grammar of Old High German:

$$8.2 \quad \begin{bmatrix} + \text{ obstruent} \\ + \text{ coronal} \\ - \text{ strident} \\ - \text{ continuant} \end{bmatrix} \rightarrow [- \text{ voice}]$$

Rule 8.2 is then altered in later grammars of Old High German to Rule 8.2′: [− continuant] in the structural analysis is replaced by [α continuant], and [− voice] in the structural change is replaced by [α voice].

$$8.2' \quad \begin{bmatrix} + \text{ obstruent} \\ + \text{ coronal} \\ - \text{ strident} \\ \alpha \text{ continuant} \end{bmatrix} \rightarrow \begin{bmatrix} \alpha \text{ voice} \\ - \text{ continuant} \end{bmatrix}$$

($d > t$ and þ $> d$.)

This alteration is also a simplification because (as can be motivated independently) variables such as alpha are higher-valued in the simplicity metric than specified pluses and minuses. In counting Rule 8.2′ as a simplification of Rule 8.2, a restriction must be placed on what happens in the structural change as well as the structural analysis. As a first step in this direction let it be assumed that features in the structural change of the original rule retain their same value in the structural change of the simplified rule except for the feature which receives an alpha. This accounts for the presence of [−continuant] in the structural change of Rule 8.2′: it was present in the structural change of Rule 8.2, and it is "kept" without change of value in the structural change of Rule 8.2′.

This example illustrates the most common mechanism that, apparently, underlies covarying shifts of the drag chain kind: simplification, though of a kind not encountered before. Like other kinds of simplification such as deletion of a feature in the structural analysis of a rule, it may be interpreted as a generalization. Here a rule originally operating on a single segment is generalized to operate on an additional segment in the same natural class. The effect is that of a drag chain.

PHONOLOGICAL SPACE / 197

A second example of a drag chain comes from the Yiddish dialects of Northern Poland. Proto-Eastern-Yiddish is reconstructed by Herzog (1965: 163–164) with the short and long vowel systems:

$$
\begin{array}{cc} i & u \\ e & o \\ & a \end{array} \qquad
\begin{array}{cc} \bar{\imath} & \bar{u} \\ \bar{e} & \bar{o} \end{array}
$$

Of the subsequent changes undergone by these vowels in the dialects of Southern Yiddish, three are of interest here. In chronological order they are:

(1) Fronting of $\breve{u} > \breve{\ddot{u}}$
(2) Unrounding of $\breve{\ddot{u}} > \breve{\imath}$
(3) Raising of $\bar{o} > \bar{u}$

The fronting of $\breve{u} > \breve{\ddot{u}}$ is clearly an innovation in Southern Yiddish, though a very thorough-going one. It cannot be ascribed to any areal influence. The parallel fronting development in Slavic never extended beyond the Ukraine (Herzog 1965:165), and no coterritorial or bordering language such as Lithuanian shows parallel changes. On these grounds Herzog regards the change $\breve{u} > \breve{\ddot{u}}$ as a "first cause" explaining subsequent developments. Thus the raising of $\bar{o} > \bar{u}$ stands in a drag chain relation to the fronting of $\bar{u} > \bar{\ddot{u}}$:

$$
\begin{array}{cc}
 & 1 \\
\bar{\imath} & \leftarrow \bar{u} \\
 & \quad \uparrow 2 \\
\bar{e} & \bar{o}
\end{array}
$$

These changes can be explained in terms of rule simplification as follows. First, we assume that Rule 8.3 was added as an innovation in Southern Yiddish:

$$
8.3 \quad \begin{bmatrix} V \\ + \text{ long} \\ + \text{ round} \\ + \text{ high} \end{bmatrix} \rightarrow [-\text{ back}]
$$

(Rule 8.3 fronts $\bar{u} > \bar{\ddot{u}}$.)

Rule 8.3 is then simplified by replacing [+ high] in the structural analysis by [α high] and replacing [− back] in the structural change by [− α back]. The resultant rule now affects both back rounded vowels, creating the drag chain $\bar{u} > \bar{\ddot{u}}$ and $\bar{o} > \bar{u}$:

$$8.3' \quad \begin{bmatrix} V \\ + \text{ long} \\ + \text{ round} \\ \alpha \text{ high} \end{bmatrix} \rightarrow \begin{bmatrix} - \ \alpha \text{ back} \\ + \quad \text{high} \end{bmatrix}$$

Again, the feature [+ high] in the structural change of Rule 8.3′ is not an arbitrary insertion. It was present in the structural change of the original innovation Rule 8.3, and is carried over into the structural change of the simplification Rule 8.3′.

Rule 8.3, which we take as the original innovation in Southern Yiddish, also serves as a basis for the fronting of short $u > ü$. More commonly rules become simplified by loss of a feature in the structural analysis. We assume that some dialects of Southern Yiddish simplified Rule 8.3 this way by suppressing the feature [+ long] in the structural analysis and giving a rule in which both long $ū > ǖ$ and short $u > ü$:

$$8.3'' \quad \begin{bmatrix} V \\ + \text{ round} \\ + \text{ high} \end{bmatrix} \rightarrow [- \text{ back}]$$

Both rules 8.3′ and 8.3″ spread throughout the Southern Yiddish region so that eventually all dialects of Southern Yiddish had rules changing $ŭ > ü̆$ and $ō > ū$. This assumption of a wave-like spread is supported by the fact that Western Transcarpathian Yiddish, which has many features in common with Southern Yiddish proper, has Rule 8.3″ but not Rule 8.3′ (Herzog 1965:170).

The segments $ǖ$ and $ü$ from Rule 8.3″ subsequently are unrounded in Southern Yiddish and merge with inherited $ī$ and i. At this point there is restructuring of the underlying segments; /ū/ and /u/ are replaced in the lexicon by /ī/ and /i/. Consequently, Rule 8.3″ and the rule unrounding $ǖ > ī$ are lost from the grammar, and the secondary plural formations characteristic of Southern Yiddish emerge: e.g. $kū : kī$ 'cow, cows' becomes $kī$ 'cow' with the variant plurals $kī/kīəs/kīən$ (Herzog 1965:167).

The analysis of these Old High German and Yiddish examples suggests a single mechanism underlying causally related shifts: alpha-variable simplification of a previous innovation. This may be too hasty a conclusion based on insufficient evidence, or it may be just wrong. Let us consider an alternative analysis of the Old High German example which, though a simplification, is not the same form of simplification presented earlier.

Assume as before that Rule 8.2 ($d > t$) was an innovation in the grammar subsequent to the rule shifting $p\ t\ k$. Assume further that a rule changing $þ > ð$ was then added to the grammar as an independent innovation:

$$8.4 \quad \begin{bmatrix} + \text{ obstruent} \\ + \text{ coronal} \\ - \text{ strident} \\ + \text{ continuant} \end{bmatrix} \rightarrow [+ \text{ voice}]$$

The assumption that we are dealing with two separate innovations is support-ed by the facts of subsequent development. The Upper German dialect (Bavarian and Alemannic) simplified Rule 8.2 by deleting the feature [+ coronal] in the structural analysis; the resulting rule changes *b d g > p t k*. Likewise, there was an Old High German lenition of spirants (*frühalthoch-deutsche Spirantenschwächung*) that eventually affected the whole natural class *f þ s h*; this, we assume, was a simplification of Rule 8.4 obtained by deleting the feature [+ coronal].

This suggests that some grammars of early Old High German contained both Rule 8.2 and Rule 8.4 as separate rules. We note, however, that the two rules have much in common: they differ in the structural analysis only in the feature *continuant*; the result of Rule 8.2 is a dental stop *t*, and the result of Rule 8.4 is a dental fricative *ð*. A child whose linguistic experience is provided by (adult) grammars with the two separate rules could simplify his grammar by collapsing them into the single rule given earlier as Rule 8.2′. The "drag chain" aspect is the result, almost casual as it were, of the child's including the feature [− continuant] in the structural change of Rule 8.2′.

Several conclusions may be drawn from examples like these. First, the kind of linked shift called "drag chain" does occur. Two such shifts were discussed here, and King (1969) provides others from a Portuguese dialect, New York City English, and Germanic. Second, "drag chains" seem to be special cases of simplification in the rule component of the grammar, and the greater simplicity of drag chains can be shown formally in generative grammar. Only incidentally is any kind of phonemic symmetry attained; indeed, if the second analysis of the Old High German example is correct, only incidentally is a drag chain itself attained, precisely when a partic-ular feature is retained in the structural change of the conflation of two rules.

If the explanations proposed here are correct, drag chains are in essence not radically different from other more usual types of simplification such as the deletion of a feature in the structural analysis of a rule or the simple conflation of two rules. Markedness, and in particular "linking" (Chomsky and Halle 1968:419–435), may play a role not investigated here.

Note that generative phonological theory does not force us to assume a single specific mechanism underlying drag chains. Simplification is responsible, but not one unvarying form of simplification. If it can be shown that drag chains are in fact uniformly produced by a single mechanism, this would point to an inadequacy in our phonological theory. We would then be required to alter the theory so that it would predict just that single mechanism for drag chains.

8.2 QUANTITATIVE SOURCES OF PHONOLOGICAL CHANGE

So far this chapter has been concerned only with *qualitative* sources for the inception of phonological change: simplicity, markedness, and phonetics. Linguists have suggested that at least some phonological changes have their origin in *quantitative* factors: frequency of occurrence of segments, the entropy associated with a phonetic system, and functional load. George Kingsley Zipf's Principle of Relative Frequency is one of the most well-known efforts to bring statistical factors to bear on the initiation of sound change (cf. Zipf 1929, 1965).

According to Zipf, every sound has a measure of "conspicuousness." The sound d^h is more conspicuous than d because d^h has all that d has plus aspiration. The sound d is more conspicuous than t because d has all that t has plus voice. (The underlying notion of markedness is evident in Zipf's speculations.)

Let us now suppose that some sound, say d, occurs very frequently in a language. According to Zipf, since people would be accustomed to hearing d frequently, they would not insist on a clear pronunciation of it, so that d would tend to weaken into the less conspicuous sound t. Suppose, on the other hand, that some sound, say t, has a very low frequency. Since t's are so infrequent and inconspicuous, people would be inclined to spend more effort on pronouncing them conspicuously; and t might take on more conspicuousness and change into t^s or t^h, both more conspicuous than t.

According to Zipf's Principle of Relative Frequency, each sound has a lower and a higher threshold frequency. A sound changes when it exceeds either its lower threshold (i.e. becomes too infrequent) or its higher threshold (i.e. becomes too frequent). Zipf used this principle to explain a number of changes, e.g. the Grimm's Law changes $p\ t\ k > f\ \not{p}\ x$, $b^h\ d^h\ g^h > b\ \eth\ g$, $b\ d\ g > p\ t\ k$, and the High German Consonant Shift $p\ t\ k > p^f\ t^s\ k^x$.

Since Zipf was unable to determine the critical threshold frequencies independently, his principle is vitiated by circularity. It is not so easy, however, to dispose of the underlying notion that statistical data such as frequency are important in phonological change. Sapir (1921:194) observed that sounds tend to drift through merger into positions statistically more secure, and other linguists have concurred.

Probably the most serious attempt to explain phonological change by quantitative measures is associated with the concept of *functional load* or *functional yield*. This term is customarily used in linguistics to describe the extent and degree of contrast between linguistic units, usually autonomous phonemes. For example, the functional load of the opposition /p/ $\neq$ /b/ in

English is high while that of /š/ ≠ /ž/ is low: there are many minimal pairs for the first opposition, few for the second.

The role of functional load in phonological change is most extensively discussed by André Martinet. The basic idea (Martinet 1955:54) is that oppositions bearing low functional loads should be less resistant to merger than those with high functional loads. This conclusion seems intuitively sound. If every occurrence of /ž/ in English became /š/ no great confusion would result; this would not be true if /t/ merged with /d/. If merger opens the possibility of communication failure because homonyms are created, and if communication must go on in spite of phonological change, then it seems intuitively evident that there should be some kind of upper limit on permissible mergers. Functional load would seem to offer such a limit.

The major hindrance to testing the pertinence of functional load to phonological change is the problem of just what to measure. Is it the functional load of phonemes occurring in the lexicon? Or is it the functional load, in some sense or other, of rules? Most scholars who have used the concept in historical explication have thought of functional load as measuring the amount of work by which autonomous phonemes keep utterances apart. King (1967a) has shown that functional load in this somewhat primitive sense is irrelevant to phonological change: loss of phonemic contrasts is neither impeded nor favored by functional load.

This is not to say that functional load in a more general formulation would be necessarily irrelevant to phonological change. It seems likely that there is some kind of upper limit on phonological change and linguistic change in general. If, say, a rule has a high functional load in that it applies to a large number of possible forms in a language, the rule might therefore not be lost from the grammar in the process of grammar acquisition. Similarly, there must be some constraint on how drastically an added rule can affect the output of a grammar. No doubt the child learning his language incorporates into his grammar all sorts of rules that if retained into adulthood would make his speech incomprehensible. Such potential freak rules, if they occur, must be filtered out by something in the language acquisition device of the child. This filter may be related to functional load in some form or another, but at present we can hardly be precise about such matters or even about the right questions to ask.

At our current state of knowledge, it seems unlikely that frequency of occurrence has much to do with phonological change. If statistics were relevant to phonological change, there should be evidence that these statistics are part of what a speaker "knows" about the phonology of his language— part of his competence. This is clearly not true in any gross sense since speakers of a language do not generally have even approximately correct ideas about the frequency of sounds in their language. And currently no evidence shows that statistical information in some more subtle sense is a part of the speaker's competence.

8.3 DRIFT

The term *drift* has been used in a variety of ways in linguistics. In the context of historical linguistics it usually means a tendency inherent in a related group of languages to develop in particular ways and to continue developing in these ways over several generations even when the languages are no longer in contact (Hockett 1948, Klima 1965:429, Sapir 1921: Chap. 7).

Many cases of drift are manifestations of simplification occurring independently in languages of the same family. An instance is the loss of terminal devoicing in Yiddish. One cannot well speak of a definite drift in German dialects here since the majority of them have kept a devoicing rule. Yet loss of this rule has occurred in German dialects other than Yiddish, in particular in some dialects of German in northern Switzerland (Zürich German has no rule of terminal devoicing). There is no question of borrowing here since the Yiddish of Eastern Europe was geographically and culturally isolated from these other German dialects during the period of its formation. Dialects that originally had a rule of final devoicing have independently undergone simplification of the same kind.

Seen in this light nothing about drift is particularly mystical. Simplification is a fact of language development, and its roots lie in the child's acquisition of language. It is a universal option. It is not surprising that some daughter languages should undergo identical but independent simplifications of a rule inherited in common from the parent language. They might lose the rule or the same feature in the structural analysis of the rule, but in either case the same process, simplification, is at work.

SUPPLEMENTARY READING

King, Robert D. 1967. "Functional Load and Sound Change." *Language* 43.831–853.

Martinet, André. 1955. *Économie des changements phonétiques.* Berne: A. Francke.

Moulton, William G. 1961. "Lautwandel durch innere Kausalität: die ostschweizerische Vokalspaltung." *Zeitschrift für Mundartforschung* 28.227–251.

9

SCRIBAL PRACTICE

A good deal of historical linguistics begins with and is accompanied by the interpretation of written records. This is particularly true of the languages on which the traditional methods of comparative linguistics were originally used: the Indo-European, many of which have some kind of literary tradition going back a millenium or more.

It would be very nice, therefore, if we could formulate a theory of scribal practice for interpreting written records, a theory that tells the linguist what kinds of linguistic representations scribes write or, at the very least, tend to write. Any strong form of such a theory is out of the question as will be readily apparent to anyone with experience of texts from even a few centuries ago in languages like English, Spanish, or German. Nor is it by any means obvious that a weaker form of such a theory, say a theory that predicts in a statistical sense what scribes *tend* to write, would stand up for long against the huge amount of confusing data that all the historical records of the world's languages provide.

Therefore nothing very significant can be said in this chapter about the relation between scribal practice and linguistic theory. But the subject is not necessarily devoid of all interest. There is a negative, a corrective value in inquiring into some of the linguistic problems underlying scribal practice and assessing certain notions that have gained currency, in particular the claim that linguistically naive scribes strive for what is basically an autonomous phonemic writing system all things being equal.

The following discussion is limited to "alphabetic" writing systems (cf. Hill 1967). An alphabetic writing system is a set of discrete symbols together with a set of associated rules that permit a native speaker to determine the correct pronunciation of words and groups of words from given spellings. Alphabets may be categorized according to their level of phonological representation. A morphophonemic writing system has for alphabet the set of morphophonemic entities in the language, and the associated rules are the phonological rules which phonetically interpret lexical items spelled in morphophonemes. This kind of writing system is the nearest analogue in practice to a generative phonology that recognizes only two significant levels of phonological representation: the systematic phonemic (roughly equivalent to the morphophonemic level in writing systems) and the systematic phonetic. An autonomous (taxonomic) phonemic writing system would be composed of the set of autonomous phonemes in the language, and the spelling rules would be the set of process statements about which allophone of a particular phoneme is to be selected in which environment. Even a phonetic script is conceivable with an alphabet of the set of IPA symbols plus required diacritics. In this case no set of rules specific to the language would be needed.

Disregarding the third possibility, which has never been observed in practice except by linguistically naive spelling reformers, we are left with two clear-cut possibilities for an alphabetic script: a morphophonemic and an autonomous phonemic. Some kind of additional requirement must be placed on both types so that a native speaker can spell as well as read. That is, an acceptable writing system must not merely permit a native speaker to determine the correct pronunciation given a word written in the appropriate alphabet; it must also enable him to recover a serviceable spelling of the word he wants to write. In terms of the linguistic theories underlying writing systems, there must be some way of deducing the abstract representation (morphophonemic or autonomous phonemic) of a word when all the native speaker knows is how the word sounds and possibly what words it is related to grammatically.

In practice, no writing system ever falls neatly into one or the other of the two groups. Modern English, as well as many other modern scripts, is morphophonemic to a large degree. *Line/lineal, crime/criminal, crisis/critical* are all spelled with *i* for the vowel under stress which is [ay] or [ɪ]. This is morphophonemically correct since these segments in the grammar of English are derived from the same underlying systematic phoneme /ī/. English orthography fails to be morphophonemically consistent, however, having such spellings as *profound/profundity*, where *ou* spells [aw] and *u* spells [ʌ] though both are from underlying /ū/. Likewise, the first *s* in *crisis* is from underlying /t/.

German spelling is morphophonemic with unusual consistency. It writes voiced obstruents denoting the underlying form in, for example, *Wald* 'forest', *halb* 'half', *König* 'king'. It does not mark length in many positions where only long vowels can occur, as before voiced obstruents in *sagen* [zaːgən] 'to say' and *haben* [haːbən] 'to have', and it does usually mark length in positions where it is not predictable, e.g. *Kahn* [kaːn] 'skiff' versus *kann* [kan] 'he can'. (*h* marks vowel length in the first instance, the doubling of *n* marks its absence in the second.) But German, like English, marks too much in its orthography to be completely morphophonemic. To cite only one example, German marks vowel length (usually with an *h*) in most final vowels even though such length is predictable: *sah* [zaː] 'he saw', *Floh* [floː] 'flea'.

Both English and German fail to qualify as autonomous phonemic writing systems largely for the same reasons that make them morphophonemic in many respects. An autonomous phonemic writing system would spell *crime/criminal* something like *kraym/krimənəl*. Similarly, if the invariance condition in autonomous phonemic practice is observed (Chomsky 1964:93–95), all final voiceless obstruents in German would have to be assigned to phonemically voiceless obstruents. Thus, *Wald, halb,* and *König* would have to be spelled *valt, halp,* and *könich* as was frequently done in Middle High German. For the same kind of reason length would have to be marked in *sagen* and *haben*, perhaps *zāgən* and *hābən*.

Though the third possibility, a purely phonetic script, was dismissed above, allophonic differences are marked in some scripts. Bolivian Quechua has had several different writing systems proposed, some of which compete down to the present. In all of them five vowels *i e a o u* are used, though in native Bolivian Quechua words *i* and *u* are in complementary distribution with *e* and *o*: *e* and *o* preceding and following post-velar obstruents, *i* and *u* elsewhere. Yet this difference is consistently marked even in native Quechua words. The Spanish influence is of course responsible. The fact that the majority of Quechua speakers are bilingual gives them a control over the orthographic representation of the allophones of /i/ and /u/ that would not be possible in a monolingual situation. Likewise, in written records from the history of a language, some spellings, in particular inconsistent ones, may be phonetic.

Thus, even in languages written today we can find few examples of strictly morphophonemic or autonomous phonemic writing systems. The earlier the linguist goes, the more frustrated are his efforts to account completely for scribal practice and writing systems. Scribes are rarely so puristic as to write consistently. The insidious and persistent influence of the written tradition, the uncertain literacy of many scribes, opaque shifts in scribal practice, slips of the pen, inconsistency pure and simple—all join to subvert any strong theory attempting to explain what all scribes at all times in all languages have written.

Counter evidence is easily found to either of the claims "Scribes tend to write morphophonemically" or "Scribes tend to write autonomous phonemes." Such diverse languages as Latin and Old English or Old High German had vowel length, both systematic or autonomous phonemically, yet almost no one wrote it with any kind of reasonable consistency. (An exception in Old High German was the learned scholar Notker Labeo of the monastery St. Gall, who introduced a length mark into German and used it with great consistency; cf. Section 4.5.) Even stronger counter evidence to either of these two claims comes from the history of Norse and the Runic alphabet.

The earliest attested Runic alphabet, the Older Futhark, had 24 characters. One of these, $\dot{e}$, is rare in Nordic inscriptions, and both its etymological and phonetic assignment are uncertain. Excepting this one symbol, the Older Futhark can be arranged as follows:

i	u		p	t	k		r	R	
e	o		b	d	g		j	w	
	a		f	þ	s	h			
			m	n					

Though the dating of this and other Runic alphabets is rather uncertain, the best opinion places the use of the Older Futhark in Norse inscriptions at A.D. 400–600 (Arntz 1935:138).

From approximately A.D. 650 onward the Older Futhark begins to shrink in number of symbols until by 800 it has been reduced to sixteen, giving the *Younger Futhark*:

i	u		b	t	k		r	R
	a		f	þ	s	h		
	ã		m	n				

i is used in place of *i, e,* and *j* in the Older Futhark; *u* is used for both *u* and *o* as well as *w*; *b* is used in place of *p* and *b*; *t* replaces both *t* and *d*; and *k* is used for older *k* and *g*.

Now there is not a shred of evidence that this radical change in the alphabets corresponds to any phonological reduction of the number of segments in the language. On the contrary, we are quite certain that the number of phonetic entities in Runic Norse increased during the period in question, due primarily to the umlaut rule in Norse which produced at least the new phonetic segments $\ddot{\bar{u}}$ $\bar{\ddot{o}}$ $\tilde{æ}$ $\mathfrak{z}$. None of these vowels was expressed in the Younger Futhark until the invention (around 1100) of the "dotted" runes, in which diacritics were used for the new umlaut vowels much as two dots designate the front rounded counterpart $\ddot{u}$ of u.

The set of systematic phonemes has remained constant over this period in two of the Nordic languages, Old Norwegian and Old Icelandic, and probably in all of them. New rules, notably the umlaut rules, have been added to the grammar, but no restructuring has taken place. During this period the number of autonomous phonemes has either remained constant (that is, the phonetic causes of umlaut were still present) or increased markedly (assuming all the umlaut variants of vowels became phonemic).

In other words, whatever happened between 600 and 800 in Nordic, the number of phonemic vowel segments could not have decreased, whether by "phonemic" one means systematic or autonomous. Nor is there evidence that the number of phonetic vowels decreased. Yet the number of vowel symbols decreased from five to three with a marginal fourth one ($\tilde{a}$). Similarly, the Older Futhark had six symbols for what in most positions were stops: b d g and p t k. In the Younger Futhark only three stops are noted in the orthography, b t k. Again, no comparative or internal evidence suggests that this in any way reflects what was happening to the phonology of these languages.

Runic Norse is admittedly a somewhat special case because runes were never used for lengthy texts. But they were used for inscriptions, many of which consist of several words and even complete sentences. As the Runic data stand, they provide counter evidence to any linguistically motivated theory of scribal practice that can be dreamed up, in particular to the two most obvious theories that scribes tend to find adequate representations for morphophonemes or autonomous phonemes. One is tempted to forget the whole business or to agree in despair with Holger Pedersen (1962:236) that there is "something psychological in this, a sort of indolence."

Where does this leave us in our effort to make sense of what scribes do or do not write? It should leave us with a very sober assessment of our ability to perceive what must have psychologically preceded the instant when scribe put quill to parchment. We should be very wary of any claim that "Scribes tend to write x's, and when they don't write x's, something else must have disturbed the essential process."

Claims such as this must underlie anyone's work with written records, however, even if no strong case can be made for a particular theory. Since the development of structural linguistics in the 1930's, it has generally been argued that scribes tend toward designation of autonomous phonemes. Most discussion has been of the question of allophonic spellings: Do scribes ever designate allophones consistently? This was the major point in the disagreement on scribal practice between Hockett (1959) and Stockwell and Barritt (1961). The claim itself—that scribes will, in the absence of strong pressure to do otherwise, tend to write autonomous phonemes—has been widely accepted ever since the famous Twaddell (1938) article in which the presence or absence of umlaut designation in the orthography of Old High German was linked to the status of the umlaut vowels as phonemes or allophones.

The predominant theory of scribal practice is: Unless culturally prescribed spelling has gained considerable currency or unless scribes have a strong tendency to keep orthographic designation of allomorphy to a minimum, scribes will write autonomous phonemes. Differences in spelling will never correlate exclusively with allophonic differences. Only when allophonic variants have become phonemic through loss of the phonetic conditioning factor does the possibility of their orthographic representation emerge, and new symbols for the new phonemes will eventually be created unless the force of spelling tradition is strong enough to defeat any innovation.

Twaddell's article on Old High German illustrates most of the implications of this theory. According to Twaddell umlaut was allophonic in the Old High German period: any back vowel /ă ŏ ŭ/ had front allophones when followed in the next syllable by $\breve{\imath}$ or j (neglecting here "secondary" umlaut). None of these allophonic variants was represented at all in Old High German orthography. The umlaut of short $\breve{a}$ was designated consistently as e, however, because, according to Twaddell, the umlaut allophone of original /ă/ had early in Old High German been reassigned to the phoneme /e/ on the basis of phonetic similarity. By Middle High German times the umlaut-producing factors $\breve{\imath}$ and j had either disappeared or merged to schwa, so that the umlaut vowels were promoted from allophonic to phonemic status and their orthographic representation became possible. And indeed in the course of the Middle High German period we do find new symbols emerging and being used increasingly for the new vowel phonemes. In summary, Twaddell's argument is that umlaut in Old High German was allophonic (except for the umlaut of short $\breve{a}$) and hence not represented in the orthography; in Middle High German it was phonemic and hence subject to representation.

If, as generative phonologists have argued, the autonomous phoneme has no place in the representation of a speaker's competence, it has a tenuous claim to psychological reality. And if this is so, it would be very surprising to find any impressive correlation between the units that scribes tend to write and autonomous phonemes. Is it possible to formulate a theory of scribal practice more in accord with the organization of language and grammar proposed in generative grammar?

The following proposal is intended as a step in that direction. In the absence of a strong nonnative orthographic influence, scribes devise symbols for the underlying systematic phonemic segments of the language. They tend to alter the existing orthography (1) when restructuring has occurred or (2) when innovations in the grammar (rule additions) have produced segments phonetically close to other surface-level segments which have a stable graphemic representation. In the event of little or no restructuring, there is little or no orthographic reform.

This theory suggests that scribes write symbols identifiable with different levels of representation from the systematic phonemic down to the systematic phonetic. Scribal inconsistency usually occurs in just those cases where representing underlying (systematic phonemic, morphophonemic) segments conflicts with representing phonetic segments produced by rule that are identifiable with other graphemic sources. That in general the morphophonemic representation wins out is to a large extent what is usually meant by "orthographic conservatism."

Such a theory goes part way toward reducing orthographic "lag," the divergence between what has taken place in the phonology of a language and its orthographic representation. Generally speaking, autonomous phonemics requires more frequent restructuring in the history of a language than does generative phonology. Generative rules can be carried along for a long time without restructuring, whereas restructuring (i.e. promotion of a segment from allophonic to phonemic status) occurs in autonomous phonemics whenever phonetic conditioning is lost. In generative phonology the loss of phonetic conditioning does not necessarily involve restructuring.

The case of High German umlaut analyzed in detail in Section 4.5 may serve as a preliminary test of the two claims: that scribes seek an adequate autonomous phonemic writing system, and that they write in accord with the theory just proposed (that is, they attempt essentially a morphophonemic writing system). Old High German provides a good test for several reasons. It is documented quite well from about the eighth century A.D. on, it was not shackled by a fixed orthographic tradition, and it underwent a number of well-understood changes both phonetic and phonemic during its documented history. It is also especially suitable since Twaddell's novel explanation of it ushered in a new era of historical linguistics under structural ministration.

In Section 4.5 the historical development of attested Old High German was divided into four stages, I–IV, in each of which phonetic umlaut was present. Umlaut vowels in underlying systematic phonemic representations were not present in any of them, but it was assumed in Section 4.5 that umlaut vowels at the systematic phonemic level were present in at least late Middle High German. From the point of view of autonomous phonemics, the umlaut of short *ă* was phonemic in Old High German Stage I. In Stage II, which is defined by the addition of a rule removing umlaut-producing *j*'s, a large number of the umlaut variants became phonemic. By Stage III most of the remaining umlaut variants had become autonomous phonemic;

and by Stage IV, the point at which we begin to speak of Middle High German, all umlaut vowels were autonomous phonemic. Note that if one requires the condition of strong invariance, which is roughly equivalent to the statement "A segment assigned to a phoneme in any of its occurrences must be regarded as an allophone of that phoneme in all of its occurrences," then umlaut in Old High German was already phonemically present for *all* vowels in Stage II.

Also, in Old High and Middle High German (Kratz 1960), there is no trace of umlaut designation of umlauted occurrences of $\bar{a}$, $\breve{o}$, or *ou*. In a handful of cases the umlaut of *u* and *uo* is marked, and the umlaut of $\bar{u}$ is marked fairly regularly beginning in the eleventh century (approximately Stage III). Middle High German begins to show attempts at designation of all the umlaut variants, though with far from complete consistency (cf. Steiner 1969).

Table 9.1, which summarizes the progress of umlaut and its orthographic designation, demonstrates the weakness of the traditional notion that scribes tend to designate autonomous phonemic entities. The orthographic lag is considerable, in the vicinity of four centuries. On the other hand, the presence of umlaut in underlying segments and the orthographic designation of umlaut stay much closer together. The umlaut of short $\breve{a}$ is designated even in Stage I because [e] (the phonetic realization of /$\breve{a}$/ under umlaut) was phonetically closer to [ɛ] (whose graphemic source was *e*) than to [a] (the nonumlaut realization of the grapheme *a*). Similarly, the designation of the umlaut of $\bar{u}$ in Stage III resulted from an historical coincidence. The old diphthong *iu* became [ü:] at this time, furnishing the Old High German scribes with a useful designation for the umlaut of $\bar{u}$, which also was [ü:]. In these two cases, then, phonetic/graphemic congruence overrode morphophonemic considerations.

TABLE 9.1

UMLAUT DESIGNATION

Stage and Time	Autonomous Umlaut Present?	Underlying Umlaut Present?	Written Designation
I			
−800	Only $\breve{a}$	No	Only of $\breve{a}$
II			
800–950	Yes, all vowels	No	Only of $\breve{a}$
III			
950–1050	Yes, all vowels	No	$\breve{a}$, some $\bar{u}$
IV			
1050–1150	Yes, all vowels	No	$\breve{a}$, some $\bar{u}$
Middle High German			
1150–	Yes, all vowels	Yes	Yes

This example points up some of the explanatory possibilities that emerge from a theory of scribal practice based more nearly on generative phonology. As mentioned repeatedly throughout this chapter, any theory of scribal practice is fraught with difficulties since we are dealing with a phenomenon conditioned by many extra-linguistic factors. No theory can explain the practice of every scribe, but a theory embedded within generative phonology stands a good chance of explaining more than does the unquestioned assumption that scribes tend to write autonomous phonemes.

The force of the argument so far has been against the position that scribes try to capture specifically the autonomous phonemic level of representation. This is one possibility, a logical one in view of phonology that recognizes no separate autonomous phonemic level of representation intermediate in abstractness between the systematic phonemic and systematic phonetic levels. There may, however, be reasons why scribes, out of all the people consciously concerned with language, would tend to devise autonomous phonemic representations. There may even be good reasons, as the following considerations suggest, why the autonomous phoneme occupies a position in scribal practice though not in the competence of a speaker.

One crucial point that distinguishes generative phonology from autonomous phonemics concerns the recoverability of phonological (phonemic) representations given phonetic representations. All theories of phonology agree that two contrastive phonetic representations must have distinct phonological representations (Postal 1968:8). The acceptance of the converse condition (among others) separates autonomous phonemics from systematic generative phonology. That is, autonomous phonemics accepts and generative phonology rejects the condition that given two distinct phonological representations, their phonetic representations are necessarily contrastive.

In order to fulfill this latter condition autonomous phonemics has observed such criteria of analysis as nonoverlapping, invariance, the principle of "once a phoneme always a phoneme," and so on. If we insist on a one-to-one mapping between phonemics and phonetics, we must observe some condition that permits recovery of the unique phonological representation associated with a given phonetic representation.

Let us consider briefly an illustration from German. As has been discussed in previous chapters, German has a rule devoicing obstruents in word-final position. The two words *Rad* 'wheel' and *Rat* 'advice' are both pronounced [ra:t]. *Rad*, however, manifests an underlying voiced /d/ in phonological alternation: *Rades* [ra:dəs] 'of the wheel', *Räder* [re:dər] 'wheels'. The *t* in *Rat*, on the other hand, undergoes no alternation in other forms: *Rates* [ra:təs] 'of the advice'. To a generative phonologist the facts are clear; *Rad* has the underlying form /rad/, *Rat* has the underlying form /ra:t/, and we have such derivations as:

Underlying Forms:	/rad	radəs	ra:t	ra:təs/
Devoicing Rule:	rat	. . . . .	. . . .	. . . . . .
Phonetic Forms:	[ra:t	ra:dəs	ra:t	ra:təs]

(The occurrence of length in vowel of [ra:t] 'wheel' and [ra:dəs] is predictable, as has been mentioned elsewhere in discussing German, and the underlying forms cited here have been simplified to expedite the present discussion.)

Thus, the phonetic form [ra:t] is a realization of both /rad/ and /ra:t/. The phonemic representation is distinct, and no condition in generative phonology requires this to be otherwise. In at least some variants of autonomous phonemics, however, this analysis would be improper since it violates the condition that distinct phonemic representations must necessarily have distinct phonetic representations. What is incorrect is the phonemic form of [ra:t] 'wheel', in particular the assignment of its [t] to phonemic /d/. Since [t] in at least some occurrences must be assigned unambiguously to /t/, as in *Rat* and *Rates*, in [ra:t] 'wheel' it should also be assigned to /t/. Those theories of autonomous phonemics requiring this would have the following relations between phonemic (underlying) forms and phonetic (allophonic) forms:

Underlying Forms:	/ra:t	radəs	ra:t	ra:təs/
Phonetic Forms:	[ra:t	ra:dəs	ra:t	ra:təs]

Looked at this way, it becomes clear why scribes might unconsciously arrive at some variant of an autonomous phonemic representation. A scribe's job is to devise a spelling system that makes it possible to convert unambiguously a word written on paper into spoken utterance. But if the scribe also is to teach others how to spell (that is, to teach others how to represent unambiguously on paper an isolated word whose pronunciation they know) and if it is desirable for spellings to be as phonetically concrete as possible, then he must adopt some form of the principle "once a phoneme always a phoneme." The scribe might reason that since [ra:t] 'wheel' and [ra:t] 'advice' are identical phonetically, they should be spelled the same. From the strictly phonetic point of view, there is no reason why [ra:t] pronounced in isolation should sometimes be spelled *Rad*, sometimes *Rat*.

Whether this is in fact an approximation of what scribes do when they write is open to question—like everything else in scribal practice. Middle High German scribes were to a large extent autonomous phonemic. They would have written the equivalent of *Rat* for both 'wheel' and 'advice'; for example, they wrote *walt/waldes* 'forest, of the forest', *rat/rades* 'wheel, of the wheel', *tac/tage* 'day, days'. Modern German has gone back to a morphophonemic spelling system in this regard: *Wald/Waldes, Rad/Rades, Tag/Tage*.

The *spelling reformers* seem to make the best autonomous phonemicists. The anonymous author of the Icelandic First Grammatical Treatise, written approximately in the second quarter of the twelfth century, is an example par excellence, and the strikingly modern aspects of his work have been appropriately recognized (Haugen 1950). In some ways his analysis of Icelandic is an exemplary autonomous phonemic analysis; for example, it relies heavily on the use of phonetic-level minimal pairs.

The work of other spelling reformers follows, often quite consciously, some condition corresponding to biuniqueness. Friedrich Klopstock, a German poet of the late eighteenth century and an enthusiastic participant in the spelling reform mania that afflicted Germany at the time, states explicitly as one of his rules that: "No sound can have more than one letter, and no letter may represent more than one sound" (cf. King 1967b:371). Despite his avowed acceptance of a form of the biuniqueness principle, Klopstock proceeded to violate it wherever biuniqueness conflicted with simplicity of analysis (King 1967b:373).

Scribal practice is not a satisfying field for the linguist. The harder one works with extensive data, the harder scribal practice is to explain in any consistent way. The considerations in this chapter are intended not to explain scribal practices, for no theory does this very well, but to suggest new perspectives for viewing the problems of scribal practice.

SUPPLEMENTARY READING

Hockett, Charles F. 1959. "The Stressed Syllabics of Old English." *Language* 35.575–597.

Stockwell, Robert P. and C. Westbrook Barritt. 1961. "Scribal Practice: Some Assumptions." *Language* 37.75–82.

Twaddell, W. Freeman. 1938. "A Note on Old High German Umlaut." *Monatshefte* 30.177–181. Reprinted in *Readings in Linguistic I*, ed. Martin Joos (New York: American Council of Learned Societies, 1958).

10

EPILOGUE

We are now in a better position to suggest answers to the basic question posed in the Prologue: Why should anyone care about historical linguistics?

A blunt answer, but maybe the best all things considered, would be: if you still feel the need to ask that question, historical linguistics is not for you; do something else in linguistics. I think, however, that a stronger case can be made for historical linguistics, namely that general linguistic theory is greatly enriched by the inclusion of the facts of historical change in its accountability. This heightens the significance of both general linguistics and historical linguistics in ways that have not hitherto been much in evidence. An example will help illustrate what is at stake here.

A crucial concept in generative phonology is simplicity. Given two solutions that cover the same ground, we choose one on the basis of descriptive adequacy, generality, intuitive soundness, and various other criteria. We then formulate rules in accordance with a measure of preferability that formally reflects these criteria; this is known as the simplicity metric. Often enough there is no problem in deciding which of two rules to regard as the simpler. Most linguists would agree that a rule stating "*A* becomes *B* in the environment before *i*" is less general, less natural than a rule stating "*A* becomes *B* in the environment before all front vowels *i e æ*." The simplicity metric should record this difference in a formal, countable way, so as to say that the second formulation of the rule is simpler (higher-valued) than the first.

It is fairly obvious which of these two rules is simpler. But the situation is not always so clear, as the following case (from Bach 1968) shows. Should the rule "*A* becomes *B* either before or after *C*" count as more simple (more general) or less simple (less general) than either of the two separate rules "*A* becomes *B* before *C*" and "*A* becomes *B* after *C*." That is, what is the simplicity relation of the rule:

$$10.1 \quad A \rightarrow B / \left\{ \begin{array}{c} \underline{} C \\ C \underline{} \end{array} \right\}$$

to the rules:

$$10.1' \quad A \rightarrow B / \underline{} C$$

and:

$$10.1'' \quad A \rightarrow B / C \underline{}$$

Intuitively Rule 10.1 seems more general than the other two somewhat similar rules; a rule carrying out a change either before or after something seems more general than rules effecting that change just before (but not after) or just after (but not before) the something in question. But does any other kind of evidence clinch the argument that 10.1 is simpler than 10.1' and 10.1"?

Suppose there are, as one can demonstrate in this case, a number of historical changes in which a rule of the form 10.1' or 10.1" has been replaced in the grammar by a rule of the form 10.1. Does this replacement have any relevance to what originally was a question, purely synchronic if you will, about which of two rules should be regarded as the simpler?

Our answer to this depends on our answer to a prior question: Should linguistic theory be responsible for the data of linguistic change? The answer to this is not mandatory. If we decide to answer No, then the facts of historical change simply have no bearing on the question of which rule is simpler. The two questions are unrelated: one has to do with a decision to be made about simplicity, the other is an historical event of no further interest.

If we answer this basic question in the affirmative, however, then the historical evidence becomes just as relevant to the question of simplicity as any purely synchronic data; and the testimony of historical change becomes binding on the formulation of theory. We know that simplification is a basic mechanism of change. Grammars become simpler over time, not less simple. Historical linguistics shows that rules of the form "*A* becomes *B* before *C*" and "*A* becomes *B* after *C*" (if they change at all) are replaced by the rule "*A* becomes *B* either before or after *C*." Development in the reverse direction does not occur. This evidence, as strong as any from synchrony, shows that a single either-before-or-after rule is simpler, more general than either of the other two rules separately, and the historical evidence has given strong support to a decision to be made in phonological theory.

Similarly, one can motivate on strictly synchronic grounds the decision to value variables higher than pluses or minuses; that is, Rule:

$$10.2 \quad [+ \text{obstruent}] \rightarrow [\alpha \text{ voice}] / \underline{\quad\quad} \begin{bmatrix} + \text{obstruent} \\ \alpha \text{ voice} \end{bmatrix}$$

should count as more general than either Rule:

$$10.2' \quad [+ \text{obstruent}] \rightarrow [- \text{voice}] / \underline{\quad\quad} \begin{bmatrix} + \text{obstruent} \\ - \text{voice} \end{bmatrix}$$

or Rule:

$$10.2'' \quad [+ \text{obstruent}] \rightarrow [+ \text{voice}] / \underline{\quad\quad} \begin{bmatrix} + \text{obstruent} \\ + \text{voice} \end{bmatrix}$$

To secure independent motivation for this decision one would look to the historical evidence and seek to show that grammars with Rule 10.2′ or Rule 10.2″ are replaced by grammars with Rule 10.2. The historical evidence has bearing on synchronic questions other than simplicity. Kiparsky (1968b) discusses some of these questions, among them the relevance of historical evidence to our choice of distinctive features and to underlying representations.

These are simple examples of the sort of benefit that accrues to the linguist who extends the domain of accountability of linguistic theory to include linguistic change. It illustrates what general linguistic theory has to gain from historical linguistics and what benefits accrue to both synchrony and diachrony from the conception of linguistic change as grammar change.

But perhaps the effort to defend historical linguistics this way is misplaced. I have emphasized the potential contributions of historical linguistics to linguistic theory in order to emphasize that a formal and substantive theory of language—generative grammar in particular—is greatly enriched by broadening its evidential base to include historical change. But let this not conceal what should be obvious: historical linguistics is per se rich, fascinating, and rewarding. It is not a dead field, the musty province of pedants and philologists. Its core is the most intriguing and dynamic feature of language —*change*. And one cannot approach the study of historical linguistics without venturing into the frontier fields of linguistic research: child learning of language, psycholinguistics in general, bilingualism, the sociology of language change.

Much work needs to be done in historical transformational syntax. Too few languages, especially non-Indo-European ones, have been analyzed thoroughly in historical generative grammar. Far too little is known about constraints on what kinds of change can occur, and certain kinds of change, notably semantic, have not been investigated at all. No large scale investigation of linguistic change has used generative grammar as the theoretical basis. Grammar change of a more comprehensive scope needs to be studied. Are there causal relationships between changes in different components of the grammar, specifically between syntactic and phonological change? Is all phonological change phonetic (e.g. assimilatory) in origin? Are there phonological changes that can be reasonably stated at and only at the autonomous phonemic level of representation? If so, they would require reassessment of the role of the autonomous phoneme in the competence of the speaker.

This book has attempted to present historical linguistics as it has been affected by the theory of generative grammar. Traditional problems have been restated in terms of generative grammar, with many of the traditional questions answered. In the process new perspectives have invited us to further research and further refinement of our theory of language and linguistic change. But that's what historical linguistics is all about, and why it needs no apologies.

BIBLIOGRAPHY

Arntz, Helmut. 1935. *Handbuch der Runenkunde*. Halle/Saale: Max Niemeyer Verlag.

Bach, Emmon. 1964. *An Introduction to Transformational Grammars*. New York: Holt, Rinehart & Winston, Inc.

Bach, Emmon. 1967. "*Have* and *Be* in English Syntax." *Language* 43.462–485.

Bach, Emmon. 1968. "Two Proposals Concerning the Simplicity Metric in Phonology." *Glossa* 2.128–149.

Becker, Donald A. 1967. *Generative Phonology and Dialect Study: An Investigation of Three Modern German Dialects*. Unpublished doctoral dissertation, University of Texas at Austin.

Behaghel, Otto. 1928. *Geschichte der deutschen Sprache* (5th ed.). Berlin and Leipzig: Walter de Gruyter.

Benveniste, Émile. 1948. *Noms d'agent et noms d'action en indo-européen.* Paris: Adrien Maisonneuve.

Benveniste, Émile. 1962. *Hittite et indo-européen.* Paris: Adrien Maisonneuve.

Bloomfield, Leonard. 1933. *Language.* New York: Holt, Rinehart & Winston, Inc.

Bonfante, Guliano. 1945. "On Reconstruction and Linguistic Method." *Word* 1.83–94, 1.132–161.

Braine, Martin D. S. 1963. "The Ontogeny of English Phrase Structure: The First Phase." *Language* 39.1–13.

Brown, Roger, and Colin Fraser. 1963. "The Acquisition of Syntax," in *Verbal Behavior and Learning,* eds. Charles N. Cofer and Barbara Musgrave. New York: McGraw-Hill Book Company.

Brunner, Karl. 1965. *Altenglische Grammatik* (3rd ed.). Tübingen: Max Niemeyer Verlag.

Campbell, Alistair. 1959. *Old English Grammar.* Oxford: Clarendon Press.

Chafe, Wallace L. 1959. "Internal Reconstruction in Seneca." *Language* 35.477–495.

Chafe, Wallace L. 1961. Review of Hoenigswald (1960). *Language* 37.113–120.

Chomsky, Noam. 1957. *Syntactic Structures* (= *Janua Linguarum* 4). The Hague: Mouton & Co.

Chomsky, Noam. 1964. "Current Issues in Linguistic Theory," in Fodor and Katz (1964).

Chomsky, Noam. 1965. *Aspects of the Theory of Syntax.* Cambridge, Mass.: The M.I.T. Press.

Chomsky, Noam, and Morris Halle. 1965. "Some Controversial Questions in Phonological Theory." *Journal of Linguistics* 1.97–138.

Chomsky, Noam, and Morris Halle. 1968. *The Sound Pattern of English.* New York: Harper & Row, Publishers.

Closs, Elizabeth. 1965. "Diachronic Syntax and Generative Grammar." *Language* 41.402–415. Reprinted in Reibel and Schane (1969).

Dyen, Isidore. 1963. "Why Phonetic Change Is Regular." *Language* 39.631–637.

Ervin, Susan M. 1964. "Imitation and Structural Change in Children's Language," in *New Directions in the Study of Language,* ed. Eric H. Lenneberg. Cambridge, Mass.: The M.I.T. Press.

Fodor, Jerry A., and Jerrold J. Katz, eds. 1964. *The Structure of Language: Readings in the Philosophy of Language.* Englewood Cliffs, N.J.: Prentice-Hall, Inc.

Fourquet, Jean. 1952. "The Two E's of Middle High German: A Diachronic Phonemic Approach." *Word* 8.122–135.

Gabelentz, Georg von der. 1901. *Die Sprachwissenschaft.* Leipzig: Chr. Herm. Tauchnitz.

Gilliéron, Jules. 1915. *Pathologie et thérapeutique verbales.* Paris: Champion.

Gilliéron, Jules. 1918. *Génealogie des mots qui désignent l'abeille.* Paris: Champion.

Hall, Robert A., Jr. 1950. "The Reconstruction of Proto-Romance." *Language* 26.6–27. Reprinted in Joos (1958).

Halle, Morris. 1962. "Phonology in Generative Grammar." *Word* 18.54–72. Reprinted in Fodor and Katz (1964).

Harms, Robert T. 1966. "Ugric Reflexes of the Uralo-Jukaghir Focus System." Unpublished paper. Published in 1967 in Hungarian: "Az uráli-jukagír fókuszrendszer ugor megfelelöi," in *A magyar nyelv története és rendszere* (= *Nyelvtudományi értekezések* 58), eds. S. Imre and I. Szathmári. Budapest: Akadémiai Kiadó. Pp. 94–103.

Harms, Robert T. 1967. "Split, Shift, and Merger in the Permic Vowels." *Ural-Altaische Jahrbücher* 39.161–198.

Harms, Robert T. 1968. *Introduction to Phonological Theory.* Englewood Cliffs, N.J.: Prentice-Hall, Inc.

Haugen, Einar I. 1950. *First Grammatical Treatise; the Earliest Germanic Phonology* (= *Language* Monograph No. 25). Baltimore: Linguistic Society of America.

Heffner, Roe-Merrill S. 1960. *General Phonetics.* Madison: The University of Wisconsin Press.

Hermann, Eduard. 1931. *Lautgesetz und Analogie.* Berlin: Weidmannsche Buchhandlung.

Herzog, Marvin I. 1965. *The Yiddish Language in Northern Poland* (= *International Journal of American Linguistics* 31, No. 2, Part III). Bloomington: Indiana University; and The Hague: Mouton & Co.

Hill, Archibald A. 1967. "The Typology of Writing Systems," in *Papers in Linguistics in Honor of Léon Dostert,* ed. William M. Austin. The Hague: Mouton & Co.

Hockett, Charles F. 1948. "Implications of Bloomfield's Algonquian Studies," *Language* 24.117–131. Reprinted in Joos (1958).

Hockett, Charles F. 1958. *A Course in Modern Linguistics.* New York: The Macmillan Company.

Hockett, Charles F. 1959. "The Stressed Syllabics of Old English." *Language* 35.575–597.

Hockett, Charles F. 1965. "Sound Change." *Language* 41.185–204.

Hoenigswald, Henry M. 1944. "Internal Reconstruction." *Studies in Linguistics* 2.78–87.

Hoenigswald, Henry M. 1946. "Sound Change and Linguistic Structure." *Language* 22.138–143. Reprinted in Joos (1958).

Hoenigswald, Henry M. 1950. "The Principal Step in Comparative Grammar." *Language* 26.357–364. Reprinted in Joos (1958).

Hoenigswald, Henry M. 1960. *Language Change and Linguistic Reconstruction.* Chicago: University of Chicago Press.

Hoenigswald, Henry M. 1964. "Graduality, Sporadicity, and the Minor Sound Change Processes." *Phonetica* 11.202–215.

Jakobson, Roman. 1931. "Prinzipien der historischen Phonologie." *Travaux du Cercle Linguistique de Prague* 4.247–267. Reprinted in Jakobson (1962).

Jakobson, Roman. 1941. *Kindersprache, Aphasie und allgemeine Lautgesetze.* Uppsala: Almqvist & Wiksells Boktryckeri. Reprinted in Jakobson (1962).

Jakobson, Roman. 1962. *Selected Writings I: Phonological Studies.* The Hague: Mouton & Co.

Joos, Martin. 1950. "Description of Language Design." *Journal of the Acoustical Society of America* 22.701–708. Reprinted in Joos (1958).

Joos, Martin. 1952. "The Medieval Sibilants." *Language* 28.222–231. Reprinted in Joos (1958).

Joos, Martin, ed. 1958. *Readings in Linguistics.* New York: American Council of Learned Societies.

Katz, Jerrold J., and Jerry A. Fodor. 1963. "The Structure of a Semantic Theory." *Language* 30.170–210. Reprinted in Fodor and Katz (1964).

Katz, Jerrold J., and Paul M. Postal. 1964. *An Integrated Theory of Linguistic Descriptions.* Cambridge, Mass.: The M.I.T. Press.

Keller, Rudolf E. 1961. *German Dialects.* Manchester: Manchester University Press.

Keyser, Samuel J. 1963. Review of Kurath and McDavid (1961). *Language* 39.303–316.

King, Robert D. 1967a. "Functional Load and Sound Change." *Language* 43.831–852.

King, Robert D. 1967b. "In Defense of Klopstock as Spelling Reformer: A Linguistic Appraisal." *Journal of English and Germanic Philology* 66.369–382.

King, Robert D. 1968. "Root versus Suffix Accent in the Germanic Present Indicative." *Journal of Linguistics* 4.247–265.

King, Robert D. 1969. "Push Chains and Drag Chains." *Glossa* 3.3-21.

Kiparsky, Paul. 1965. *Phonological Change.* Unpublished doctoral dissertation, Massachusetts Institute of Technology.

Kiparsky, Paul. 1967. "A propos de l'histoire de l'accentuation grecque." *Langages* 8.73–93.

Kiparsky, Paul. 1968a. "Tense and Mood in Indo-European Syntax." *Foundations of Language* 4.30–57.

Kiparsky, Paul. 1968b. "Linguistic Universals and Linguistic Change," in *Universals in Linguistic Theory*, eds. Emmon Bach and Robert T. Harms. New York: Holt, Rinehart & Winston, Inc.

Klima, Edward S. 1964. "Relatedness between Grammatical Systems." *Language* 40.1–20. Reprinted in Reibel and Schane (1969).

Klima, Edward S. 1965. *Studies in Diachronic Transformational Syntax*. Unpublished doctoral dissertation, Harvard University.

Kratz, Henry. 1960. "The Phonemic Approach to Umlaut in Old High German and Old Norse." *Journal of English and German Philology* 59.463–479.

Krause, Wolfgang. 1963. *Handbuch des Gotischen* (2nd ed.). Munich: Verlag C. H. Beck.

Kurath, Hans, and Raven I. McDavid, Jr. 1961. *The Pronunciation of English in the Atlantic States*. Ann Arbor: The University of Michigan Press.

Kuryłowicz, Jerzy. 1945–1949. "La nature des procès dits 'analogiques'." *Acta Linguistica* 5.15–37. Reprinted in Kuryłowicz (1960).

Kuryłowicz, Jerzy. 1958. *L'accentuation des langues indo-européennes*. Wrocław–Kraków: Polish Academy of Sciences.

Kuryłowicz, Jerzy. 1960. *Esquisses linguistiques*. Wrocław–Kraków: Polish Academy of Sciences.

Kuryłowicz, Jerzy. 1964. "On the Methods of Internal Reconstruction," in *Proceedings of the Ninth International Congress of Linguists*, ed. Horace G. Lunt. The Hague: Mouton & Co.

Labov, William. 1963. "The Social Motivation of a Sound Change." *Word* 19.273–309.

Labov, William. 1965. "On the Mechanism of Linguistic Change," in *Georgetown University Monograph Series on Languages and Linguistics*, No. 18, ed. Charles W. Kreidler. Washington, D.C.: Georgetown University Press.

Lakoff, George. 1965. *On the Nature of Syntactic Irregularity* (= Report No. NSF-16 to the National Science Foundation). Cambridge, Mass.: The Computation Laboratory of Harvard University.

Lakoff, Robin T. 1969. *Abstract Syntax and Latin Complementation*. Cambridge, Mass.: The M.I.T. Press.

Lamb, Sidney. 1966. "Prolegomena to a Theory of Phonology." *Language* 42.536–573.

Lane, George S. 1949. "On the Present State of Indo-European Linguistics." *Language* 25.333–342.

Lerch, Eugen. 1925. "Über das sprachliche Verhältnis von Ober- zu Unterschicht." *Jahrbuch für Philologie* 1.70–124.

Lightner, Theodore M. 1968. "On the Use of Minor Rules in Russian Phonology." *Journal of Linguistics* 4.69–72.

Malkiel, Yakov. 1967. "Each Word Has a History of Its Own." *Glossa* 1.137–149.

Malkiel, Yakov. 1968. "The Inflectional Paradigm As an Occasional Determinant of Sound Change," in *Directions for Historical Linguistics*, eds. Winfred P. Lehmann and Yakov Malkiel. Austin: The University of Texas Press.

Mańczak, Witold. 1958. "Tendances générales des changements analogiques." *Lingua* 7.298–325, 7.387–420.

Mandelbaum, David G. 1949. *Selected Writings of Edward Sapir*. Berkeley and Los Angeles: University of California Press.

Marchand, James W. 1956. "Internal Reconstruction of Phonemic Split." *Language* 32.245–253.

Martinet, André. 1952. "Function, Structure, and Sound Change." *Word* 8.1–32.

Martinet, André. 1955. *Économie des changements phonétiques*. Berne: A. Francke.

McNeill, David. 1966. "Developmental Psycholinguistics," in *The Genesis of Language*, eds. Frank Smith and George A. Miller. Cambridge, Mass.: The M.I.T. Press.

Moulton, William G. 1960. "The Short Vowel Systems of Northern Switzerland." *Word* 16.155–182.

Moulton, William G. 1961a. "Zur Geschichte des deutschen Vokalsystems." *Beiträge zur Geschichte der deutschen Sprache und Literatur* (Tübingen) 83.1–35.

Moulton, William G. 1961b. "Lautwandel durch innere Kausalität: die ostschweizerische Vokalspaltung." *Zeitschrift für Mundartforschung* 28.227–251.

Moulton, William G. 1962. "Dialect Geography and the Concept of Phonological Space." *Word* 18.23–32.

Naert, Pierre. 1941. "Des mutations *ct, cs > pt, ps; gn > mn* et *mn > un* en roumain." *Acta Linguistica* 2.247–257.

Passy, Paul. 1891. *Étude sur les changements phonétiques et leurs caractères généraux*. Paris: Firmin–Didot.

Paul, Hermann. 1960. *Prinzipien der Sprachgeschichte* (6th ed.). Tübingen: Max Niemeyer Verlag.

Pedersen, Holger. 1962. *The Discovery of Language* (= *Linguistic Science in the Nineteenth Century*), trans. John W. Spargo. Bloomington: Indiana University Press.

Pike, Kenneth L. 1951. *Axioms and Procedures for Reconstructions in Comparative Linguistics—An Experimental Syllabus*. Norman, Okla.: Summer Institute of Linguistics.

Postal, Paul M. 1968. *Aspects of Phonological Theory*. New York: Harper & Row, Publishers.

Prokosch, Eduard. 1939. *A Comparative Germanic Grammar*. Philadelphia: Linguistic Society of America.

Reibel, David A., and Sanford A. Schane, eds. 1969. *Modern Studies in English: Readings in Transformational Grammar*. Englewood Cliffs, N.J.: Prentice-Hall, Inc.

Röll, Walther. 1966. "Das älteste datierte jüdisch-deutsche Sprachdenkmal." *Zeitschrift für Mundartforschung* 33.127–138.

Rousselot, L'Abbé. 1892. "Les modifications phonétiques du langage étudiées dans le patois d'une famille de Cellefrouin (Charente)," Part 3. *Revue des patois Gallo-Romans*, Vol. 5. Paris: H. Welter.

Sapir, Edward. 1921. *Language*. New York: Harcourt, Brace & World, Inc.

Sapir, Edward. 1926. "A Chinookan Phonetic Law." *International Journal of American Linguistics* 4.105–110. Reprinted in Mandelbaum (1949).

Sapir, Edward. 1929. "Male and Female Forms of Speech in Yana," in *Donum Natalicium Schrijnen*. Nijmegen–Utrecht: Dekker & Van de Vegt. Reprinted in Mandelbaum (1949).

Sapir, Edward. 1949. "Notes on Judeo-German Phonology," in Mandelbaum (1949).

Saussure, Ferdinand de. 1959. *Course in Modern Linguistics*, trans. Wade Baskin. New York: The Philosophical Library, Inc.

Schuchardt, Hugo. 1885. *Über die Lautgesetze. Gegen die Junggrammatiker*. Berlin: Oppenheim.

Sommerfelt, Alf. 1923. "Note sur les changements phonétiques." *Bulletin de Société de Linguistique* 24.138–141. Reprinted in Sommerfelt (1962).

Sommerfelt, Alf. 1962. *Diachronic and Synchronic Aspects of Language*. The Hague: Mouton & Co.

Spitzer, Leo. 1922. *Hugo-Schuchardt Brevier*. Halle (Saale): Max Niemeyer Verlag.

Stanley, Richard. 1967. "Redundancy Rules in Phonology." *Language* 43.393–436.

Steiner, Rulon B. 1969. *Umlaut und Vowel Length Designation in Middle High German*. Unpublished master's thesis, University of Texas at Austin.

Stockwell, Robert P., and C. Westbrook Barritt. 1955. "The Old English Short Digraphs: Some Considerations." *Language* 31.372–389.

Stockwell, Robert P., and C. Westbrook Barritt. 1961. "Scribal Practice: Some Assumptions." *Language* 37.75–82.

Szemerényi, Oswald. 1960. *Studies in the Indo-European System of Numerals.* Heidelberg: Carl Winter.

Trager, George L., and Henry L. Smith, Jr. 1957. *An Outline of English Structure* (= *Studies in Linguistics* Occasional Papers, No. 3). Washington, D.C.: American Council of Learned Societies.

Twaddell, W. Freeman. 1938. "A Note on Old High German Umlaut." *Monatshefte für Deutschen Unterricht* 30.177–181. Reprinted in Joos (1958).

Vasiliu, Emanuel. 1966. "Towards a Generative Phonology of Daco-Rumanian Dialects." *Journal of Linguistics* 2.79–98.

Vendryes, Joseph. 1925. *Language,* trans. Paul Radin. London: Routledge & Kegan Paul Ltd.

Wang, William S-Y. 1965. "Two Aspect Markers in Mandarin." *Language* 41.457–470.

Wang, William S-Y. 1967. "Phonological Features of Tone." *International Journal of American Linguistics* 33.93–105.

Wang, William S-Y. 1968. "Vowel Features, Paired Variables, and the English Vowel Shift." *Language* 44.695–708.

Wang, William S-Y. 1969. "Competing Changes As a Cause of Residue." *Language* 45.9-25.

Watkins, Calvert. 1962. *Indo-European Origins of the Celtic Verb.* Dublin: The Dublin Institute for Advanced Studies.

Weinreich, Uriel. 1954. "Is a Structural Dialectology Possible?" *Word* 10.388–400.

Weinreich, Uriel. 1963. "Four Riddles in Bilingual Dialectology," in *American Contributions to the Fifth International Congress of Slavists,* Vol. 1. The Hague: Mouton & Co. Pp. 335–359.

Weinreich, Uriel, William Labov, and Marvin I. Herzog. 1968. "Empirical Foundations for a Theory of Language Change," in *Directions for Historical Linguistics,* eds. Winfred P. Lehmann and Yakov Malkiel. Austin: The University of Texas Press.

Weir, Ruth H. 1962. *Language in the Crib.* The Hague: Mouton & Co.

Whitney, William D. 1883. *The Life and Growth of Language.* New York: D. Appleton and Company.

Zipf, George K. 1929. "Relative Frequency As a Determinant of Phonetic Change." *Harvard Studies in Classical Philology* 40.1–95.

Zipf, George K. 1965. *The Psycho-Biology of Language.* Cambridge, Mass.: The M.I.T. Press.

INDEX

226